Physical Medicine and Rehabilitation

Rehabilitation of Sports Injuries

Jeffrey A. Saal, M.D.
Guest Editor

Volume 1/Number 4 November 1987

HANLEY & BELFUS, INC. Philadelphia

STATE OF THE ART REVIEWS

Publisher: HANLEY & BELFUS, INC.
210 South 13th Street
Philadelphia, PA 19107

PHYSICAL MEDICINE AND REHABILITATION: State of the Art Reviews   ISSN 0888-7357
November 1987 Volume 1, Number 4   ISBN 0-932883-43-5

PHYSICAL MEDICINE AND REHABILITATION: State of the Art Reviews is published quarterly
by Hanley & Belfus, Inc., 210 South 13th Street, Philadelphia, Pennsylvania 19107.

POSTMASTER: Send address changes to PHYSICAL MEDICINE AND REHABILITATION:
State of the Art Reviews, Hanley & Belfus, Inc., 210 South 13th Street, Philadelphia, PA 19107.

This issue is Volume 1, Number 4.

The Editor of this publication is Linda C. Belfus.

CONTENTS

iii

The biomechanics of the shoulder in the throwing motion need to be understood in order to formulate an approach to treatment. The anatomy, biomechanics, and muscular physiology of the shoulder, as well as rehabilitation procedures for specific injuries, are discussed and illustrated.

This chapter formulates the rationale for the rehabilitation of lumbar spine disorders in the injured athlete. Treatment programs are outlined that advance from initial acute treatment to refined programs for specific injuries and sport types.

Medical advances in diagnosis, surgical technique, bracing, and rehabilitation, as well as a better understanding of the biomechanical and clinical consequences of a torn anterior cruciate ligament, have provided more consistently successful results and greater patient satisfaction. This chapter presents the surgical rationale and rehabilitation protocol for the management of the patient with a repaired or reconstructed anterior cruciate ligament.

This chapter focuses on the proper management of head injuries in the athletic setting, with special emphasis on sideline decision making. The injury protocol that is presented is directed at assisting team physicians in managing athletes with head injuries, especially those with mild injuries who wish to return to play. The principles addressed may also be applied to other athletic head injuries.

Based on accepted goals, a systematic approach to the preparticipation examination is proposed, including what should and what should not be included in the standard examination. Attention is focused on how the basic examination can and should be modified to meet individual needs resulting from differences in age, sport, or health.

CONTRIBUTORS

Stephen J. Anderson, M.D.
Clinical Assistant Professor, Department of Pediatrics, University of Washington School of Medicine, Seattle, Washington

Michael F. Dillingham, M.D.
Team Physician, San Francisco 49ers, San Francisco, and Santa Clara University, Santa Clara, California; Clinical Assistant Professor of Surgery, Stanford University, Stanford, California

Gary S. Fanton, M.D.
Staff Physician, Sports, Orthopedic and Rehabilitation Medicine Associates, Portola Valley, California; Orthopedic Consultant, San Francisco 49ers, San Francisco; Team Physician, San Jose Golddiggers, College of San Mateo, and DeAnza College; Company Physician, San Jose-Cleveland Ballet; Chairman, Section of Orthopedic Surgery, Sequoia Hospital, Redwood City, California

Jeffrey A. Saal, M.D.
Staff Physician, Sports, Orthopedic and Rehabilitation Medicine Associates, Portola Valley, California; Associate Clinical Professor, Physical Medicine and Rehabilitation, University of California at Irvine, Irvine, California; Team Physician, Santa Clara University, Santa Clara, California; Consulting Team Physician, San Francisco 49ers, San Francisco, California

Joel S. Saal, M.D.
Staff Physician, Sports, Orthopedic and Rehabilitation Medicine Associates, Portola Valley, California

Mark J. Sontag, M.D.
Staff Physician, Sports, Orthopedic and Rehabilitation Medicine Associates, Portola Valley, California; Team Physician, San Mateo Junior College and San Mateo High School, San Mateo, California

Jeryl J. Wiens, M.D.
Staff Physician, Sports, Orthopedic and Rehabilitation Medicine Associates, Portola Valley, California; Consulting Team Physician, San Francisco 49ers, San Francisco, California

PUBLISHED ISSUES 1987

Volume 1, Number 1   **Orthotics**
Edited by J.B. Redford, M.D.
Kansas City, Kansas

Volume 1, Number 2   **A Primer on Management for Rehabilitation Medicine**
Edited by F. Patrick Maloney, M.D.
Little Rock, Arkansas

Volume 1, Number 3   **Medical Complications of Spinal Cord Injury**
Edited by Mark N. Ozer, M.D. and
James K. Schmitt, M.D.
Richmond, Virginia

FUTURE ISSUES, 1988–1989

Rehabilitation of the Alcoholic
Edited by Curtis Wright, M.D.
Baltimore, Maryland

Home Care
Edited by Jay Portnow, M.D.
Braintree, Massachusetts

Rehabilitation of Spinal Cord Injuries
Edited by Milan R. Dimitrijevic, M.D.
Houston, Texas

Head Trauma
Edited by Nathan Cope, M.D. and
Lawrence Horn, M.D.
Washington, D.C. and
Philadelphia, Pennsylvania

Geriatric Rehabilitation
Edited by Roy Erickson, M.D.
New Britain, Connecticut

Subscriptions and single issues available from the publisher—Hanley & Belfus, Inc., Medical Publishers, 210 South 13th Street, Philadelphia, PA 19107 (215) 546-7293.

PREFACE

The rehabilitation of sports injuries requires a sound scientific rationale. Fad treatments or poorly conceived surgery with irrational or nonexistent postoperative rehabilitation programs have no place in sports medicine. This issue of **PM&R: STARs** on the rehabilitation of sports injuries contains information that should be of value to practicing physicians, physical therapists, and athletic trainers who treat injured athletes. The general principles covered in chapter 2 are intended to be a matrix for all sports-related rehabilitation programs. The chapters on flexibility, strength, and aerobic and nonaerobic training detail currently available scientific understanding. The guidelines setting forth criteria for return to play are intended to assist responsible professionals in this difficult decision, which of course has to be made based on individual circumstances.

The paper on lumbar spine rehabilitation introduces a set of principles that can guide programs in physical therapy. The concept of ''training therapy'' rather than ''pain control therapy'' is discussed. The scientific and clinical rationale for stabilization exercises is described in exquisite detail. The articles on shoulder, cervical spine, and brachial plexus injury rehabilitation are carefully reasoned reviews that are designed to emphasize practical information. The article on head injury is intended to guide the side-line physician in proper decision-making based upon careful clinical reasoning. Dr. Anderson's paper on the preparticipation examination covers the approaches to and pitfalls of this well-intended but often misdirected process. Tremendous advances in postoperative knee rehabilitation are in evidence in Dr. Fanton's article, which should serve notice to surgeons to keep these patients moving.

Accurate diagnosis and early aggressive rehabilitation, as appropriate, are stressed throughout this issue. Significant voids exist in the science of sports medicine and such voids have led to the dissemination of confusing and conflicting misinformation. More research is obviously needed in the field of rehabilitation of sports injuries, but the principles and applications presented here are based on the state of the art and the state of the science available at this time. I hope that this issue provides a thought-provoking experience, as well as a useful reference, for all those who choose to read its pages.

JEFFREY A. SAAL, MD
GUEST EDITOR

JEFFREY A. SAAL, MD

THE PHYSIATRIC AND ORTHOPEDIC TEAM CARE APPROACH TO SPORTS MEDICINE

Reprint requests to Jeffrey A. Saal, M.D., Sports, Orthopedic and Rehabilitation Medicine Associates, 3250 Alpine Rd., Portola Valley, CA 94025.

Sports medicine is a multidisciplinary and multidimensional discipline. Its breadth crosses the boundaries of all medical specialties. In the subspecialty area of neuromusculoskeletal injury the pathways of the physiatrist and orthopedic surgeon cross. Over 10 years ago it became obvious to me that an ideal marriage was potentially available between these two specialties. It was my presumption that a synergistic medical relationship could be developed that would enable a higher level of sophisticated care to be delivered to the injured athlete. It appeared that a void in musculoskeletal medical care had developed. Where does the patient with back pain, neck pain, shoulder pain, elbow pain or other physical pain go to seek medical attention? If it is to the general medical physician who is hindered by a lack of training and expertise in managing musculoskeletal problems, invariably an analgesic and NSAID is prescribed with the nonspecific recommendation of rest. After that course of action does not alter the pain process, the patient is referred to the orthopedic surgeon.

The surgeon is able to determine quickly that the problem is not surgical in nature and advises the patient to keep resting and taking medication. When the patient asks what the next course of action is if the current plan fails, the surgeon tells the patient if the pain becomes intolerable he can operate. As the patient leaves the doctor's office it is not quite clear what the surgeon will operate upon and by what method, but it is clear to the patient that returning to the surgeon's office means more drugs or surgery. Where does the patient turn now? The rheumatologists are occupied with immunologic problems, so that pathway will not work. Enter the physical medicine specialist (physiatrist), who by virtue of training, background, and interest is capable and willing to help this patient.

The physiatrist's background and training in neuromuscular physiology, bio-mechanics, orthotics and bracing, and scientific approaches to rehabilitation have a tremendous amount to offer in the field of sports medicine. The vast majority of sports injuries are nonsurgical and by their very nature require rehabilitation. Who is better equipped to deliver this service than the physiatrist? The orthopedic surgeon has been traditionally recognized as the sports medicine physician. Given their training in traumatology, they are well equipped to handle knee ligament and meniscal injuries and the like, but they are neither interested nor trained to manage the myriad of soft tissue injuries and neural injuries sustained by athletes. With the physical fitness explosion non–team-affiliated athletes began suffering soft tissue–type overuse injuries that necessitated attention. Knowledge of the biomechanics of injury and rehabilitation techniques was necessary to adequately treat these inherently nonsurgical problems. Based upon the premise that surgeons should do what they do best and are most suited to do by virtue of their training, physiatrists should concentrate on those problems in which they are most capable. A scheme was developed for surgeons to see surgical problems and for physiatrists to see clinical problems that necessitated diagnostic workups and nonoperative rehabili-tation care plans. An open environment for constant interchange between the prac-titioners was fostered so that no one was practicing in a vacuum. The only goal was to supply the best level of care possible. It was on this basis that SOAR (Sports Orthopedic and Rehabilitation Medicine Associates) was founded. Patients were often evaluated on multiple occasions by both the physiatrist and the surgeon, depending how the care plan was evolving. Thus a multidisciplinary team concept of care evolved.

For example, a 25-year-old woman runner presents to the office with a chief complaint of lateral knee pain, which began after running and vigorous aerobic workouts. She is initially seen by the orthopedic surgeon to rule out internal de-rangement of the knee. Upon careful questioning the patient reports that the pain is posterolateral and occasionally radiates to the lateral calf region. She also elab-orates a history of 3 years of chiropractic care for low back pain and intermittent buttock pain. The orthopedic surgeon asks the physiatrist to evaluate the patient to determine if the knee pain is referral zone pain or "true" knee pain. After the physiatric evaluation a diagnosis of L5 radiculopathy is established and the patient is begun on a lumbar spine rehabilitation program. Surgery of the knee is not performed, the posterolateral knee pain is resolved, and the patient is delighted with the result. This outcome is certainly preferable to one that reads like this: knee arthrogram negative, "exploratory" arthroscopy with "trimming" of the lateral cartilage, persistent postoperative lateral knee pain, "pain" patient.

Another typical example is the tennis player referred for a rotator cuff injury, but who, after initial evaluation, is noted to have signs of an incipient C6 radicu-lopathy that has led to shoulder girdle muscle weakness and secondary rotator cuff pathology. The physiatric evaluation unraveled the cause of the pain and allowed an appropriate care plan to be developed. If only a surgeon examined this patient, the approach may very well have been surgical.

The orthopedic surgeons in this multidisciplinary milieu have been alerted to look for and suspect referral zone pain patterns, and the physiatrists have been trained to evaluate joints for surgical pathology. The physiatrists are taught the appropriate timing and indications of surgical interventions for the various injuries.

Most important, the physiatrists are taught to interact with the surgeons in a non-threatening team approach.

The orthopedic surgeons, on the other hand, are taught to think like physiatrists. Functional evaluation is stressed as well as structural diagnostics. Surgical decision making is predicated on a thorough understanding not only of the structural pathology, but also on the social profile and goals of the injured athlete. The surgeons supervise their own patients' protocols for postoperative rehabilitation, whereas the physiatrists manage their own cases. Postoperative rehabilitation problems are evaluated by the physiatrist, but the patient is still the surgeon's case. Case "dumping" is absolutely discouraged. The athletes and the coaches look upon both the surgeon and the physiatrist as team physicians and are equally at ease having either on the sideline administering medical care. Only after the physiatrist is fully trained in evaluation of all types of injury is he asked to "fly solo" on the sidelines. Knee ligament injuries with resultant instability and the triage of fractures are two areas in which the physiatrist must be brought up to speed.

There is no doubt the system works. The individual athletes and the teams that have been managed this way all agree that the level of care is the best that they have experienced. The completeness and thoughtfulness of the process are recognized and commented upon by patients. On the surface, the principles are simple, but one should beware. Egos must be smoothed and thoughtful physicians must be teamed. Each must understand the other's specialty and guidelines. Each team member must be willing to learn and grow. Playing to each other's strengths is fundamental, and learning to trust the other's clinical judgment is imperative.

When things click, everyone is happy. The surgeons are doing what they do best and enjoy the most, and the physiatrists are placed in a role they enjoy and can excel in. The ultimate beneficiary of the system is the patient, as it should be. Is that not the goal of all medical care systems?

JEFFREY A. SAAL, MD

GENERAL PRINCIPLES AND GUIDELINES FOR REHABILITATION OF THE INJURED ATHLETE

Reprint requests to Jeffrey A. Saal, M.D., Sports, Orthopedic and Rehabilitation Medicine Associates, 3250 Alpine Rd., Portola Valley, CA 94025.

By virtue of the physiatrist's background and training, he or she becomes an ideal practitioner of sports medicine. The physiatrist must apply a background in and knowledge of anatomy and pathophysiology of musculoskeletal injury and combine this with an understanding of modern rehabilitative procedures. Experience is an extremely important ingredient. To successfully treat and rehabilitate the injured athlete, experience must be gained in dealing with athletes competing in a variety of sports and at varying levels of competition. For instance, it is difficult to treat the injured tennis player if one is not well versed in the biomechanics of the tennis serve and the mechanical characteristics of the equipment utilized. Therefore, it is imperative for the physiatrist with an interest in sports medicine to become familiar with the biomechanics of running, throwing, swimming, and jumping.[53] Practical experience can be gained by working with local teams and by participating in sports injury clinics. The sports medicine practitioner also is responsible for educating the community about prevention of injury and selection of proper equipment, proper training methods, and the use and abuse of ergogenic aids.

LEVELS OF COMPETITION

Goal setting is an important aspect of rehabilitative care. In the field of athletic medicine, goals can be defined based upon the type of injury and the competition level of the injured athlete.

The first competition level is the *recreational* athlete. This level comprises two types: the occasional recreational athlete (e.g., an individual who runs or plays tennis two or three times a week but does not compete in formal events) and the competitive recreational athlete (e.g., a serious athlete involved in ongoing training to improve performance while competing in races or matches, and whose needs and desires to return to competition are extremely high).

The next level of competition is the *institutional* level, comprising high school and university athletes who have commitments to their institutions and to their teams, are motivated to improve, and because of their athletic and academic calendars are on tight training schedules. Decisions regarding care must consider scheduling needs as well as the school seniority status of the competitor. The college senior participating in his or her last year of a sport with no intention of continuing in the professional ranks has goals different from those of a junior in high school competing for a collegiate scholarship.

The *professional* athlete is under pressure to perform and to continue to participate at a high level of efficiency. Team sports such as baseball, basketball, and football have organized sports medicine programs for team members. The nonaligned athletes—such as track and field participants, tennis players, and motorcycle racers—usually do not have organized health care and pursue this on an individual basis.

The final category of competition level is the *Olympic* athlete. This is a special individual who has chosen to put aside other goals and endeavors in his or her life to participate in Olympic competition. These individuals do not always have financial support and often do not have medical insurance. The donation of time and effort to Olympic athletes can be a rewarding experience both for the athlete and the sports medicine physician. Because Olympic athletes have only one opportunity to perform, their performance must be at the highest level attainable. The rehabilitation goals for these individuals, therefore, are geared toward the "moment of truth."

The age and sex of athletic participants require consideration in planning treatment goals and strategies. Unique physiologic as well as emotional issues in the pediatric athlete must be addressed in the rehabilitative care plan.[30,36] The geriatric population participates in athletic endeavors, most frequently tennis, golf, and walking. The rehabilitation of senior citizens should also be goal-oriented to enable them to maintain health and fitness. The female athlete has special problems, specifically bone mineralization and endocrinologic disorders.[10,26] Bone mineralization may predispose the female athlete to stress fractures as well as overuse injuries, both of which must be considered in rehabilitative care. Specific questions regarding exercise during pregnancy and postnatal periods must also be considered.[46]

PATHOPHYSIOLOGY OF INJURY AND HEALING

An adequate understanding of how injuries affect living tissue and how healing occurs is extremely important. During the first 7 days after an injury, the acute inflammatory process is in full force. Hemorrhage and infiltration of cellular elements occur at a rapid pace. This period of time should be looked upon as a productive phase and should not be unduly interrupted. The chemical mediators of the inflammatory response include prostaglandins, kallikreins, and bradykinins, which mediate the process and set the stage for the development of pain, effusion, and edema. The initial phases of the inflammatory response are reparative and necessary. However, continuation of the initial inflammatory response beyond the initial healing phases can be destructive and, therefore, deleterious to the outcome. The goal of initial rehabilitative procedures is to limit and curtail the inflammatory response and to treat the sequelae of pain, effusion, and immobility.

Two weeks following an injury (days 7–21) are marked by collagen proliferation produced by the newly infiltrated fibroblasts and cellular fibrin matrix. The collagen fibers are initially laid down in a random pattern. Unless specific stresses are placed upon the healing tissue to force the tissue to comply with Wolff's law, the newly produced collagen will become useless scar tissue.[1,2] Stretching of collagen tissue forces the collagen fibrils to become aligned in an organized pattern and, therefore, enhances range of motion and limits exuberant and unnecessary scar formation.[3] Elastin fibers, which are the most prominent component of ligaments (70–80% of the dry weight of the ligamentum nuchae), serve an important role in the maintenance of the tensile strength of tissue.[72] Stretching of ligamentous tissue has been demonstrated to cause proliferation of elastin fibrils. Ligamentous tissue that has been immobilized has no elastin fibrils and, therefore, poor tensile strength.[3,14,54]

Muscle strength and loss of strength secondary to immobility and injury are well recognized.[11,12,52] Inflammation and joint effusion are also important inhibitors of muscle strength and can cause rapid atrophy of juxta-articular musculature.[18,23] Loss of strength leads to delays in the rehabilitation process and in the return to full participation.

Several key points can be garnered from an understanding of the inflammatory process and its sequelae. First, the initial phase of healing following the injury is an important restorative process, which if inappropriately shortened by the early injudicious use of corticosteroids, will interfere with normal tissue healing.[40,66] This can lead to weakened support structures and prolonged disability. If the initial phase is prolonged, it will lead to excessive edema and scar formation as well as pain, loss of motion, and weakness. Administration of nonsteroidal anti-inflammatory agents within 24 hours after an ankle inversion injury has been shown to speed rehabilitation and to have no adverse effect on the mechanical integrity of tissue.[72]

The second key point concerns the proliferative phase of the inflammatory process. Early mobilization during this phase enhances normal collagen and elastin fiber deposition. Early mobilization also strengthens tendons and ligaments.[69,70] If prolonged immobilization occurs in this phase, soft tissue contracture and poor nutrition to intraarticular tissues result.[1] Therefore, shortening of the proliferative phase sets the stage for beginning functional rehabilitation.

The mechanism of sports-related injury can be divided into three categories: overuse, direct contact, and soft-tissue failure. The common factor in *overuse* injuries is repetitive microtrauma to an anatomic structure.[7] Frictional forces, tractional forces, and cyclical loading forces may cause secondary inflammation of involved structures, resulting in pain and disability. An example of frictional force is bursal inflammation over a bony prominence. An example of tractional force is plantar fasciitis in a runner.[17] An example of cyclical loading forces is stress fracture of a lower extremity.[48]

An example of a sports injury by *direct contact* is acromioclavicular joint separation in a football player secondary to direct impact to the shoulder girdle.

Soft tissue failure is the mechanism by which a single violent muscular contraction or effort can injure a structure without specific overuse and without contact. Examples are a pulled hamstring and rupture of an Achilles tendon.

PRINCIPLES OF REHABILITATION

The goal of rehabilitation is to restore an optimal state of health and function. Functional restoration must take into account the type, age, and level of performance of the athlete, the structure injured, the athlete's level of conditioning prior to the injury, and the level of conditioning to which the athlete must return. The rehabilitation process can be divided into the following phases, each of which is part of an overall plan to restore optimal function: (1) control of the inflammatory process, (2) control of pain, (3) restoration of joint range of motion and soft tissue extensibility, (4) improved muscular strength, (5) improved muscle endurance, (6) development of specific sports-related biomechanical skill patterns (i.e., coordination retraining), (7) improved general cardiovascular endurance, and (8) maintenance programs.

Surgical Planning.   The appropriate timing of surgical referral is an integral part of the rehabilitation continuum. Ongoing evaluation of the injured athlete allows the physician to develop reasonable therapeutic goals and guidelines.[22] Decisions regarding surgery must start with an accurate diagnosis. Careful workups—which include thoughtful radiographic radionuclide bone scans, electromyograms, and arthrograms—may be indicated according to the specific site and severity of the injury. The diagnostic algorithm for each injury will not be provided here, as it is beyond the scope of this article, but it should be familiar to all sports medicine physicians. It is important to obtain a social profile of the injured athletic to determine his or her goals and needs before surgical intervention is planned. Problems that obviously require surgical management such as grade III ligament injuries should be referred immediately to the surgeon on the sports medicine team. Injuries that do not respond to nonoperative rehabilitation should also be referred to a surgeon for consultation.

The SAID Principle.   The SAID principle—Specific Adaptation to Imposed Demands—is an important concept in sports rehabilitation. The SAID principle states that the body responds to a given demand with a specific predictable adaptation.[4] Therefore, if one can define the specific goals of the rehabilitation process, then the program designed can be tailored to meet that need. For instance, identifying a weak supraspinatus muscle in a throwing athlete with rotator cuff tendinitis and impingement syndrome necessitates strength training isolated to that particular muscle group as part of the rehabilitation process.[5]

The Team Approach.   Careful communication between the sports medicine physician and the trainer and/or physical therapist will ensure a good outcome. The team approach to sports medicine improves care. The partnership of a thoughtful sports-minded surgeon and a physiatric team member is invaluable.

The Timing of Rehabilitation.   The rehabilitation process begins immediately after injury and is terminated only when the injured athlete can successfully return to his or her previous level of competition. Carefully outlining rehabilitation goals prior to embarking upon a functional restoration program will eliminate the athlete's frustration and discouragement. The establishment of a precise diagnosis is the key to unlocking the rehabilitation plan. An improper or imprecise diagnosis can lead to major pitfalls in the treatment regimen. Early intervention results in control of inflammatory processes and speeds the recovery of normal articular and soft tissue range of motion. Early exercise enhances the early development of muscular strength, which has been shown to correlate with the development of stronger ligaments and tendons.[38,54,69,70]

These principles have long been applied to other rehabilitation situations and are well-known to the practicing physiatrist. One organizes the phases of rehabilitation for an injured athlete in the same manner as for a spinal-cord-injured patient—by the establishment of therapeutic goals. As in other forms of rehabilitation, the key ingredient to success appears to be the maintenance of motivation in the injured individual.

Phase I: Control of Inflammatory Process

The control of inflammation that occurs secondary to an injury can best be accomplished by the early application of ice, combined with elevation of the structure. Cryotherapy is the cornerstone in rehabilitation of the injured athlete. The purpose of cryotherapy is to control edema and to reduce pain. Ice can be applied in the form of crushed ice in a plastic bag, in an iced immersion tub, or as ice massage. The use of crushed ice in a plastic bag is specifically applicable to an acutely injured knee. The extremity is elevated, and ice is applied directly to the knee and held on with an Ace bandage. Limiting the initial development of joint effusion will speed the recovery process.[1] Ice is applied for 12 to 15 minutes, followed by a rest period, then reapplication. Immersion tubs are applicable to subacute injuries of the calf or hamstring. Ice massage finds its greatest use in the treatment of tendinitis, especially prior to and after exercise.[63]

The prescription of rest is also an important component of the treatment process during the inflammatory phase. The amount of rest should be specifically prescribed to the injured athlete and guidelines for progressive activity established. Non-weightbearing of the involved lower extremity during this early phase curtails inflammation. Likewise, the use of a sling or splint in the upper extremity serves the same purpose. Compression wrapping is also effective early after injury. The use of a horseshoe-shaped compression wrap on an ankle that has sustained an inversion sprain may significantly reduce edema.[21] When compression is combined with the other early components of treatment—which may include ice, elevation, rest, immobilization, and non-weightbearing—early control of the inflammatory process can be gained.

Nonsteroidal anti-inflammatory medications are extremely useful during this initial phase, and appear to speed recovery by curtailing the inflammatory response and controlling pain. During the acute phase of injury, glucocorticoids must be used cautiously. Their powerful anti-inflammatory effect may inhibit the normal healing process and thereby actually prolong rehabilitation.[34,40,66] For example, an acutely torn ligamentous structure would be harmed by the systemic or local application of corticosteroid during the first seven days. During the proliferative phase of the inflammatory process, especially after 14 to 21 days, the use of glucocorticoids can reduce an unchecked inflammatory response and control edema. The injection of glucocorticoids into tendon sheaths, bursae, and joints can rapidly reduce inflammation; however, the careful timing of these procedures is imperative. The infiltration of a tendon itself with glucocorticoids should be avoided. The Achilles tendon and patellar tendon have been reported to rupture after injection with corticosteroid.[40] On the other hand, injection into a tendon sheath, such as an inflamed abductor pollicis longus tendon, can markedly reduce inflammation and speed rehabilitation. Direct intratendinous injection of corticosteroid into the rotator cuff should be avoided. Injection of corticosteroid into the subacromial bursa combined with careful injection into the biceps tendon sheath as it rests in the intertubercular groove can reduce inflammation in the peritendinous structures. Injection of corticosteroid for muscle pulls, either during the acute or subacute stages, is not generally useful. However, if one can identify a specific area of restricting fibrosis in the musculotendinous unit in the subacute to the chronic phase, careful injection of corticosteroid followed by friction massage can be beneficial. The intraarticular injection of corticosteroid into a joint with synovitis in an individual who has had a previous osteochondral injury can be effective.

Continuation of nonsteroidal anti-inflammatory therapy throughout all phases of rehabilitation is often necessary. Careful monitoring for the development of side effects is strongly advised.[29]

Electrical galvanic stimulation (EGS) is useful in the reduction of edema. Pulsed, galvanic current coupled with ice is an effective means of controlling early edema.[8] Higher pulse rates of 75 per second and above will produce a tetanic muscle contraction and can be used to control acute pain. Lower frequencies of 1–5 Hz are useful in chronic pain control.[43] Iontophoresis can be a useful means for delivering corticosteroids to superficial inflamed soft tissue structures.[27,28] This technique can be applied in cases of patellar tendinitis, Achilles tendinitis, and wrist extensor tendinitis with lateral elbow pain and occasionally rotator cuff injuries.

During the later phases of the inflammatory process, ultrasound may be employed to enhance local circulation to remove the by-products of the inflammatory process, although the key role of ultrasound during this phase appears to be enhancement of soft tissue extensibility, thereby facilitating early motion. Phonophoresis can also be a successful way of delivering corticosteroids to superficial structures.[31,32] Patients tend to find phonophoresis more comfortable than iontophoresis.

Contrast baths are an ideal way to reduce resistant edema during the later phases of the inflammatory process. This is useful in soft tissue injuries about the ankle.

The duration of phase I is determined by edema and effusion control. Once joint effusion can be eliminated or minimized and interstitial edema controlled, the later phases of the rehabilitation process can proceed. Occasionally arthrocentesis is required to remove an excessive or stubborn knee joint effusion. The presence of hemarthrosis of the knee following an acute injury is a strong indicator of anterior cruciate ligament tear.[19]

Phase II: Control of Pain

The approach to pain control following a sports-related injury is similar to that of control of inflammation. Ice, rest, immobilization, and non-weightbearing are important components. Throughout the rehabilitation process, pain needs to be controlled. The use of ice is often the most successful approach. Applying ice prior to and after strengthening workouts is also beneficial.

Non-steroidal anti-inflammatory medications may be useful for the control of pain. Acetylsalicylate should be avoided during the early phases of injury. This is due to its antiplatelet activity, which persists for the life of the platelet, versus nonsteroidal anti-inflammatory agents in which the antiplatelet effect is entirely dose-related.[29] Opiate and nonopiate analgesic medications may be necessary during the very early phase of the post-injury treatment but should be used judiciously.

Transcutaneous nerve stimulation is a useful modality for treatment of acute pain following injury. The control of pain by transcutaneous nerve stimulation allows the injured athlete to participate in range of motion and strengthening programs. Acupuncture may be employed to control both acute post-injury pain as well as pain that limits function during the rehabilitation process. Acupuncture may also be used in lieu of examination of a joint under anesthesia to aid in the diagnosis of suspected acute knee and ankle ligament injuries. Acupuncture can be an extremely useful and reliable tool. Transcutaneous nerve stimulation and acupuncture raise the level of endorphins in the central nervous system.[62]

Protection of the injured structure can be accomplished by taping, padding, or bracing. In an unstable knee, a cast brace or knee immobilizer is useful. For an injured ankle, rigid taping combined with a compressive wrap serves a protective function. The use of slings to limit arm motion in acute acromioclavicular joint injuries may help to control post-injury pain. Cervical spine injuries that result in segmental instability necessitate immobilization until bone and soft tissue healing is sufficient to limit instability. A cervical collar may be worn to control pain from cervical facet or ligamentous injury. The period of immobilization or protection of the injured area must be adjusted for each injury. Careful reevaluation during the early phases of the program will inform the decision to continue or discontinue taping, bracing, or protective equipment.

Phase III: Restoration of Joint Range of Motion and Soft Tissue Extensibility

Prior to commencement of a strengthening program, the joint range of motion and soft tissue flexibility must be improved. Limited range of motion may result from muscular spasm, soft tissue tissue contracture, intraarticular blockade, and pain. The cause of the loss of motion will determine the treatment regimen.

Ice and electrical stimulation may help to alleviate muscle spasm. Ultrasound followed by a stretching program and friction massage is recommended for treating soft tissue contracture. Intraarticular blockade may be caused by a locked meniscus, for example, which requires operative intervention, or may be secondary to intraarticular fibrosis. Pain that inhibits joint motion may mimic intraarticular pathology. Alleviation of pain by TENS, acupuncture, or local anesthetic infiltration can aid in diagnosis, break the pain cycle, and enhance motion.

Range of motion programs may be classified as passive, active assistive, and active programs. In addition, a full flexibility program should be started after joint range of motion is attained. During the initial phases of range of motion restoration, careful passive techniques are utilized. This requires a skilled therapist and a cooperative patient. Static stretch and proprioceptive neuromuscular facilitation techniques, such as contract relax, the contraction of contralateral extremity and contraction of antagonistic muscle, can all be effective.[51,67] The use of the stationary bicycle to enhance knee range of motion by frequently adjusting the seat height is valuable. Active assistive range of motion should begin as early as the patient can tolerate it and is especially useful when the patient is not in the therapy gymnasium. Active assistive programs are effective for shoulder injuries; pulleys help to enhance motion. Active range of motion exercise can begin as the individual reaches the limits of normal range. The athlete should be taught specific exercises to ensure that a full range of motion is attained. The full flexibility program geared to attain maximal soft tissue flexibility can be started at the end of this phase.

The presence of instability must be noted and taken into consideration. Obviously, when a joint is unstable, vigorous range of motion exercises in certain planes are not advisable. For example, in anterior glenohumeral dislocation, abduction and external rotation should be avoided during the first 6 weeks of rehabilitation. Subsequently the gradual stretching of the anterior capsule can be accomplished, but theoretically the maintenance of some level of anterior capsule contracture may be of benefit to prevent further recurrences.[6] A hinged cast brace can be beneficial for a grade II medial collateral ligament injury.

Phase IV: Improved Muscular Strength

After the injured athlete has regained range of motion, phase IV begins. There are times when phase III and phase V treatment principles are used concurrently (for example, early isometric strengthening after ankle injury even prior to normalizing joint range of motion). In most cases, the patient is advised to gain at least 75% of range of motion before beginning strengthening programs. There are four basic types of strengthening programs: manual resistance, isometric, isotonic, and isokinetic. The exercises can be further subdivided into concentric contractions and eccentric contractions. Special programs for specific muscle groups have been designed. The limits of performance must be persistently extended to improve muscle strength. The rate of improvement appears to depend upon the willingness of the subject to overload.[16,20]

Isometric exercises comprise the initial phase of the strengthening program. The isometric phase can be carried out early on, while protecting joint motion. Manual resistance exercises begin once the joint can be moved. The therapist uses carefully graded manual resistance to act as the progressive resistor. As the patient is able to accomplish manual resistance exercises with comfort, the therapist notes the range that is appropriate to work within. It is important that the contractions be carried out in the pain-free range.[45]

When the patient has progressed through the manual resistance program and isometric program, pain-free ranges may be adjusted. Isometric contractions are optimally held for 5–6 seconds, with a rest period of between 10 and 20 seconds to ensure proper muscle blood flow and to remove the substrate of muscular contraction. The isometric contraction should be carried out frequently during the day, utilizing sets of 10–12 repetitions.[4] The goal is to transfer isometric strength development to the isotonic and/or isokinetic programs. Individuals who perform isometric exercises more frequently develop greater endurance, which transfers to progressive resistive exercises.

The concept of specificity of exercise should be kept in mind. Because dynamic muscle contraction is necessary in most athletic endeavors, merely training the muscle with static contractions (i.e., isometric contractions), even though this method can increase absolute static strength,[166] may not be transferable to the playing field.[4,33,41,42]

After the patient can successfully perform isometric and manual resistance exercises, either isotonic or isokinetic exercises are started. Isokinetic exercises are often preferable during this phase of the strengthening program because of the ability to control speed while maintaining force.[44,49] Studies have demonstrated that participants in both isokinetic and isotonic training programs eventually reach the same degree of absolute strength but that the participants in the isokinetic program reach that goal sooner with less post-workout soreness.[56]

The establishment of strength maintenance programs following the structured and supervised rehabilitation program is important. Teaching baseball pitchers and tennis players to maintain a level of strength in their supraspinatus muscles and to stretch their rotator cuffs has been found to be extremely useful in the prevention of recurrent rotator cuff injuries.[5,37,59]

The postsurgical patient must have a carefully planned program. Careful attention must be paid to the type of surgery and the healing time postoperatively. Specific programs for rehabilitation of the individual who has undergone an anterior cruciate repair or reconstruction have been developed by a variety of authors.[50,55,61,64,65] This topic is addressed in the chapter on postoperative knee rehabilitation.

Phase V: Improved Muscular Endurance

Costill has demonstrated the necessity for integrating strength and endurance programs into the muscle rehabilitation portions of the program. Because there is a specific response to the type of exercise performed, an exercise program must be tailored to the needs of the individual.[33] Steadman has employed a group of exercises that challenge the muscles in three different ways.[65] High-repetition, moderate-weight sets are performed initially, followed by rapid, low-resistance repetition until fatigue occurs. The last step is to hold an isometric contraction for approximately 1 minute. This type of program improves not only absolute strength but endurance, and enhances the anaerobic endurance required for burst-type activities.[15] Gaining muscle endurance entails stressing the aerobic pathways and improves the oxidative enzyme capacity of slow-twitch muscle fibers.[20] This necessitates higher-repetition work at lower weight levels.[9,13] These muscle endurance sets are useful as maintenance programs as well. Isolating the specific muscle contractions to be used for endurance training is based upon the knowledge of the particular sports activity.

The threshold of change in the development of muscular endurance is unclear. Therefore, the degree of intensity placed upon the muscle cannot be clearly defined. In one study, strength scores improved significantly when preceded by a program utilizing high-repetition work. Therefore, it would seem appropriate to start the athlete on a high-repetition, low-weight program before embarking on a higher resistance program.[22] This appears to allow time for cellular adaptation to occur and enhances the eventual strength gains of the participant.

The use of the stationary bicycle with variable resistance is extremely beneficial in a lower extremity muscle endurance program. Swimming and other hydrotherapy programs are useful in an upper extremity muscular endurance program. The maintenance of muscle endurance has been demonstrated to be a significant factor in the prevention of injury. It is not uncommon to see injuries occur late in competition or on the last ski run of the day. This appears to be related to depletion of oxidative enzymes in slow-twitch fibers, leading to fatigue of the musculature and inability of the musculature to protect the joint.[24]

Phase VI: Development of Specific Sports-Related Biomechanical Skill Patterns

To begin phase VI of the program the athlete has gained joint range of motion and soft tissue flexibility. He or she has increased muscular strength and improved muscular endurance. Work has also been undertaken to improve the speed of contraction with the use of high-speed lifting techniques. The athlete is now ready to begin specific training or retraining in the development of biomechanical and neurophysiologic skill patterns necessary for the specific sport.

The concept of specificity of exercise states that there is poor carryover from one type of exercise to another. In other words, to train an athlete who needs power, strength, and skill in running with only pool training would be inappropriate due to the poor carryover from the pool exercises to his land needs. As alluded to previously, the use of isometric strengthening solely as a strength development technique trains that particular muscle to obtain a static concentric contraction at that particular joint angle.[45,57] Therefore, strengthening activities must be carried out through the full arc of motion, and specifically through the full arc of motion utilized in the particular sporting endeavor. Training the enzyme systems that are physiologically necessary for the neuromuscular skeletal system to carry out its function should precede this phase. The neurophysiologic learning process to develop coordinated skill patterns is based upon constant repetition with careful attention to perfect the movement.[25,35] Substitution patterns must be avoided to reduce the possibility of a substitution engram occurring. Substitution patterns arise when certain muscle groups are either weak or inflexible or there is not full joint and soft tissue range of motion available to carry out the perfect movement. The most efficient engram pattern occurs with slow methodical repetition with minimal forced application. As the movement is carried out with greater degrees of precision, the speed and force can be increased. While the speed and force are being increased, it is imperative to watch for the development of substitution patterns. If substitution patterns develop, the speed and force must be reduced. Force should be minimized and replaced by coordinated movements of associated articulations to perform the movement.[35] An example of this would be the throwing motion. The acceleration of the throwing arm is most efficiently accomplished by trunk rotation. The rotator cuff muscles are utilized as stabilizers of the glenohumeral joint in order to maintain instantaneous center of rotation of the humerus and glenoid.[39] If excessive force is applied by the shoulder girdle musculature during the throwing motion, overuse injuries will occur as well as poor accuracy and early fatigue.[5,59,60]

The redevelopment of running and cutting skills after lower extremity injury is carried out in a similar fashion. The use of rolling slant boards to retrain proprioception of the ankle joint has been found to be useful in the rehabilitation of the ankle after repeat inversion sprains.[21] Careful progressive running should be carried out initially with fast walking and attention to gait style, eliminating possible substitution patterns and asymmetry. After the individual can carry out a normal gait pattern, then slow running is begun. Slow running is limited to the speed that can be accomplished pain-free without causing recurrent joint effusion and without using substitution patterns. The individual then advances to faster running. Fast running is done initially on soft surfaces such as grass or a track. A track appears to be better for this technique because of the constancy of terrain, which is not always obtainable on grass surfaces. The use of protective equipment such as ankle taping or knee bracing during this phase is continued. The athlete should gradually increase the stride length. After the patient can successfully run at 75% of maximum speed without pain or recurrent swelling, lazy S's and figure eights are begun slowly. The figure eights are made closer and run tighter and tighter as the athlete actually begins to start cutting. After this is successfully achieved, specific agility drills are performed, jumping in and out of obstacles and jumping on top and over obstacles such as automobile tires and wooden boxes. The amount of jumping depends upon the sport. The use of plyometric exercises appears to be valuable in this phase.[25] Ski racers obviously have a greater need for this type of training technique than do long-distance runners.

High-speed sprinting is also started during this phase followed by high-speed cutting. The progression through these running phases should be carried out slowly and methodically, and is best accomplished under the direction of a skilled physical therapist, athletic trainer, or coach. The principles outlined above should be carefully adhered to in order to avoid the development of substitution patterns. The recurrence of pain and/or swelling during this phase may necessitate medical reevaluation.

Similar programs have been devised for swimmers using kickboards and by progressively lengthening the stroke patterns. Careful technique is stressed and speed is the last element to be refined.

If the athlete is part of an organized athletic program, work with the coaching staff is helpful during this phase. The coach should look for specific flaws in technique which can be retrained to establish the necessary coordination engrams.

Coaches and therapists must stress the repetition of only precise movements. The repetition of imprecise movements is deleterious to the performance of the athlete and may potentially expose the individual to reinjury. Psychological support from the coaching staff, treating physician, and therapist/trainer is exceedingly important during this phase. The athlete must regain confidence during this reacculturation program.

Phase VII: Improved General Cardiovascular Endurance

During the entire functional restoration program, we have tried not to allow the injured athlete to remain sedentary. At the earliest possible moment, either stationary bicycle exercises or pool exercises are begun. The aerobic capacity of the athlete should not be allowed to drop during the early phases of the program. This particular phase, therefore, is more of a "topping off" of the aerobic needs of the athlete. The aerobic needs of a soccer player are different from those of a football lineman. A football lineman operates mostly in the anaerobic category, whereas a soccer player places great demands on the aerobic enzymatic system. The cardiovascular reconditioning program should be tuned to the sport. Long-distance swimmers and sprint swimmers should be trained in the pool doing their particular stroke, whereas running athletes should be trained using running programs. Consistency is the key to the development of aerobic capacity. Rapid dropoffs in aerobic capacity occur with cessation of this type of training. A five-times-per-week aerobic program of at least 30 minutes per session, with the athlete exercising at greater than 75% percent of heart rate, is recommended. Obviously, special precautions must be taken in middle-aged athletes, who may have preexisting cardiac disease. The early recognition of possible cardiovascular abnormalities or disease is important.[47,58,68,71]

Substitution of one aerobic program for another during the rehabilitation program is often necessary. Early in a program, swimming may be the aerobic program of choice. Later, the athlete progresses to running in the pool, and finally to a running program, as described in the Skills section. Some athletes may not be able to resume previous levels of activity and will be forced to switch from running activities to bicycling and/or swimming training on a permanent basis. Bicyclists are able to use stationary turbo trainers in order to use their bicycles indoors or they can use standard stationary bike equipment. The Schwinn Airo-Dyne bicycle, which couples arm and leg motion, is a beneficial form of aerobic training. This bicycle enables the athlete to use large muscle groups in the upper and lower extremities in varying patterns. Rowing machines, seated pedal cycles, stair steppers, and cross-country ski machines are other useful ways to improve aerobic function.

After the completion of all these phases of training, maintenance programs for flexibility, strength, and aerobic maintenance are designed.

Criteria for Return to Play

One of the most important and difficult decisions the sports medicine physician faces is deciding when to allow the athlete to return to activity and at what level. The basic guidelines provided below are discussed in greater detail in the following section. When the athlete has:

1. full range of motion,
2. normal strength,
3. normal neurologic examination,
4. no persistent swelling,

    5. no unchecked joint instability,

    6. ability to run without pain,

    7. been instructed in proper warmup, flexibility, and strength program,

    8. been instructed in proper use of ice and heat,

    9. been instructed regarding proper taping and bracing to protect the injured area,

    10. been instructed to report increases in pain and post-exercise swelling to the physician and/or trainer and coaching staff,

    11. not taking corticosteroid or analgesic medications, and

    12. been informed regarding the risks of future injury and disability as it relates to the injury and the chosen sport.

The guidelines presented above are broad and general and may not precisely fit every clinical circumstance. For instance, the loss of the end ranges of motion in an injured metacarpal joint or a previously operated-upon knee may not militate against competition. The strength requirements for return to competition are also not absolute. After a neurologic insult such as a brachial plexus injury, regaining full strength prior to returning to activity is necessary as is a normal neurologic examination. But a patient who has undergone anterior cruciate reconstruction may be able to return to competition at $80+\%$ of strength, compared with the opposite side, if movement retraining shows no functional deficiencies. Small amounts of swelling can be tolerated; however, a continually effused ankle and knee indicates that the athlete should not return to activity. Joint instability that is braced, taped, or well-compensated for by muscular mechanisms is not a contraindication for return to athletics, whereas unchecked joint instability noted during movement retraining is.

When the athlete returns to activity, drugs that significantly alter the perception of pain should be eliminated. Corticosteroids and opiate analgesics fall into this category. There are arguments against the use of nonsteroidal anti-inflammatory drugs, but in my opinion they can be utilized in the athlete who returns to activity. Running without pain is a criterion for most sports, but obviously has no bearing on water sports, equestrian activities, or weight lifting.

SUMMARY

The general principles of rehabilitation presented will allow one to design a thoughtful and rational care plan. These guidelines are intended to assist the decision-making process but need to be adapted to each individual. The level of competition and the social profile of the athlete are important factors that color all decisions in this regard. The whole scheme is predicated upon accurate diagnosis and early intervention. Rehabilitation programs and their rationale are presented for each anatomic area in the chapters that follow.

REFERENCES

1. Akeson WH: An experimental study of joint stiffness. J Bone Joint Surg 43A:1022–1034, 1961.
2. Akeson WH, Amiel D, LaViolette D: The connective tissue response to immobility: A study of chrondroitin-4 and 6-sulfate and dermatan sulfate changes in periarticular connective tissue of control and immobilized knees of dogs. Clin Orthop 51:183–197, 1967.
3. Akeson WH, Wo SLY, Amiel D, et al: Connective tissue response to immobility. Clin Orthop 93:356–362, 1973.
4. Allman FL: Exercise in sports medicine. *In* Basmajian JV (ed): Therapeutic Exercise, 9th ed. Baltimore, Williams and Wilkins, 1984.
5. Aronen JG: Shoulder rehabilitation. Clin Sports Med 4:477–493, 1985.
6. Aronen JG, Regan K: Decreasing the incidence of recurrence of first-time anterior shoulder dislocations with rehabilitations. Am J Sports Med 12:283–291, 1984.

7. Beck JL, Day RW: Overuse injuries. Clin Sports Med 4:553, 1985.
8. Blackburn TA: Rehabilitation of anterior cruciate ligament injuries. Orthop Clin North Am 16:244–249, 1985.
9. Bonde-Petersen F, Grandal H, Hansen JW, Hvid N: The effect of varying the number of muscle contractions on dynamic muscle training. Eur J Appl Physiol 18:468–473, 1966.
10. Bonen A, Keitzer HA: Athletic menstrual cycle irregularity: Endocrine response to exercise and training. Phys Sportsmed 7:83–95, 1984.
11. Booth FW: Time course of muscular atrophy during immobilization of hind limbs in rats. J Appl Physiol 43:656–661, 1977.
12. Booth FW, Seider MJ: Effects of disuse by limb immobilization on different muscle fiber types. *In* Pette D (ed): Plasticity of Muscle. New York, de Gruyter, 1980.
13. Burger RA: Optimal repetitions for the development of strength. Res Q 33:334–338, 1962.
14. Chvapil M: Physiology of Connective Tissue. London, Butterworth Publishers, Inc., 1967.
15. Costill DL, Coyle EF, Fink WF, et al: Adaptations in skeletal muscle following strength training. J Appl Physiol 46:149, 1976.
16. Costill DL, Fink WJ, Habansky AJ: Muscle rehabilitation after knee surgery. Phys Sportsmed 5:71–74, 1977.
17. D'Ambrosia RD, Drez D: Orthotics. *In* D'Ambrosia RD, Drez D: Prevention and Treatment of Running Injuries. Thorofare, NJ, Charles B. Slack, 1982.
18. DeAndrade JR, Grant C, Dixon AS: Joint distention and reflex muscle inhibition in the knee. J Bone Joint Surg 47:313–322, 1965.
19. DeHaven KE: Diagnosis of acute knee injuries with hemarthrosis. Am J Sports Med 8:9–14, 1980.
20. DeLateur BJ: Exercise for strength and endurance. *In* Basmajian JV (ed): Therapeutic Exercise, 9th ed. Baltimore, Williams and Wilkins, 1984.
21. Derscheid GL, Brown WC: Rehabilitation of the ankle. Clin Sports Med 4:July 1985.
22. Dickinson AD, Bennett KN: Therapeutic exercise. Clin Sports Med 4:417–429, 1985.
23. Edstrom L: Selective atrophy of red muscle fibre in the quadriceps in long-standing knee-joint dysfunction. J Neurol Sci 11:551–559.
24. Ericksson F: Anatomical, histological and physiological factors in experienced downhill skiers. Orthop Clin North Am 7:159–165, 1976.
25. Fahey TD: Physiological adaptation to conditioning. *In* Fahey TD (ed): Athletic Training: Principles and Practice. Mayfield Publishing Co., 1986.
26. Frisch RE, Wyshak G, Vincent L: Delayed menarche and amenorrhea in ballet dancers. N Engl J Med 303:17–19, 1980.
27. Gangarosa LP, Park N, Wiggins CA, Hill JM: Increased penetration of nonelectrolytes into mouse skin during iontophoretic water transport (iontohydrokinesis). J Pharmacol Exp Ther 212:1980.
28. Glass JM, Stephen RL, Jacobson SC: The quality and distribution of radiolabeled dexamethasone delivered to tissue by iontophoresis. Int Soc Trop Dermatol 19:519–525, 1980.
29. Goodman AG, Gilman LS, Gilman A: The Pharmacological Basis of Therapeutics, 6th ed. New York, Macmillan 1980, p. 686.
30. Grana WA, Kriegshauser LA: Scientific basis of extensor mechanism disorders. Clin Sports Med 4:247–257, 1985.
31. Griffin JE, Touchstone JC: Ultrasonic movement of cortisol into pig tissues. Am J Phy Med Rehabil 44:77–84, 1965.
32. Griffin JE, Touchstone JC, Liu AC: Ultrasonic movement of cortisol into pig tissue. Am J Phys Med Rehabil 44:20–25, 1965.
33. Halling A, Dooley J: The importance of isokinetic power and its specificity to athletic conditions. Athletic Training, Summer 1979, pp. 83, 86.
34. Halpern AA, Horowitz BG, Nagel DA: Tendon ruptures associated with corticosteroid therapy. West J Med 127:378–432, 1977.
35. Harris FA: Facilitation techniques and technological adjuncts in therapeutic exercise. *In* Basmajian JV (ed): Therapeutic Exercise, 9th ed. Baltimore, Williams and Wilkins, 1984.
36. Harvey JS Jr: Overuse syndromes in young athletes. Clin Sports Med 2:595–607, 1983.
37. Hawkins RJ, Hobeika PE: Impingement syndrome in the athletic shoulder. Clin Sports Med 2:391–405, 1983.
38. Hirsch G: Tensile properties during tendon healing. Acta Orthop Scand 153(Suppl):1–145, 1974.
39. Jobe FW, Tibone JE, Perry J, Moynes D: An EMG analysis of the shoulder in throwing and pitching. Am J Sports Med 11:3–5, 1983.
40. Kennedy JC, Baxter-Willis R: The effects of local steroid injections on tendons: A biochemical and microscopic correlative study. Am J Sports Med 4:11–18, 1976.
41. Knapik JJ, Wright JE, Mawdsley RH, Braun JM: Isokinetic isometric and isotonic strength relationships. Arch Phys Med Rehabil 64:77–80, 1983.

42. Knapik JJ, Wright JE, Mawdsley RH, Braun J: Isometric, isotonic, and isokinetic torque variations in four muscle groups through a range of joint motion. Phys Ther 63:939–947, 1983.
43. Lampe GN, Mannheimer JS: Clinical Transcutaneous Electrical Nerve Stimulation. Philadelphia, F.A. Davis, 1984, pp. 210–212.
44. Lesmes GR, Costill DL, Coyle EF, Fink WJ: Muscle strength and power changes during maximal isokinetic training. Med Sci Sports 10:266–269, 1978.
45. Lindh M: Increase of muscle strength from isometric quadriceps exercise at different knee angles. Scand J Rehabil Med 11:33–36, 1979.
46. Lutter JM: Health concerns for women runners. Clin Sports Med 4:615, 1985.
47. Maron BJ, Roberts WC, McAllister HA, et al: Sudden death in young athletes. Circulation 62:218–229, 1980.
48. McBryde AM: Stress fractures in runners. Clin Sports Med 4:635, 1985.
49. Moffroid M, Whipple R, Hofkoch J, et al: A study of isokinetic exercise. J Am Phys Ther Assoc 49:735–747, 1969.
50. Montgomery JB, Steadman JR: Rehabilitation of the injured knee. Clin Sports Med 4:333–343, 1985.
51. Moore MA, Hutton RS: Electromyographic investigation of muscle stretching techniques. Med Sci Sports 12:322–329, 1980.
52. Muller EA: Influence of training and of inactivity on muscle strength. Arch Phys Med Rehabil 51:449–462, 1970.
53. Nicholas JA, Grossman RB, Hershman EB: The importance of a simplied classification of motion in sports in relation to performance. Orthop Clin North Am 8:499, 1977.
54. Noyes FR: Functional properties of knee ligaments and alterations induced by immobilization: A correlative biomechanical and histological study in primates. Clin Orthop 123:210–242, 1977.
55. Paulos L, Noyes FR, Grood E, Butler DL: Knee rehabilitation after anterior cruciate ligament reconstruction and repair. Am J Sports Med 9:140–149, 1981.
56. Pipes TU, Wilmore J: Isokinetic vs. isotonic strength training in adult men. Med Sci Sports Exercise 7:262–274.
57. Rasch PJ, Morehouse LE: Effect of static and dynamic exercises on muscular strength and hypertrophy. J Appl Physiol 11:29–1957.
58. Raskoff WJ, Goldman S, Cohn K: The "athletic heart." JAMA 236:158–162, 1976.
59. Richardson AB: Overuse syndromes in baseball, tennis, gymnastics and swimming. Clin Sports Med 2:379–390, 1983.
60. Richardson AR: The biomechanics of swimming: The shoulder and knee. Clin Sports Med 5:1986.
61. Sherman WM, Pearson DR, Plyley MJ, et al: Isokinetic rehabilitation following surgery: A review of factors which are important to developing physiotherapeutic techniques following knee surgery. Am J Sports Med 10:155–161, 1981.
62. Sjolund BH, Terenius L, Eriksson M: Increased cerebrospinal fluid levels of endorphins after electroacupuncture. Acta Physiol Scand 100:383, 1977.
63. Stanish WD, et al: Tendinitis: analysis and treatment. Clin Sports Med 4:593–608, 1986.
64. Stanitski CL: Rehabilitation following knee injury. Clin Sports Med 4:495–511, 1985.
65. Steadman JR: Rehabilitation after knee ligament surgery. Am J Sports Med 9:294–296, 1980.
66. Sweetham R: Corticosteorid arthropathy and tendon rupture. J Bone Joint Surg 51B:397–398, 1969.
67. Tanigawa MC: Comparison of the hold-relax procedure and passive mobilization on increasing muscle length. Phys Ther 52:725–735, 1972.
68. Thompson PD, Stern MP, Williams P, et al: Death during jogging or running. JAMA 242:1265–1267, 1979.
69. Tipton CM, James SL, Mergner W: Influence of exercise in strength of medial collateral ligaments of dogs. Am J Physiol 218:894–902, 1970.
70. Tipton CM, Schild RJ, Tomanek RJ: Influence of physical activity on the strength of knee ligaments in rats. Am J Physiol 212:783–787, 1967.
71. Virmani R: Jogging, marathon running, and death. Hosp Phys 18:A28–A39, 1982.
72. Woo SLY, Matthews JV, Akeson WH, et al: Connective tissue response to immobility: A correlative study of biochemical and biomechanical measurements of normal and immobilized rabbit knees. Arthritis Rheum 18:257–264, 1975.

JOEL S. SAAL, MD

FLEXIBILITY TRAINING

Reprint requests to Joel S. Saal,
M.D., Sports, Orthopedic and Rehabilitation Medicine Associates,
3250 Alpine Rd., Portola Valley, CA
94025.

Stretching has become a popular prelude to most athletic events. Flexibility training is widely accepted as an essential part of any conditioning program and has been promoted as a means of avoiding injury and improving perfor-mance.[18,19,20,28,35,39,51,56,76,91,92,104] A consider-able sport experience and theoretical basis support the importance of adequate flexibility in all ath-letes.[2-4,9,28,29,39,95,96] Flexibility training is a two-edged sword, however, as it is not without risk, having the potential to cause significant injury if performed incorrectly.[91,95,96,97] It must be ap-proached within a program outlined for the spe-cific needs of the individual athlete's body and sport.

The nature of flexibility is complex, with an interplay of connective tissue biophysics, the neu-rophysiology of motor control, and human joint kinematics. A flexibility training program should be approached with a view toward the full com-plement of tissues that must be stretched. Al-though flexibility clearly plays a role in sports injury and performance,[1,5,7,16,18,20,24,28,29,35,56,63,67,76,79,82,83,91,92,96,104,113,118] there is conjec-ture regarding optimal stretching methods, indi-cations, and measurement. While a great deal of information is available in basic science, the clin-ical literature is less precise. There is, however, an adequate basis for necessitating flexibility training and for establishing criteria for safe and effective stretching programs.

DEFINITION

For the purposes of this chapter, flexibility is defined as follows: the total achievable excur-sion (within limits of pain) of a body part through its potential range of motion. This includes the range of motion not only of the major joint in-volved but also of all contiguous joints and soft tissues. For example, shoulder girdle flexibility includes glenohumeral, scapulothoracic, sternoclavicular, acromioclavicular, sternocostal, and costochondral motion, as well as soft tissues of the anterior chest wall (including intercostal musculature). It also includes the periscapular and intrinsic shoulder musculature, and the above-mentioned joints' capsules and attendant ligamentous support.

It is important to clearly establish the differences between flexibility and joint laxity. Flexibility refers to extensibility of periarticular tissues to allow normal or physiologic motion of a joint or limb. Laxity refers to the stability of a joint, which is dependent upon its supporting structures (ligaments, capsule, and bony continuity). Excessive laxity could result from chronic injury or congenital hyperelasticity (e.g., Ehlers-Danlos syndrome) of stabilizing capsular structures with the presence of positive instability maneuvers (e.g., anterior drawer in knee or ankle, talar tilt, etc.). In general and for the purposes of this chapter, the term ''flexibility'' refers to the degree of normal motion and ''laxity'' to the degree of abnormal motion of a given joint.

Adequate flexibility implies an ideal state of length and elasticity of the structures crossing joints and affecting single or multiple joint motion (such as the hamstring muscle crossing the hip and knee joints). The goal of a flexibility training program is to develop adequate flexibility without causing injury or excessive joint laxity. To accomplish this, the program must consider the axis and potential range of motion of the joints involved. This potential range includes all planes of motion of a given joint (within physiologic limits of boundary tissues). Flexibility training includes stretching and mobilization. The term stretching is used to define an activity that applies a deforming force along the plane of linear motion of a joint. It can be performed safely up to the limits of comfortable tension. The term mobilization describes the application of force along the rotational or translational planes of motion of a joint. It should be performed along the lines of geometry of the joint and within the planes of stability of the joint. Theoretically, joint capsular structures as well as nonarticular structures have a basic requirement to maintain optimal elasticity. In the injured athlete, this may assume an even greater significance. A combination of these activities is necessary for complete flexibility training.

DETERMINANTS OF BODY FLEXIBILITY

The determinants of normal joint mobility includes both static and dynamic factors. Among the static factors are the type and state of collagen subunits in the tissue, types of intervening tissue (i.e., ligament, tendon, muscle, loose connective tissues), presence or absence of inflammation and, within limits, the temperature of the tissue. The dynamic factors include voluntary muscle control variables, the length-tension ''thermostat'' of the muscle-tendon unit, and the presence or absence of painful or other inhibitory factors associated with injury. Each of these will be discussed individually in the context of its contribution to flexibility and normal joint mobility.

The muscle tendon unit is probably the most important target site of flexibility training. It is the basic functional effector unit of motion and must withstand forces greater than body weight delivered over a small area. It is also the major site of injury related to lack of flexibility.[18–20,24,29,60] The muscle tendon unit includes the full length of the muscle and its supporting tissue, the full length of the tendon and tendon bone junction, as well as the muscle-tendon junction. Specific studies of the forces delivered to these structures separately have not been performed, and precisely which structures are lengthened with each given stretching maneuver is not known. There is conjecture about the relative contribution of various individual tissues, the most widely accepted view being that the greatest role is played by muscle, followed by loose (areolar) connective tissue, then dense connective tissue (ligament and tendon).[13,42,64,65,93,100,101,102] Each of these tissues has the capacity to lengthen in response to an applied force as shown in in-vivo and in-vitro animal studies.[40,42,45,54,55,65,66,68,106,108]

Although muscle differs structurally from the other components of the stretch, there is evidence that its mechanical behavior is in part due to its connective tissue components,[13,93] with some qualification as to what degree this behavior exists in intact muscle under conditions of physiologic loading. Sapega argues that muscle behaves primarily in this manner.[93] However, in the awake and alert state, muscle is not relaxed enough or electrically silent at all levels to behave purely in this manner. This is evident in the effectiveness of physiologic maneuvers aimed at neural inhibition for facilitating stretch.[57,63,72,81,105] Additionally, the bending stiffness of the trunk is greater in the alert than in the anesthetized state, presumably because of dynamic muscle factors (static contraction) rather than material stiffness.[94] Hill theorized that muscles' elastic properties were due to an elastic component in parallel to the contractile component.[46,47]

Of the tissues involved in a stretch, muscle probably has the largest capacity for percent lengthening.[51,55,101,102] One study demonstrated a ratio of 95% to 5% for muscle tendon length change.[101] However, the capacity of a given tissue for absolute lengthening is not necessarily equivalent to the importance of that tissue in a stretching program. In this regard, tendon may have the greatest significance. Despite its limited capacity for lengthening (2–3% of its length compared with approximately 20% for muscle),[27,40,101,102,120] tendon must withstand repeated stresses that require it to be maintained at its optimal length and elasticity. Similarly, fibrous joint capsules supply a significant percentage of overall stiffness of a joint[55] and, therefore, have a minimum requirement for an applied stretching force.

IMPORTANCE OF FLEXIBILITY

The inability to clearly define injuries by a "gold standard" diagnostic test has made it difficult to draw definitive conclusions regarding the relevance of any of the interventions used in daily practice on all levels of sports medicine. Although it has been demonstrated that the application of flexibility programs can prevent muscle injuries,[1,28,29,85] it has been difficult to document the full extent of the observed empirical benefit of flexibility on injury prevention (further divided into major knee injuries, tendinitis, and muscle tears), performance enhancement, and rehabilitation of sports surgeries.

The relationship between degree of flexibility and the occurrence of major knee injuries (ligament disruption, internal derangement) has received a great deal of attention in the literature. The results, however, are far from conclusive. Nicholas[85] demonstrated a correlation between five tests of laxity/flexibility and the occurrence of third-degree muscle strains and major knee injuries in a group of professional football players. There was an increased relative incidence of major knee injuries in players with increased joint laxity and an increased incidence of muscle tears in players with poor flexibility. There was no clear separation between flexibility and laxity, however, and subsequent attempts by other authors gave conflicting results. Subsequent studies[36,58,82] found a wide variation between subjective assessment of joint laxity between different trained examiners and results contrary to those of Nicholas. Numerous clinical studies to date (both prospective cohort studies and retrospective cross-sectional studies) display a general agreement that the major predictive factor for joint injury was a previous joint injury or the presence of excessive joint laxity, and not necessarily inadequate flexibility.[28,29,36,39,58,60,96] A prospective study of a flexibility program in soccer players showed a correlation of improved range of motion and a decrease in muscle tears.[28] Additionally, this study revealed poorer flexibility in hip range of motion in soccer players than in age-matched controls. A more recent review of all studies of soccer injuries[60] suggested an important role for flexibility in the prevention of injury, especially in older players. Muscle strain and tendinitis are more common in older and less flexible soccer players, and up to 11% of all injuries are related to poor flexibility.[28,60]

There are major injuries as a direct or an indirect result of inadequate flexibility that were not evaluated by any of these studies. There is a detailed biomechanical evidence to show that lower extremity flexibility is needed for prevention of lumbar spine injuries.[32,33] Indeed, there is report of increased frequency of spondylolysis/spondylolisthesis in kindreds with severe hamstring inflexibility.[89] In a given individual with a history of back injury, flexibility plays a vital role in reducing further stresses on the spine. Adequate cervical spine mobility and flexibility in both uninjured and injured athletes is important to allow for the normal function of this very complex structure. However, no systematic evaluation of the role of flexibility in spine injury prevention in athletics has been performed. An anthropometric analysis of adolescents with and without back pain found a significant association of lower extremity inflexibility and back symptoms.[31] In the industrial setting, Cady found an inverse relationship between the degree of flexibility and the incidence of back injuries and Workers' Compensation costs in a cohort study of firefighters placed on a fitness program.[12] Considering the high incidence of spine injury and related complaints that exist on all levels of organized football, this is an area that needs investigation.

It is again important to distinguish between flexibility and laxity in reference to cervical spine injuries in football. Adequate soft tissue flexibility and intervertebral joint mobility do not imply lack of muscular strength or stability. Improved flexibility allows for a better dynamic stability, which is critical for the prevention of cervical spine injury. In this setting, the presence of adequate flexibility in no way militates against adequate stability.

There are areas of inflexibility common to a large percentage of athletes that contribute to excessive forces at the intervertebral joints, the knee, and the ankle. The iliopsoas and anterior hip soft tissues are frequently overlooked and directly contribute to excessive torque at the intervertebral disk if their inflexibility does not allow for full excursion at hip extension. This requires greater pelvic rotation both in the transverse and the sagittal planes, transferring increased force across the lower lumbar disk spaces.[32,33] The hip rotators have a similar role in indirect injury prevention. The sternoclavicular and costoclavicular joints, in combination with the anterior chest and chest wall soft tissues are important for adequate rotation at the level of thoracic spine, in maintenance of thoracic and cervicothoracic posture, and in the prevention of untoward traction on neurovascular structures in the thoracic outlet. This is an area without a quantifiable measure of range of motion or a controlled evaluation for injury prevention.

In the setting of injury, flexibility takes on an even more crucial role in the function of the athlete. Where strength has been lost, or pain limits force production, the resistance offered by soft tissues can lead to abnormal movement patterns. The abnormal excursions of joints allows for further adaptive shortening of soft tissues as well as excessive forces on joints, thereby establishing a vicious circle. This is especially common in the spine and shoulder girdle. Restoration of adequate flexibility on a regional basis along with specific strength and movement training is the cornerstone of physical rehabilitation. There are, however, situations in which withholding stretching is in order. Joint instability should not be treated by mobilization and aggressive stretching. A hypermobile structure requires stabilization, not mobilization. This is an issue commonly faced in spine and shoulder rehabilitation. In the presence of anterior instability of the shoulder, stretching the posterior capsule while allowing for adaptive shortening of the anterior capsule is the program of choice. Conversely, a frozen or severely hypomobile joint requires mobilization (for a capsular stretch) as well as stretch of extra-articular structures. Following ankle sprains it is crucial to restore the normal anterior ankle glide at the tibio-talar joint. This is accomplished by a combination of mobilization in an anteroposterior plane as well as stretching in the Achilles tendon and medial structures. In general, these principles govern the major use of flexibility within rehabilitation of sports and other musculoskeletal injuries.

There appears to be less controversy regarding the importance of inflexibility of soft tissues (i.e., muscle and tendon) in the pathogenesis of tendinitis than in the etiology of major joint injury. It is considered by many researchers to play a causative role in Achilles tendinitis. However, the mechanism of its role is not clear. Although biomechanical properties of tendon have been shown to involve a change in fiber pattern following application of stretching force in vitro, the in vivo event is not certain.[19] The sites of tendinitis have been demonstrated to coincide with areas of relatively lower blood flow than neighboring portions of tendon.[20,70] There are no data to prove that flexibility training alters that blood flow per se. As previously mentioned, the relative change in length with an applied stretching force for tendon is much smaller than for muscle. Although common stretching maneuvers may deliver some force to the tendon itself, the majority of deformation probably occurs in the muscle bellies.[16,51,101,102] The force generated at the tendon insertion increases in a nonlinear manner as the elasticity of intervening tissues along the lever arm of force decreases.[18–20] However, the symptomatic improvements noted with flexibility programs in the treatment of tendinitis may be largely due to a change in muscle function, rather than simply to a change in the biomechanical profile of the tendon substance. Despite the mechanical uncertainties, flexibility training appears to be valuable in the treatment and prevention of many sites of tendinitis.

Despite the interest on the part of many experts, there exists little experimental documentation of enhancement of sport performance by improved flexibility. A program of sprint training combined with flexibility training failed to show a significant improvement in running speed compared with sprint training alone.[36] There is, however, a physiologic basis upon which speed, strength, and agility may be improved with ideal flexibility. The performance of fine and repetitive motor control requires a delicately balanced sensitivity of proprioception (''muscle-tendon memory'') as transmitted through a complex arrangement of receptors in series and in parallel within the muscle and connective tissue architecture. Owing to the plastic nature of collagen-based connective tissue, a regularly applied stretching force will affect the fiber array of collagen and thereby determine the mechanical properties of the musculotendinous or ligament-bone unit. Similarly, the arrangement of tension control receptors and effectors within muscle would also be directly affected by an applied stretching force. I would advance that an ideal state of flexibility in the individual would heighten the sensory feedback mechanism to the athlete's advantage of increased proprioceptive accuracy and sensitivity.

Some variables in performance—such as grace, ease of movement, fluidity, and style—are difficult to measure in a quantitative or isolated manner. These play a specific performance role in dance, gymnastics, and ice and figure skating, but they are becoming more influential in an overall sense of ability in sports like basketball, football and soccer.[16] The feedback system of joint proprioceptor and pressure sensors, and the interplay of musculotendinous receptors of stretch (Golgi-tendon, intrafusal) underlie this aspect of performance.

It should be noted that delayed muscular soreness may be altered by a flexibility program. Although the etiology of this troublesome condition is controversial and probably multifactorial, there is some evidence that it can be prevented and treated by static stretching.[22,24] Enhancement of the force of muscle contraction has been demonstrated in prestretched muscle, with an increase relative to the degree of pre-stretch.[10,11,14,15,18,19,100] Training methods based upon elastic stretch followed by immediate contraction have been developed to capitalize on this observed effect. Although Cavagna demonstrated that the greater amount of work performed could not be accounted for purely on the basis of the elastic property of muscle, this type of activity places a greater stress upon the elastic component.[14] A study of the effect of intense flexibility training on the function profile of knee extensors revealed no change in maxiumum force of contraction, but significant improvement was seen in speed of repetitive isometric contractions, relaxation time, and stride frequency on treadmill running.[51] The optimization of muscle performance by improvement in flexibility, therefore, has a theoretical basis.

BIOPHYSICAL ASPECTS OF FLEXIBILITY

The manner in which muscle and connective tissue respond to stretching is a direct reflection of their structure and chemistry. Although they differ in their overall structure, there are similarities that allow each of these tissue types to respond to stretching with a permanent (lasting, but not irreversible) elongation. Muscle is arranged on a cellular level as overlapping filaments of actin-myosin, with a varying number of tropomyosin cross-bridges (Fig. 1). These are enclosed within the sar-colemma (muscle cell membrane) delineating individual myofibrils. The myofibrils are arranged in parallel and series within a sequence of connective tissue layers (endomysium, perimysium, then epimysium) to form the whole muscle. Within an individual myofibril, the contractile units are divided into sarcomeres (Fig. 1).

Connective tissue is largely composed of a collagen fibers, which are made up to individual fibrils composed of an overlapping arrangement of tropocollagen subunits (Fig. 2). The collagen fibers are combined with a smaller number of elastin fibers woven as a mesh within a matrix ground substance composed of varying amounts of proteoglycans and numbers of fibroblasts. The collagen fibers are found in a wavy, longitudinal arrangement in ligament, and in a more parallel arrangement in tendon. In areolar connective tissue (loose connective tissue that surrounds other structures such as organs or tendons and muscle) the fibers are oriented in a more random fashion, resulting in slightly different physical properties (i.e., increased deformation with low-level force). There are specific subtypes of collagen depending on the specific tissue, with differing physical properties. In general, tendon and ligament are composed of type-I collagen. There are a few specialized structures, such as ligamentum flavum and ligamentum nuchae, that contain a greater amount of elastic tissue.

Connective tissues are, for the most part, sparsely cellular in their mature state. They are, however, metabolically active tissues, relying upon the continued syn-thesis of specialized matrix substances (proteoglycans) and collagen turnover for the maintenance of their specific function. There is, to some degree, a natural order in connective tissue; it has an inherent tensile force and will naturaly shorten to the

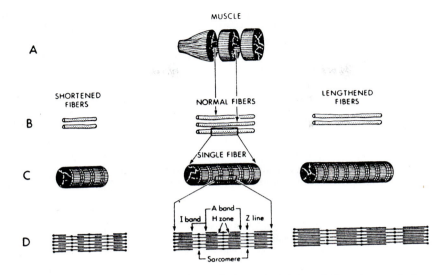

FIGURE 1. The structure of normal muscle (center) and the relative changes that occur when a muscle undergoes changes due to a shortened position (left) or lengthened position (right). *A*, Skeletal muscle composed of single fibers (cells). *B*, Single fibers. *C*, Single fiber enlarged to show myofibrils; note decreased and increased sarcomere numbers in the shortened and lengthened fibers, respectively. *D*, Myofibril enlarged to show contractile proteins of the sarcomere (actin and myosin myofilaments); note increased and decreased sarcomere length in the shortened and lengthened fibers, respectively. Both neurophysiologic (alteration in sarcomere length) and structural (change in sarcomere number) adaptations are presented. (Adapted from Gossman.[40])

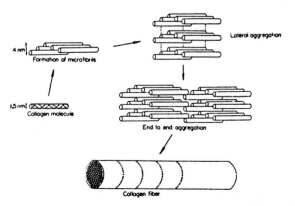

FIGURE 2. Formation of the five-membered microfibril and its potential for lateral and end-to-end aggregation to form fibers. (Adapted from Nimni.[86])

shape in which it is maintained if not subjected to an outside deforming force on a regular basis.[65,86–88] This occurs through the continuous remodeling of collagen, the turnover of collagen molecules, and the production and removal of the proteoglycan matrix.[3,4,87,88] This entire process is accelerated in the presence of wound healing (the entire spectrum of injury).[61,86,88,119,120]

It is the viscoelastic properties (exhibits features of both fluid and solid nature) of connective tissue and the contractile-elastic properties of muscle that determine their response to stretching. Muscle and connective tissue (tendon and connective tissues surrounding muscle) are aligned in series along the axis of an applied stretch. Muscle has been described mechanically as composed of contractile and elastic elements[46] arranged in parallel.[53] Huxley and Simons[53] demonstrated this feature to be secondary to the cross bridges of actin and myosin. As mentioned earlier, muscle can respond to an applied force with permanent elongation. Animal studies have demonstrated that this is due to an increase in the number of sarcomeres. Additionally, this affects the contractile nature of the muscle, with an increase its peak tension at a longer resting length.[37,38,106,108,115] Muscle at rest has a constant tendency to shorten, based upon its contractile element. Animal studies have shown that this results in permanent shortening, most likely due to a reduction in the number of sarcomeres.[106,108,115]

Similarly, connective tissues will adapt its structure based upon the forces to which it is subjected. Both tendon and ligament have been demonstrated to respond to regularly applied force (exercise versus immobilization) with increased strength/ weight ratios.[2–4,9,67,86,87,109,117] The improved strength is due to both increased proteoglycan content and collagen cross links.[67,86,87,109,117] The organization of fibers is related to the amount of applied forces, with a more random organization of fibers in the absence of outside force. Both the strength and elasticity of tendon and ligament are reduced in this state.[18,19,66,86] Connective tissue responds to stretch in a viscoelastic manner.[45,54,66,103,111] This describes characteristics of reversible (elastic) and plastic (nonreversible) deformation. These properties have been entensively studied in tendon, in both animal and ex-vivo human studies.

In the laboratory, when tendon is subjected to a tensile force, its response is depicted graphically by a stress force (force per unit area) strain (percent length change/ original length). As shown in Figure 3, this is not a linear function. There is a greater deformation at low loads, followed by a rapid increase in stress until rapid deformation occurs (rupture). The initial change is related to the gradual elongation of elastic fibers, along with the straightening of the wavy arrangement of collagen fibers. This is followed by rupture of smaller collagen fibers with disruption of cross links. The shape of this curve can be altered by prestretching the tendon. The stiffness of the tendon varies inversely with its length. Therefore, a tendon of greater length will show greater flexibility.[19] Within the initial part of the curve, the deformation is time-dependent, a feature known as creep (percent length change/time at constant applied force). A low load applied for a prolonged time will produce a greater length change than a large force applied rapidly.[19,45,65,103,111] The amount of force required is also influenced by temperature, local blood flow, and nutritional state.[64,65,68] On this basis one can conclude that a stretching program should include the regular application of forces in a gradual and prolonged manner, with an adequate tissue temperature. Since the presence of inflammation will also affect the response, attention to the injury must be appropriately maintained.

MUSCLE FACTORS

Whole muscle is a heterogeneous structure, with components of varying flexibility. Following the external to internal organization, each muscle contains an

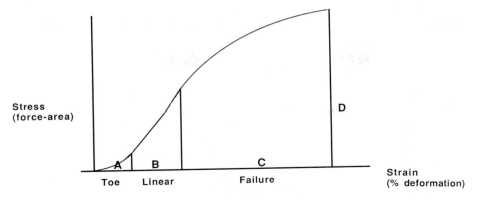

FIGURE 3. Representative stress/strain deformation curve for tendon. A = toe, B = linear deformation, C = failure (individual fibrils), D = rupture. (Adapted from Stromberg.[103])

outer connective tissue sheath (epimysium), inner connective tissue sheaths surrounding fiber groups (perimysium), individual fibers (endomysium), and the sarcolemma (membrane that delineates individual fibers). These cells, known as extrafusal fibers, are innervated by alpha-motoneurons. These are the contractile elements and determine the power of the muscle. In parallel with these fibers are the intrafusal fibers (muscle spindles). They are innervated by gamma-motoneurons and, although given a contractile function, serve the purpose of length/tension control for the muscle as a whole (Fig. 4).[6,27] Their length and tension are determined by the input of the gamma-motoneuron, whose activity in turn is influenced by numerous factors, including suprasegmental input via descending cerebellar and cortical tracts, segmental input through direct sources (muscle tension and force development via the segmental innervation by alpha-motoneuron) and indirect sources (overlap of cutaneous afferents and receptors of multiple types). In this manner, there can be multiple simultaneous inputs to the determination of muscle length and tension at a given time. Additionally, there are receptors in the musculotendinous unit (Golgi-tendon organ) that operate in a fail-safe manner (all or none) at the point of critical stresses to the structure, delivering inhibitory input, preventing further muscle contraction (therefore, allowing lengthening and facilitating relaxation). This has been referred to by some[7,104] as the inverse stretch reflex. The intrafusal fibers operate on a continuous basis, adjusting length via speed and force considerations (a more slowly applied stretch elicits less response from the muscle spindles).[6,27] When the muscle spindle is stretched, it sends impulses to the spinal cord, reflectively causes the muscle to contract. If the stretch is maintained (longer than 6 seconds) the Golgi tendon organ will fire, causing relaxation.[6,27,96] This has direct implications for slow, prolonged stretching and for specific adaptations of stretching techniques. The resetting of the length/tension baseline in muscle may be achieved by applying a stretch in this manner.

The length- and tension-setting physiology is the basis for the use of neuromuscular facilitation techniques. These techniques were first developed as a means of increasing strength in paralyzed limbs but soon gained an increasing utility in

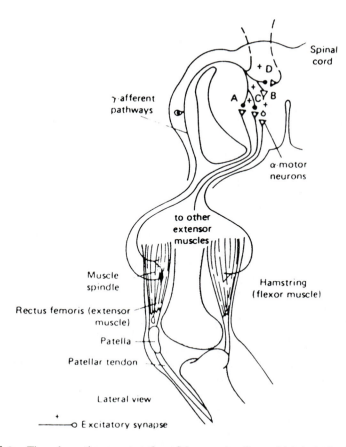

FIGURE 4. The schematic representation of the stretch reflex, which is the basis of control of the length/tension ratio. Alpha motor neuron innervates extrafusal muscle fibers. Gamma motor neuron innervates intrafusal muscle fibers (muscle spindles) with both suprasegmental and segmental input via IA afferent fibers. (Adapted from Brooks and Fahey: Exercise Physiology: Human Bioenergetics and Its Applications. Newy York, John Wiley and Sons, 1984.)

the treatment of spastic extremities, and subsequentally in neurally intact limbs. The reflex loops described above in combination with the Sherrington law of reciprocal inhibition (antagonist muscle group) have resulted in numerous stretching techniques with varying degrees of direct neurophysiologic rationale. The cellular and extracellular electrophysiology of the basis of these methods has been investigated by numerous researchers.[7,20,27,41,44,50,52,57,63,72,78,81,98,105,107,114] Although these methods have been demonstrated to be effective in increasing flexibility, there is conflicting evidence regarding the specific basis for the observed effect.[81] In Moore's study of female gymnasts, EMG activity during stretch was greater, as were mobility gains in the PNF group. There is evidence that a preceding muscle contraction will cause a lingering after-discharge that results in persistent muscle activation.[21,41,52,81] While this may play a facilitating role in enhancing muscle strength and contraction efficiency, it should have the opposite effect upon flexibility characteristics. It appears likely that the observed benefits are due to neural factors, although the interaction of excitatory and inhibitory activity is apparently more complex than the model drawn up to this point, with our inability to measure the specific "message" within the electric signal.

It is apparent that the precise discrete in vivo physiologic event that occurs during stretching is not known. While animal studies have demonstrated that muscle, tendon, and loose connective tissue will change physical and mechanical properties with prolonged immobilization at different lengths, it is not clear what is the correlate to human "tightness" and inflexibility (in the absence of immobilization-induced contracture). Athletic flexibility training is performed for much shorter time periods than those employed in the aforementioned studies. It is not known whether absolute length changes (secondary to protein synthesis) are involved at all in vivo. The dynamic factors affecting muscle length (i.e., muscle spindle, gamma loop, and Golgi-tendon organ) clearly play a role in the flexibility changes observed with the use of stretching programs. The changes in hamstring flexibility noted immediately after the institution of stretching program are too rapid to be accounted for on the basis of change in the number of sarcomeres or alteration in protein synthesis alone. The tremendous stiffness of tendon compared with muscle makes it unlikely that tendon length change plays any role in this phenomenon. It is unclear whether the improved flexibility occurs secondary to alteration in actin myosin cross bridges, to lengthening of other connective tissues, or to resetting of the muscular length/tension by neural factors. The relative contribution of each of these components is controversial. In the initial phases of training, neural factors probably play the major role in the observed flexibility changes. After prolonged periods of flexibility training, changes in sarcomere number may play a role in reaching the new steady-state muscle length.

FLEXIBILITY MEASUREMENT/OBJECTIVE ASSESSMENT

The measurement of flexibility is a complex task that is difficult to standardize. Measurement of joint range of motion and assessment of flexibility are not necessarily equivalent, but in a practical sense they are usually considered to be. There is good standardization of method and normal ranges recorded for static goniometric recording of single joints.[30,64,90] The equipment (goniometer) is a protractor designed for easy application to joints. Its use is relatively simple, producing quantitative results with good inter- and intra-observer reproducibility.[30] Limitations include static measurements only, single joints at a given time, and difficulty in application to certain joints (e.g., sternoclavicular and costoclavicular). To ease the application to whole body parts, Leighton designed the flexometer, which consists of a weighted circular dial with a needle enclosed, which can be strapped to the body part. Its reliability is good but not quite so high as that of the standard goniometer.[43] The electrogoniometer designed by Karpovich[59] substitutes a potentiomenter for a protractor. Its advantage is the ability to record range of dynamic motion with fair accuracy, somewhat less than static measurements. Few specific joints, however, can be measured with this device.

The measurement of trunk flexibility has special limitations and inherent difficulties. The standard goniometer is not appropriate for measuring trunk motion in the sagittal plane and is entirely inadequate in the coronal and rotational planes.[83,90] To this end, the Schober test (originally designed for spinal range of flexion and extension in patients with ankylosing spondylitis) was modified by Moll and Wright as a method of reproducible and semiquantitative compound spine movements.[78] Two marks are made along the ends of the lumbar spine, and the tape-measured distance between them is determined in flexion, neutral, and extension. Lack of a standard normal makes interpretation between the ends of range difficult to interpret clinically. Similarly, the inclinometer method was designed by Loebl.[69] An evaluation of the difference between these methods and simple "fingertip-to-floor" measurement for inter- and intra-examiner variability[74] demonstrated good reliability for the Moll and Schober tests only. "Eyeball" measurements have variability up to 30%.[83] Other methods with good reliability but requiring the use of special equipment or x-rays are available but have obvious drawbacks. At this point, it appears that for a reproducible, quantitative assessment of lumbar spine motion these tests are recommended. Disadvantages include their inapplicability to the cervical or thoracic spine, and their limitation to measurement of compound motion only (the entire thoracolumbar spine). None of these methods can assess articular mobility in the translational or rotational planes. Furthermore, they cannot measure flexibility of non-articulating soft tissue (fascia, chest wall tissue) or of joints that have motion patterns less well defined by external landmarks (i.e., intercostal, thoracic, rib/spine articulations, abdominal wall).

METHODS OF STRETCHING

Stretching techniques have evolved over the recent years to include numerous options for improving flexibility. Although each method has its share of faithful supporters, the distinct superiority of one method has not been demonstrated.[7,19,23,27,34,44,50,57,63,70–72,91,104] There are indications for the relative superiority of a given method in individual clinical situations. Prevention of injury (as in general warm-up), treatment of specific joint injury, flexibility needs in the presence of pain, and muscle spasm require modification of the basic method. The objectives of a flexibility program must be established with a perspective on the specific needs of the athlete. To obtain and maintain a level of flexibility is the general rule. Progressive daily gains in range of motion are unnecessary once a basic level has been achieved. The postures utilized are designed to optimize stretch on the target tissue while minimizing stress on vulnerable structures (most notably the spine and knees). The stretching options available can be divided into the following categories: ballistic, static, passive, and neuromuscular facilitation. Additionally, each of these methods can be combined with modalities.

Ballistic stretching employs the rapid application of force in a repeated manner in a bouncing, throwing, or jerking maneuver. This methods was the standard in the last decade but is no longer recommended. The rapid increase in force can cause injury and is less efficient than other available methods.[7,65,96,104,110]

Passive stretching is performed with a partner applying a stretch to a relaxed extremity. This method has limited usefulness because of the increased risk of injury. There must be excellent communication between the partners, with slow and sensitive application of force. Gymnasts, dancers, and football kickers and soccer players have used this method for hamstring and adductor stretching, and swimmers have used it for anterior shoulder and chest wall stretching. This method is commonly employed in the training room and physical therapy department and is safest when used in this context.

Static stretching is the easiest and probably the safest method and is recommended for preparticipation flexibility exercise in combination with warm-up. A position that applies a gradual stretch to the body part is attained and held with steady force for a period of 15–60 seconds. The duration of the applied stretch has recently suggested to be equally effective at 15 compared with 45–60 seconds.[74] This is the basis of yoga-type stretching and was advocated by deVries.[23] The added advantage of decreased muscular soreness after exercise is a factor supporting the use of static stretching methods.[24,25] Yoga-type stretching can be very effective, although specific cautions are necessary. These methods have been tested over centuries, but they carry a definite risk of injury if performed incorrectly or in the presence of certain injuries (specific joint instabilities, degenerative disk disease, especially cervical, or in association with instability).

Neuromuscular facilitation techniques have been demonstrated in numerous studies to be effective methods for stretch.[7,57,63,81,91,105] Most of these methods require an experienced partner (usually a physical therapist or trainer). Hold-relax and contract-relax (with or without agonist contraction) are the activities most frequently employed. In the experienced and attentive athlete, the contract-relax with added agonist contraction can be a very effective and safe method. For hamstring stretch, the hamstring is isometrically contracted for 5 seconds, while a gentle submaximal hip flexor contraction is maintained.[81] I recommend this method for quadriceps, hamstring, and gastrocnemius/soleus/Achilles complex. A cross-training effect has been demonstrated with PNF techniques on hip flexibility.[72] This has a direct implication for flexibility training in the contralateral immobilized leg in the injured athlete.

In addition to manipulation of the neuromuscular system to enhance flexibility, the thermal characteristics of connective tissue can be exploited to improve flexibility programs in certain circumstances. Warm-up exercises[96,111,113,116] or conduction heating methods prior to stretching take advantage of the viscoelastic nature of collagen with increased temperature within the physiologic range. Warm-up prior to stretch[116] or instead of stretch[113] failed to increase the level of flexibility except in ankle dorsiflexion, which showed significant gains beyond stretching alone. The ease of stretch and prevention of injuries was not studied, however, and this is an equally important consideration. Therefore, I recommend 5–10 minutes of warm-up activity prior to stretching. This could be in the form of light jogging, fast walking, or stationary bike work.

Cold application has been used following flexibility training exercises in order to take advantage of the thermal characteristics of connective tissue.[93] Once plastic deformation has occurred, lowering the temperature can theoretically prolong the length changes. This has not been proved to be effective, except in the setting of treatment of an injury. In this setting, muscle spasm and painful inhibition of joint and limb range of movement can be suppressed by cold application in the form of ice massage, cold immersion, or ice packs (time period for use varies with each of these methods).[27,65] The use of a vapocoolant spray has been demonstrated to be of no significant benefit for flexibility gains in the absence of treatment of the injury.[84] However, in the setting of injury where muscle spasm is a factor, this can be a very effective modality (myofascial syndromes).[27,65] Stimulation of cutaneous afferents with the coolant spray can effect muscle relaxation on a physiologic basis similar to the PNF techniques.

While there are data to suggest improved static or passive stretching when combined with ultrasound,[112] there are few data at this time to support its routine use in the absence of injury or fixed joint contracture. The ideal flexibility program should, therefore, include a combination of stretching and mobilizing techniques (''stretching'' across the long axis of the joint, and ''mobilizing'' along the translational and rotational axes). A combination of passive, static, and PNF techniques should be utilized, with specific target sites and motions for each sport. Within each sport, there will be variation of needs according to individual flexibility profiles. The program should be designed with these factors in mind and should be performed routinely: in off-season 3 times per week, and daily during the regular season. Gains in flexibility have been shown to be superior in athletes with a postactivity program.[80] Therefore, a pre- and a post-competition routine should be established. The ''after'' routine can be more specific and abbreviated, focusing on muscle groups most stressfully involved in the athletic event. Since the short-term effect of stretching diminishes significantly after 90 minutes, the program should be exercised within this time frame.[79] It should be performed for at least 15–20 minutes, as this appears to be the minimum time period for achieving adequate gains in temperature and extensibility.[8,96] I recommend five repetitions for each motion, with each extremity. The duration of ''hold'' on static stretches should be 15 seconds with the initial stretch, to 30 seconds on the last repetition. Stretches of longer duration have not been demonstrated to have increased effectiveness.[74] Self-mobilization exercises at the segmental level of the thoracic and lumbar spine are recommended for most athletes who require upper body rotation and load bearing. Finally, stretching and mobilization techniques should be exercised with careful attention to form to stay within the ''window'' of safety and effectiveness.

SUMMARY

Flexibility is a characteristic of musculoskeletal function that is more than simple joint range of motion. Flexibility training invokes a complex interaction of biophysical and neurophysiologic factors. A variety of tissue types are involved in stretching maneuvers, but the exact target site or discrete physiologic event is not completely known. While the majority of attention has been focused upon the muscle tendon unit, a complete flexibility training program should also include maneuvers aimed at improvement of joint capsule and pericapsular tissue flexibility. In the setting of athletic injury rehabilitation, especially with attendant weakness (either from pain or neurally induced), this becomes an important issue. While flexibility training is widely employed for the prevention and treatment of overuse injuries, the mechanism of its action in this setting is not well understood. Although adaptive shortening of connective tissue can occur, whether actual tissue length changes or neurally mediated relaxation plays a major role in flexibility gains is not known. At the present time there is enough epidemiologic evidence to support the routine use of flexibility training programs in most sports. No single stretching method has been shown to be singularly superior, but the evidence implies that PNF methods can achieve the greatest overall flexibility gains. Programs should include a variety of methods and must be designed with consideration of the abilities and specific needs of the athlete. Constant awareness to avoid spinal or peripheral joint injury is imperative. The major evidence regarding the influence of flexibility training on injury prevention and treatment as well as alteration of sport performance is theoretical. In the absence of controlled studies with large groups of subjects, we will have to rely on this theoretical basis to guide our use of flexibility training in the near future.

REFERENCES

1. Agre J: Hamstring injuries: Proposed aetiological factors, prevention, and treatment. Sports Med 2:21–33, 1985.
2. Akeson W, Amiel D, Abel M, et al: Effects of immobilization on joints. Clin Orthop 219:28–37, 1987.
3. Amiel D, Akeson W, Harwood F, Mechanic G: The effect of immobilization on the types of collagen synthesized in periarticular connective tissue. Connect Tissue Res 8:27–32, 1980.
4. Amiel D, Woo S, Harwood F, Akeson W: The effect of immobilization on collagen turnover in

connective tissue: A biochemical-biomechanical correlation. Acta Orthop Scand 53:325–332, 1982.

5. Anderson B: Stretching. Bolinas, CA, Shelter Publications, 1980.
6. Basmajian J: Therapeutic Exercise, 3rd edition. Baltimore, Williams and Wilkins, 1978.
7. Beaulieu J: Developing a Stretching Program. Phys Sportsmed 9:59–69, 1981.
8. Bohannon R: Effect of repeated eight-minute muscle loading on the angle of straight-leg raising. Phys Ther 64:491–497, 1984.
9. Booth F: Physiologic and biochemical effects of immobilization on muscle. Clin Orthop 219:15–20, 1987.
10. Bosco C, Komi P: Potentiation of the mechanical behavior of the human skeletal muscle through prestretching. Acta Physiol Scand 106:467–472, 1979.
11. Bosco C, Tihanyi J, Komi P, et al: Store and recoil of elastic energy in slow and fast types of human skeletal muscles. Acta Physiol Scand 116:343–349, 1982.
12. Cady L, Thomas P, Karwasky R: Program for increasing health and physical fitness of fire fighters. J Occup Med 27:110–114, 1985.
13. Casella C: Tensile force in total striated muscle, isolated fibre and sarcolemma. Acta Physiol Scand 21:380–401, 1950.
14. Cavagna G, Saibene F, Margaria R: Effect of negative work on the amount of positive work performed by an isolated muscle. J Appl Physiol 20:157–158, 1965.
15. Cavagna G, Dusman B, Margaria R: Positive work done by a previously stretched muscle. J Appl Physiol 24:21–32, 1968.
16. Corbin C: Flexibility. Clin Sports Med 3:101–117, 1984.
17. Crawford G: The growth of striated muscle immobilized in extension. J Anat 114:165–183, 1973.
18. Curwin S, Stanish W: Tendinitis: Its Etiology and Treatment. Lexington, MA, D.C. Heath and Company, 1984.
19. Curwin S, Stanish W: Tendinitis: its etiology and treatment. In Butler D, Grood E, Noyes F, Zernicke R: Biomechanics of Ligaments and Tendons. Exer Sport Sci Rev 6:125–182, 1978.
20. D'Ambrosia R, Drez D: Prevention and treatment of running injuries. In Stanish W (ed): Neurophysiology of Stretching. Thorofare, NJ, Charles Slack, 1982.
21. Devanandan M, Eccles R, Yokota T: Muscle stretch and the presynaptic inhibition of the group 1a pathway to motorneurones. J Physiol 179:430–441, 1965.
22. deVries H: Electromyographic observations of effects of static stretching upon muscular distress. Res Q 32:468–479, 1960.
23. deVries H: Evaluation of static stretching procedures for improvement of flexibility. Res Q 33:222–229, 1962.
24. deVries H: Prevention of muscular distress after exercise. Res Q 32:177–185, 1960.
25. deVries H: Quantitative electromyographic investigation of the spasm theory of muscle pain. Am J Phys Med 45:119–134, 1966.
26. Dintiman G: Effects of various training programs on running speed. Res Q 35:456–463, 1964.
27. Downey J, Darling R: Physiological Basis of Rehabilitation Medicine. Philadelphia, W.B. Saunders Co., 1971.
28. Ekstrand J, Gillquist J: The avoidability of soccer injuries. Int J Sports Med 4:124–128, 1983.
29. Ekstrand J, Gillquist J: The frequency of muscle tightness and injuries in soccer players. Am J Sports Med 10:75–78, 1982.
30. Ekstrand J, Wiktorsson M, Oberg B, Gillquist J: Lower extremity goniometric measurements: A study to determine their reliability. Arch Phys Med Rehab 63:171–175, 1982.
31. Fairbank J, Pynsent P: Influence of anthropometric factors and joint laxity in the incidence of adolescent back pain. Spine 9:461–464, 1984.
32. Farfan H, Gracovetsky S: The mechanism of the lumbar spine. Spine 6:249–262, 1981.
33. Farfan H, Gracovetsky S: The optimum spine. Spine 11:543–573, 1986.
34. Gajdosik R, LeVeau B, Bohannon R: Effects of ankle dorsiflexion on active and passive unilateral straight leg raising. Phys Ther 65:1478–1482, 1985.
35. Glick J: Muscle strains: Prevention and treatment. Phys Sportsmed 6:73–77, 1980.
36. Godshall R: The predictability of athletic injuries: An eight-year study. J Sports Med 3:50–54, 1975.
37. Goldspink D: The influence of immobilization and stretch on protein turnover of rat skeletal muscle. J Physiol 264:267–282, 1977.
38. Goldspink G, Williams PE: The nature of the increased passive resistance in muscle following immobilization of the mouse soleus muscle. J Physiol (Lond) 289:55–58, 1979.
39. Gordon N, Moolman J, Van Rensburg J, et al: The South African Defense Force Physical Training Programme. S Afr Med J 69:483–490, 1986.

40. Gossman M, Sahrmann S, Rose S: Experimental evidence and clinical implications. Phys Ther 62:1799–1808, 1982.
41. Hagbarth K, Vallbo A: Discharge characteristics of human muscle afferents during muscle stretch and contraction. Exp Neurol 22:674–694, 1968.
42. Harkness R: Mechanical properties of collagenous tissue. *In* Gould BS (ed): Treatise on Collagen. NY, Academic Press, 2(A):247–310, 1968.
43. Harris M: Flexibility. Phy Ther 49:591–601, 1968.
44. Hartley-O'Brien: Six mobilization exercises for active range of hip flexion. Res Q Exerc Sport 51:625–635, 1980.
45. Haut R, Little R: A constitutive equation for collagen fibers. J Biomech 5:423–430, 1972.
46. Hill AV: The heat of shortening and the dynamic constraints of muscle. Proc Royal Soc Lond 126(B):136–195, 1938.
47. Hill A: The mechanics of active muscle. Proc Roy Soc Lond 141(B):104–117, 1953.
48. Hill A: The series elastic component of muscle. Proc Royal Soc Lond 137(B):273–280, 1950.
49. Hill DK: Tension to interaction between sliding filaments of resting striated muscle: The effect of stimulation. J Physiol 199:367–384, 1968.
50. Holt L, Travis T, Okita T: Comparative study of three stretching techniques. Percept Mot Skills 31:611–616, 1970.
51. Hortbagyi T, Faludi J, Merkely B: Effects of intense "stretching"-flexibility training on the mechanical profile of the knee extensors and on the range of motion of the hip joint. Int J Sport Med 6:317–321, 1985.
52. Hutton R, Smith J, Eldred E: Persisting changes in sensory and motor activity of a muscle following its reflex activation. Pflugers Arch 353:327–336, 1975.
53. Huxley A, Simmons R: Mechanical properties of the cross-bridges of frog striated muscle. J Physiol Lond 218:59P–60P, 1971.
54. Jenkins R, Little R: A constitutive equation for parallel-fibered elastic tissue. Biomechanics 7:397–402, 1974.
55. Johns R, Wright V: Relative importance of various tissues in joint stiffness. J Appl Physiol 17:824–828, 1962.
56. Johnson J, Sim F, Scott S: Musculoskeletal injuries in competitive swimmers. Mayo Clin Proc 62:289–304, 1987.
57. Kabat H: Studies of neuromuscular dysfunction: The role of central facilitation in restoration of motor function in paralysis. Arch Phys Med Rehab 33:523, 1952.
58. Kalenak A, Morehouse C: Knee stability and knee ligament injuries. JAMA 234:1143–1145, 1975.
59. Karpovich PV, et al: Electrogoniometer: A new device for study of joints in action. Fed Proc 18:79, 1959.
60. Keller C, Noyes F, Buncher R: Sports traumatology series: The medical aspects of soccer injury epidemiology. Am J Sports Med 15:230–237, 1987.
61. Klein L, Dawson M, Heiple K: Turnover of collagen in the adult rat after denervation. J Bone Joint Surg 59-A:1065–1067, 1977.
62. Sherrington CS: The Integrative Action of the Nervous System. New Haven, Yale University Press, 1961.
63. Knott M, Voss D: Proprioceptive Neuromuscular Facilitation: Patterns and Techniques. New York: 1956. As cited in Basmajian J: Therapeutic Exercise, 3rd ed. Baltimore, Williams and Wilkins, 1978.
64. Kottke F, Stillwell K, Lehmann JF: Krusen's Handbook of Physical Medicine and Rehabilitation 3rd edition. Philadelphia, WB Saunders, 1982.
65. Kottke F, Pauley D, Ptak R: The rationale for prolonged stretching for correction of shortening of connective tissue. Arch Phys Med Rehab 47:345–352, 1966.
66. LaBan M: Collagen tissue: Implications of its response to stress in vitro. Arch Phys Med Rehab 43:461–466, 1962.
67. Laros G, Tipton C, Cooper R: Influence of physical activity on ligament insertions in the knees of dogs. J Bone Joint Surg 53-A:275–286, 1971.
68. Lehmann J, Masock A, et al: Effect of therapeutic temperature on tendon extensibility. Arch Phys Med Rehab 51:481–487, 1970.
69. Loebl W: Measurement of spinal posture and range of spinal movement. Ann Phys Med 9:104–111, 1967.
70. MacNab I, Rathburn M: The microvascular pattern of the rotator cuff. J Bone Joint Surg 52B, 1970.
71. Madding S, Wong J, Hallum A, Medeiros J: Effect of duration of passive stretch on hip abduction range of motion. J Ortho Sports Phys Ther 8:409–416, 1987.

72. Markos P: Ipsilateral and contralateral effects of propioceptive neuromuscular facilitation techniques on hip motion and electromyographic activity. Phys Ther 59:366–373, 1979.
73. Medeiros J, Smidt G, Burmeister L, Soderberg G: The influence of isometric exercise and passive stretch on hip joint motion. Phys Ther 57:518–523, 1977.
74. Medeiros J, Madding SW: Effect of duration of passive stretch on hip abduction range of motion. Orthop Sports Phys Ther 8:409–411, 1987.
75. Merritt J, McLean T, Erickson R: Measurement of trunk flexibility in normal subjects: Reproducibility of three clinical methods. Mayo Clin Proc 61:192–197, 1986.
76. Millar A: An early stretching routine for calf muscle strains. Med Sci Sports Exerc 8:39–42, 1976.
77. Millar A: Strains of the posterior calf musculature ("tennis leg"). Am J Sports Med 7:172–174, 1979.
78. Moll J, Wright V: Normal range of spinal mobility: A clinical study. Ann Rheum Dis 30:381–386, 1971.
79. Moller M, Ekstrand J, Oberg B, Gillquist J: Duration of stretching effect on range of motion in lower extremities. Arch Phys Med Rehab 66:171–173, 1985.
80. Moller M, Oberg B, Gillquist J: Stretching exercise and soccer: Effect of stretching on range of motion in the lower extremity in connection with soccer training. Int J Sports Med 6:50–52, 1985.
81. Moore M, Hutton R: Electromyographic investigation of muscle stretching techniques. Med Sci Sports Exerc 12:322–329, 1980.
82. Moretz J, Walters R, Smith L: Flexibility as a predictor of knee injuries in college football players. Physician Sports Med 10:93–97, 1982.
83. Nelson M, Allen P: Clamp SE DE Dombal FT: Reliability and reproducibility of clinical findings in low back pain. Spine 4:97–101, 1979.
84. Newton R: Effects of vapocoolants on passive hip flexion in healthy subjects. Phys Ther 65:1034–1036, 1985.
85. Nicholas J: Injuries to knee ligaments: Relationship to looseness and tightness in football players. JAMA 212:2236–2239, 1970.
86. Nimni ME: Collagen: Structure, function, and metabolism in normal and fibrotic tissue. Semin Arthritis Rheum 13:1–86, 1983.
87. Noyes F, Torvik P, Hyde W, DeLucas J: Biomechanics of ligament failure: An analysis of immobilization, exercise, and reconditioning effects in primates. J Bone Joint Surg 56-A:1406–1418, 1974.
88. Peacock EE: Some biochemical and biophysical aspects of joint stiffness: Role of collagen synthesis as opposed to altered mollecular bonding. Ann Surg 164:1–12, 1986.
89. Phalen GS, Dickson JA: Spondylolisthesis and tight hamstrings. J Bone Joint Surg 43-A:505–512, 1961.
90. Polley H, Hunder G: Physical Examination of the Joints. 2nd edition. Philadelphia, WB Saunders Co., 1978.
91. Sady S, Wortman M, Blanke D: Flexibility training: Ballistic, static or propioceptive neuromuscular facilitation. Arch Phys Med Rehab 63:261–263, 1982.
92. Sammarco G: Diagnosis and treatment in dancers. Clin Orthop 187:176–187, 1984.
93. Sapega A, Quedenfeld T, Moyer R, Butler R: Biophysical factors in range-of-motion exercise. Physician Sportsmed 9:57–65, 1981.
94. Scholten P, Veldhuizen A: The bending stiffness of the trunk. Spine 11:463–467, 1986.
95. Schultz P: Flexibility: Day of the static stretch. Phys Sportsmedicine 7:109–117, 1979.
96. Shellock F, Prentice W: Warming up and stretching for improved physical performance and prevention of sports-related injuries. Sports Med 2:267–278, 1985.
97. Shyne K, Dominguez R: To stretch or not to stretch? Physician Sportsmed 10:137–140, 1982.
98. Smith J, Hutton R, Eldred E: Postcontraction changes in sensitivity of muscle afferents to static and dynamic stretch. Brain Res 78:192–202, 1974.
99. Stanish W, Curwin S, Rubinovich M: Tendinitis: The analysis and treatment for running. Clin Sports Med 4:593–609, 1985.
100. Steben R, Steben A: The validity of the stretch shortening cycle in selected jumping events. J Sports Med 21:28–37, 1981.
101. Stolov W, Weilepp T, Riddell W: Passsive length-tension relationship and hydroxyproline content of chronically denervated skeletal muscle. Arch Phys Med Rehab 51:517–525, 1970.
102. Stolov W, Weilepp T: Passive length-tension relationship of intact muscle, epimysium, and tendon in normal and denervated gastrocnemius of the rat. Arch Phys Med Rehab 47:612–620, 1966.
103. Stromberg D, Wiederhielm C: Viscoelastic description of a collagenous tissue in simple elongation. J Appl Physiol 26:857–862, 1969.

104. Surburg P: Flexibility exercises re-examined. Athlet Train 37–40, Spring 1983.
105. Surburg P: Neuromuscular facilitation techniques in sportsmedicine. Physician Sportsmed 9:115–127, 1981.
106. Tabary JC, Tabary C, Tardieu C, et al: Physiological and structural changes in the cat's soleus muscle due to immobilization at different lengths by plaster casts. J Physiol (Lond) 224:231–244, 1972.
107. Tanigawa M: Comparison of the hold-relax procedure and passive mobilization on increasing muscle length. Phys Ther 52:725–735, 1972.
108. Tardieu C, Tarbary J, Tardieu G, et al: Adaptation of sarcomere numbers to the length imposed on muscle. *In* Gubba F, Marechal G, Takacs O (eds): Mechanism of Muscle Adaptation to Functional Requirements. Elmsford, NY: Pergamon Press, 1981.
109. Tipton C, James S, Mergner W, Tcheng T: Influence of exercise on strength of medial collateral knee ligaments of dogs. Am J Physiol 218:894–902, 1970.
110. Wallin D, Ekblom B, Grahn R, Nordenborg T: Improvement of muscle flexibility: A comparison between two techniques. Am J Sports Med 13:263–268, 1985.
111. Warren C, Lehmann J, Koblanski J: Heat and stretch procedures: An evaluation using rat tail tendon. Arch Phys Med Rehab 57:122–126, 1976.
112. Wessling K, DeVane D, Hylton C: Effects of static stretch versus static stretch and ultrasound combined on triceps surae muscle extensibility in healthy women. Phys Ther 67:674–679, 1987.
113. Wiktorsson-Moller M, Oberg B, Ekstrand J, Gillquist J: Effects of warming up, massage, and stretching on range of motion and muscle strength in the lower extremity. Am J Sports Med 11:249–252, 1983.
114. Wilkerson G: Developing flexibility by overcoming the stretch reflex. Physician Sportsmed 9:189–191, 1981.
115. Williams PE, Goldspink G: Changes in sarcomere length and physiological properties in immobilized muscle. J Anat 127:459–468, 1978.
116. Williford H, East J, Smith F, Burry L: Evaluation of warm-up for improvement in flexibility. Am J Sports Med 14:316–319, 1986.
117. Woo S, Ritter M, Amiel D, et al: The biomechanical and biochemical properties of swine tendons: Long-term effects of exercise on the digital extensors. Connect Tissue Res 7:177–183, 1980.
118. Wooden M: Preseason screening of the lumbar spine. J Ortho Sports Phys Ther 3:6–10, 1981.
119. Young A, Stokes M, Illes J: Effects of joint pathology on muscle. Clin Orthop 219:21–27, 1987.
120. Zarins B: Soft tissue repair: Biomechanical aspects. Int J Sports Med 3:9–11, 1982.

MICHAEL F. DILLINGHAM, MD

STRENGTH TRAINING

Reprint requests to Michael F. Dillingham, M.D., Sports, Orthopedic and Rehabilitation Medicine Associates, 3250 Alpine Rd., Portola Valley, CA 94025.

Strength training can begin only in the presence of a relatively pain-free joint with an acceptable range of motion and flexibility. The issues of strengthening to be discussed are appropriate to late-phase rehabilitation, to training for athletic competition, and for those people who wish to maintain a healthy, vigorous lifestyle or effect a significant change in their current lifestyle.

Much is known about muscle physiology in terms of energy systems, neural control, hypertrophy, and training effect. However, we still lack complete scientific agreement on the best way to apply this knowledge for optimal strength training. Adding to this dilemma is a paucity of well-controlled investigations of techniques. Available studies have often been limited by sample size, duration of the study (often made to fit a school semester or quarter), poor statistical analysis, the use of untrained subjects, and lack of control of important variables, such as the general state of nutrition and health of the subjects and the vigor with which they adhere to the exercise protocol. Additionally, assessment of strengthening requires maximal effort by a subject, which is difficult to attain for a variety of factors, including individual tolerance to pain and factors of motivation at the time of testing.

Testing of isolated muscle preparations does not correlate well with muscle behavior in vivo. The distribution and metabolic parameters of animal muscle fiber vary somewhat from those of human muscle; especially in the smaller animals used for studies, contraction velocities tend to be greater and there is a much higher tendency to have single fiber–type muscles.

The lack of a completely sound scientific basis for training technique, however, does not mean that the information available is not helpful. We hope that our presentation of basic information followed by practical applications will help in formulating a conceptual framework for strength training. However, it should also be remembered that strength training has many applications to sports.

MUSCLE FIBER TYPES

A variety of schemes have been used to classify muscle, including color (red, white), metabolic activity (oxidative-glycolytic), time to peak tension (fast, slow), and neutral (type I and type II). However, two commonly cited schemes exist at the present time. The first is based on the metabolic emphasis of the muscle: slow, fast oxidative, fast oxidative/glycolytic, and fast glycolytic. The other is a scheme based on muscle response to myofibrillar ATPase stain, which is more intense in muscle with well-developed glycolytic pathways. The naming of this scheme is neutral: type I, type IIa, type IIb, and type IIc. Type I correlates with a slow metabolic classification, and there is good, but not precise, correlation between the subtypes of type II and the three subtypes of fast muscle cited above. The later scheme, i.e., a type I and II scheme, is most commonly used today.

Fiber type is a function of the motor unit supplying the muscle and is the direct result of neural influence. Under normal circumstance, a variance from person to person and fiber type distribution is genetically controlled. Experimentally, fiber types can be changed with reinnervation and chronic electrical stimulation. As a practical matter, no significant fiber type changes have been proved in humans as a result of training. Muscle biopsy has shown, however, that high-level endurance athletes tend to have more type I fibers in some muscles, and sprint or burst-type athletes have more type II fibers. It has also been found that most human muscle is a mosaic of approximately half type I and half type II fibers. This is in contrast to the findings in animals, especially smaller animals, which may have unmixed muscles. It implies that all human muscle has capacity for both speed and strength types of work and also for endurance.

We know certain things about the various fiber types, as implied by the metabolic naming scheme. The type I slow fibers are primarily oxidative in their metabolic pathways and utilize mitochondrially-based oxidative reactions to produce large amounts of ATP. The other fiber type, the fast fibers, have a combination of oxidative (aerobic) and nonoxidative (anaerobic) metabolic pathways. Apparently, there are some fibers that have no mitochondrial or oxidative pathways, and these are described as type IIc or the fast glycolytic fibers.

The maximum velocity of shortening of a fast-twitch fiber is approximately six fiber lengths per second; of a slow-twitch fiber, approximately two fiber lengths per second. In terms of the speed on contraction, the range for most human muscle fiber is approximately 40–110 msec.

The power of the fast-twitch fiber is greater than that of the slow-twitch fiber at all velocities of shortening. The fast-twitch fiber also has a peak power approximately four times that of the slow-twitch fiber because of its greater shortening velocity. In an evenly mixed muscle at a low velocity, which would provide peak slow-twitch power, the fast-twitch fiber still provides 2.5 times the contribution of the slow-twitch fibers to total power. As a matter of fact, the mixed muscle has a peak power only 55% of that of an unmixed fast-twitch muscle of the same size. Thus, at very low velocities, slow-twitch and fast-twitch fibers can make near-equal contributions to muscle power. At moderate velocities of contraction, however, slow-twitch fibers make only a very slight contribution. For practical purposes, at high velocities of shortening, power is a function of fast-twitch fibers only, as the slow-twitch fibers' contribution is not significant. One setting in which the fast-twitch fiber and slow-twitch fiber are essentially equal in the tension they develop is the isometric contraction; however, in dynamic contractions (those allowing motion) the fast-twitch fiber is much more powerful than the slow-twitch fiber. Because of its ability to have high peak power and resistance to fatigue, the fast oxidative/type IIa fiber can sustain moderate power over a prolonged period, better even than the slow-twitch fiber. The greatest difference between fiber types, in fact, is in their potential for glycolytic metabolism. Most fast-twitch fibers have a component of oxidative enzymes equaling approximately 30–40% of the capacity of slow-twitch fibers. However, the potential for glycolytic metabolism may vary by as much as 600% between fast and slow fibers.

It is apparent that for burst-type activities requiring peak power, it is the fast-twitch fiber that must be trained. The slow fibers are important as an endurance background or base in the setting of strength training. They are also important to provide a depot for the metabolism of the anaerobic by-products (i.e., the oxidation of lactate in the mitochondrial oxidative system). An individual's genetic make-up determines the distribution of muscle fiber type and, thus, probably the potential muscle size.

METABOLISM

Brooks and Fahey state, "The design of the training regimen to improve performance in any physical activity should begin with an evaluation of which energy system or systems are involved." Energy sources are described in a variety of ways; such words as immediate, ultra-short-term, short-term, and endurance are used by a variety of different authors, but basically they are meant to describe the time duration through which an energy source is utilized. An abrupt switch from aerobic to anaerobic metabolism does not occur.

The first energy sources to be considered are most frequently described as immediate energy sources. These are ATP and creatine phosphate (CP). The ATP and CP are occasionally referred to as phosphagen.

ATP is sufficient in volume in the muscle to allow approximately one second of activity. The combination of stored ATP and CP allows approximately 5–6 seconds of activity. This represents acute-burst activity or short-sprint activity. During this time, further ATP is created by a reaction of CP plus ADP, yielding C plus ATP. However, it is probable that up to 20% of immediate energy needs are met by glycolysis. Clearly, glycolysis is not a critical metabolic pathway at this time. The immediate period has also been referred to as alactic. In a teleologic sense, this alactic period allows time for glycolytic metabolism to begin. As we know, glycolytic metabolism probably begins at about the first second of activity.

By 10 seconds into an intense activity the original phosphagen has been utilized. Glycolysis is working at a near-maximum rate. This rate is approximately 1000 times baseline in a sprint. It is this rate that makes up for the inefficiency of the anaerobic system. Glycolysis produces lactate (protons) and 3-ATP per glycogen, not the 39-ATP that would be produced oxidatively. At maximal activity, oxidative metabolism is unable to utilize more than about one tenth of the lactate produced. At 40–50 seconds, energy production may be 50% oxidative. However, a large build-up of lactate still occurs. Lactate produced by type II fast muscle is utilized by adjacent type I fibers. Oxidative metabolism obviously requires that oxygen be supplied to the muscle. The subsarcolemmal mitochondria energize the active transport processes involved in oxidative metabolism. This period of less than one minute, often described as ultra-short-term activity, therefore involves both aerobic and anaerobic metabolism, with the aerobic metabolism becoming more important toward the end of the period. However, 60% of the energy produced during this period is anaerobic.

The enzymes of the immediate energy systems and glycolytic metabolism are water-soluble and exist in the sarcoplasm near the contractile proteins to facilitate rapid activity and recovery. The enzymes of the aerobic oxidative pathways exist within the mitochondria.

Activity in the range of 5–6 minutes is referred to as short-term activity. Approximately 20% of the energy referred for this is derived from anaerobic sources. Training for this sort of activity by necessity then trains all energy systems.

In prolonged activities, the training is primarily of the endurance type. In prolonged activities, such as a 1-hour run, most of the energy provided is from aerobic metabolism.

Endurance training has very specific effects on oxidative metabolic machinery. With adequate training, mitochondrial size can increase to double baseline. As a matter of fact, it is believed now that there are a few huge mitochondria per fiber rather than many small ones; the previous idea that there were multiple mitochondria per fiber was probably an artifact of sectioning. With endurance training there is greater utilization of fat as an energy source, sparing glycogen and allowing greater endurance. There is also better clearance of blood lactate. An increased myoglobin concentration thus allows better oxygen transport into muscle. There is also an increased sensitivity to insulin and increased lipase concentration to allow more efficient utilization of energy sources. Increased stroke volume aids the oxidative metabolic pathways. Increased glycogen storage in muscle also follows.

It is clear that oxidative energy sources, thought of both as endurance and non-power in nature, are important well before one minute is sustained in intense exercise; thus they must be considered in training for speed and power activities that are intermittent, such as football and weight training, as they represent a source of recovery between bursts of activity. These factors are taken into consideration when programs are designed that allow for setting an endurance base in the plan of strength training and also for the periodicity or cycling of strength training.

We have considered the type of muscle fibers that exist and their metabolic pathways. At this point it is appropriate to consider how they work, i.e., what type of contractions occur. The first type of contraction to be considered is the isometric contraction. Isometrics, as a form of contraction and exercise have received an inordinate amount of attention because isometric contraction is easy to study in the isolated muscle preparation in the laboratory; also it was purported to be a panacea of muscle strengthening and rehabilitation. Though understanding of isometric muscle contraction is quite important, isometric exercise in terms of its use for strength training has limited utility.

Isometric contraction implies that both ends of the muscle are fixed and there is no motion in the muscle as a result of the contraction. Thus, there is no mechanical work and energy is dissipated as heat. Maximal isometric tension can be produced at 1.2 times the resting length of the muscle. It should be noted that the resting length of the muscle is the length it assumes when lying free. Isometric tension falls to 0 at the point of maximal shortening. It is also 0 at twice the resting length, since at this length actin and myosin do not overlap. A maximal isometric contraction can be held for only a few seconds, a 50% contraction can be held for approximately 1 minute, and a 10–15% isometric contraction can be held virtually indefinitely, as an aerobic activity. Isometrics, however, results in little endurance training. Hettinger and Mueller (1953) indicated that isometrics are an excellent way to strengthen muscle, but their study has not been validated. Isometric training is quite specific to the angle of the joint. It does not change muscle's ability to exert a force rapidly, and it provides little stimulus for hypertrophy or endurance in dynamic activity.

Isotonic muscle contraction is described as a constant muscle contraction with constant tension, but in fact, this rarely happens. This condition is difficult to achieve, and it is perhaps best to describe it as a dynamic muscle contraction that implies the motion of the muscle. There is a variety of subgroups under this heading, including eccentric, concentric, and isokinetic contractions.

Shortening contractions are described as concentric. Concentric shortening contractions are also described as positive contractions. External work is done as a function of the weight moved and the distance through which it is moved. The mechanical efficiency of this type of work is generally 20–25%, with 75–80% of the energy produced dissipated as heat.

Lengthening contractions are also described as eccentric, or negative; they also produce external work. Isokinetic contractions are dynamic contractions done at a controlled velocity. These have become quite popular in rehabilitation circles, because the equipment necessary to do this has become more widely available.

Under normal circumstances the resting length of muscle is under slight tension. The usual range of shortening or lengthening falls between 0.7 and 1.2 times the normal resting length. Thus, maximal tension can be achieved at ranges seen physiologically. The tension decreases with shortening and increases with lengthening. With passive stretching, elastic tension can increase up to twice that of equilibrium. Equilibrium length is described as that length obtained by an unattached muscle and at that point tension is normal. The highest force generated is with a fast eccentric contraction and the lowest with a fast concentric contraction. Eccentric contractions can generate greater force and power maximums than concentric contractions at any given velocity of stretch. In fact, an integrated EMG shows less activity for the same force level in eccentric contraction as opposed to concentric contraction. Additionally, there is less oxygen consumption and greater mechanical energy produced than for similar concentric contraction.

The greatest power is generally at 25–30% of the maximum velocity of contraction. In activity of very short duration, maximum strength is essentially the same as maximum power, i.e., work per unit time. In long events, power is a function of both strength and metabolic capacity to generate ATP.

In reviewing the potential strength of muscle, certain things need to be realized. Power equals force times the velocity of shortening. Potential power is proportional to the number of active sarcomeres in parallel. The number of sarcomeres present in a cross-sectioned specimen determines the potential maximum force generated by a muscle. Thus, the total mass in the muscle determines its power. Velocity is proportional to the number of active sarcomeres in series; thus, fiber length determines the potential maximum velocity of contraction. Looked at another way, longer muscles can contract more quickly, as there are more sarcomeres with greater shortening per unit time.

Maximum tension in a muscle is a function in its cross section, as there are more cross-bridges in parallel. It is believed that maximum tension in human muscle is approximately 1 to 2 kg per cm^2. It is important to realize, though, that in-vivo muscle does not act as it does in an in-vitro isolated pattern. Full resting length is indeed the postion of greatest possible tension, but other factors exist in vivo that modify the effect of the muscle contraction, e.g., the lever arm, the angle of pull, the insertion of origin of the muscle, and a variety of external forces. Additionally, fiber type, recruitment pattern, coordination, and speed of the cyclic pattern of agonist and antagonist all will affect what we measure or think of as strength. In a variety of subjects, muscle strength can vary 10–20% on a given day when measured with the same activity.

Thus it becomes apparent that length determines speed of contraction and that cross section determines potential maximal force. The highest power is generated at approximately one fourth the maximum velocity of contraction. These factors should be taken into consideration with training. Movements in strength training should be full-range and controlled. "Cheating" by utilizing momentum to move heavier weights than might otherwise be lifted should generally be avoided, except for the last few repetitions at fatigue level. A controlled motion of concentric and eccentric contraction is the best way to provide muscle stimulus.

RECRUITMENT

As mentioned above, muscle size in terms of cross section and velocity is not the only factor involved in power output. Coordination of neural factors—i.e., recruitment—is also critical.

Note that the force generated in a motor unit from two stimuli is greater than that generated by one stimulus of the same total strength. This is referred to as summation. At high rates of stimulation muscle cannot relax and a tetanic action, called fusion of contraction, is achieved. We also know that the fast fibers are innervated by larger motor neurons than slow fibers. Slow fibers will achieve tetanic fusion at 20 hZ and fast fibers at approximately 50 hZ. The range of stimulation for slow fibers is 5–30 hZ and for fast fibers, 30–60 hZ. In general, the number of units firing is described as recruitment and the frequency of firing as rate coding. The frequency becomes more important at higher tensions.

Certain things have been learned from integrated EMG. A voluntary isometric contraction reveals linear EMG activity relative to tension. A voluntary concentric contraction shows activity proportional to tension, but the slope is less with eccentric contraction—i.e., with an eccentric contraction it takes less excitation to get a given tension. At maximal contraction of any type, the integrated EMG is the same: all motor units are firing. A relaxed muscle reveals no integrated EMG activity. Its tone is a result of elasticity of connective and fibrous tissues. With any contraction up to maximum, new units are constantly being recruited to the point of maximum tension. Low threshold units are slow, type I; type II, fast units are high threshold. Thus, it becomes clear that maximal force uses near maximal recruitment of slow- and fast-twitch fibers during any rapid voluntary contraction. In this process there is an orderly recruitment according to size, i.e., the smallest units are recruited first. Thus, slow-twitch involvement is obligatory and mixed muscle fibers are in maximal contraction. The slow-twitch fibers have a long period and low frequency; fast-twitch fibers are more intermittent and at a higher frequency. Slow-twitch fibers are of low threshold, low conduction velocity, and long-twitch conduction time. Fast-twitch fibers are of high threshold, fast conduction velocity, and short-twitch conduction time. Because of the nature of the fast-twitch fibers, a high stimulus frequency is needed to produce a fusion tetany. Thus maximal force occurs when both slow- and fast-twitch pools are recruited, and the rate coding allows fusion tetany synchronously in each motor unit.

Practically speaking, slow contraction muscle units are first recruited in low force-demand activities. Firing frequency is low. As more strength is demanded, there is an increased frequency motor unit action potential (MUAP) firing at higher recruitment rates. The previously involved motor units thereby create a greater contraction force and new units are recruited.

With strength training it has been found that most of the increase in the integrated EMG activity occurs within the first 3–4 weeks of training. Reflex potentiation is also increased as measured by integrated EMG. Motor unit synchronization occurs most efficiently during brief maximal contractions. Motor unit recruiting order is fixed for specific moves and varies with different positions and velocity of movement. Thus, it becomes reasonable to train a muscle in more than one position, with more than one type of motion, and with near maximal contraction.

The neural coordination provided by such strength training is additive to the effects of hypertrophy and to the effects of training on energy systems. Together they facilitate the purpose of strength training, which is to accelerate a given mass more rapidly. Since neural coordination is so important to strength, it implies the need for specificity. It also implies that technique should be proper so that learned patterning is appropriate to the activity desired. It is additive to the effects of hypertrophy, which increase cross section and mass of muscle. It is additive to the effects of training and to the increase of the energy systems necessary for the strength activity.

FATIGUE

The layman's definition of fatigue is failure to maintain power output. It is important to remember that fatigue is a normal occurrence and is in a sense protective, preventing overwork, muscle overload, and excessive damage. Psychological factors, especially the individual's ability to tolerate discomfort, are involved with the perception of fatigue. Muscle discomfort is generally associated primarily with an aerobic state and accumulation of lactate. Blood flow increases with muscle contraction but starts to decrease at a maximum voluntary contraction of about 30%. As one approaches maximal voluntary contraction, blood flow may be severely reduced, thereby requiring anaerobic metabolism. With practice and mental conditioning the central nervous system can maintain full activation during this anaerobic state.

It is unlikely that neural activation plays a critical role in fatigue during normal exercise activity. Therefore, the loss of strength or power due to fatigue is a result of changes in the muscle contractile system at maximal effort. The same is true of repetitive submaximal effort. The integrated EMG activity falls with fatigue, but there seems to be a feedback mechanism that allows enough motor-unit firing to elicit the maximal possible effort, regardless of whatever level of fatigue is present. Thus, the motor-unit firing rate remains at the minimum necessary to maximally stimulate a muscle to perform its necessary task.

Fatigue occurs when the phosphagen is exhausted. Glycolysis begins in the first second of maximal exercise, and within a few seconds it contributes significantly to the energy generated. Performance at submaximal but relatively high cycle work loads depends on muscle glycogen stores, though free fatty acids contribute substrate as well. Fatigue in prolonged exercises thus occurs as a result of glycogen depletion in type I (slow/oxidative) and type IIa (fast/oxidative) fibers. In intense exercise, it is probably a result of glycogen depletion in type IIb fibers.

At the cellular level, there are probably two significant processes that contribute to muscle contractile failure. The myosin actin cross-bridges are mediated by release of calcium from the sarcoplasmic reticulum and coupling to the tropomyosin molecule. These activities are interfered with by increased hydrogen ion concentrate. Additionally, the breakage of the cross-bridges between actin and myosin requires energy from ATP. ATP generation is reduced because of reduced myosin-kinase activity at low pH and low ATP/ADP ratios.

One of the significant effects of strength training is that the athlete is taught to tolerate fatigue and discomfort with vigorous exercise. Once this is achieved with time and practice, "true muscular failure" becomes a function solely dependent on the muscle contractile elements rather than on voluntary activation of the CNS.

SEX DIFFERENCES

Beginning in childhood, males are stronger than females, generating a greater tension per volume of muscle. With the onset of puberty and of androgenic hormones, the difference between males and females increases. An adult male, in general, will be 50% stronger than a female. The fast fibers in males have a greater cross section than in females. Muscle glycogen synthesis and fat oxidative capacity in females probably do not respond to training as quickly as in males, though there is little difference in male and female fiber mix, blood lactate levels, fat metabolism, or muscle glycogen. Adult males have more muscle cell nuclei than do females, and thus a greater potential for hypertrophy. At puberty, both males and females experience an increase in lean body mass, the male moreso. An adult male has approximately ten times the androgen level as a child or female. Strengthening in an adult male occurs both by muscle hypertrophy and by recruitment. The muscle hypertrophy involves increased contractile protein mass. Children, females, and older males increase strength primarily by recruitment and do not have the capacity for muscle hypertrophy noted in adult males.

AGE DIFFERENCES

Though the elderly can increase strength through training, gains are limited. They are unable to achieve muscle hypertrophy. With age, motor units, especially type-II units that are necessary for strength and power, are lost. Additionally, the remaining muscle also suffers a decrease in enzyme activity and mitochondrial mass; thus it is able to generate less ATP per volume of muscle. There also is an increased threshold of activation of motor units and a longer recovery time. Myosin, ATP, and CP also decrease in concentration. It is noted that the decline in strength is more noticeable in trunk and legs than in arms. Maximal strength occurs at about age 20–30. At age 65 in a trained individual, strength can be approximately 80% of the lifetime maximum. Additional factors, including decreased flexibility and arthritis, also play a role with increasing age.

OVERLOAD

Overload is one of the critical principles in strength development. The neuromuscular unit is capable of adapting to appropriate stimuli. The greater the overload, the more postadaptation. Additionally, the greater the overload, the more post-exercise recovery time necessary.

There are four basic factors in overload: intensity, volume, duration, and rest. The applied stimulus should be gradual and progressive but cycled discontinuously. This will allow neural adaptation, muscle hypertrophy, and the development of stressed metabolic systems. Overload specifically increases immediate energy systems not through increased concentration of enzyme per unit volume but by increasing muscle volume by hypertrophy. It increases potential strength by increasing the cross section and mass of muscle through hypertrophy. It increases endurance capacity by increasing mitochondrial volume and by a variety of other changes in the oxidative metabolic pathway.

SPECIFICITY

Specificity is a critical factor in neuromuscular training. While overload encourages development of metabolic systems and muscle size, specificity encourages metabolic systems and, most importantly, neural coordination. Strength can be increased by activation of prime movers, better co-contraction of synergists, and increased inhibition of antagonists. Untrained persons cannot fully activate muscles, especially the high-threshold muscle motor units. Recruitment patterns of muscle are relatively patterned. We know that specificity applies to velocity of contraction, to joint position utilized during the contraction, and to the type of contraction carried out. A recruitment pattern that is established can be modified by sensory input. Thus, muscular strength in a particular activity can be accomplished by training. In strength training, it is important to practice moves. As stated before, practice should be proper so it will develop appropriate neural patterning and habits.

MUSCLE GROWTH

Muscle growth occurs primarily by enlarging the number and size of myofibrils and the associated sarcoplasm. Fiber splitting, which for some time was thought to be a source of hypertrophy, probably does not occur. Heavy resistance training increases the cross section of both type I and type II fibers; however, the increase is more marked in type II fibers, as they are involved in the adaptive response to heavy resistance training. The cross section is larger because of the addition of actin and myosin filaments at the outside of the myofibril. There is a general decrease in the concentration of mitochondria, as type II fibers are trained more specifically than type I; however, the total volume of mitochondria does increase. There may be a slight decrease in the sarcoplasm:myofibril ratio. There is no change in capillary:fiber ratio. Glycogen is not depleted by heavy resistance training, and there is no change in the number of muscle fibers.

Connective tissue increases are proportional to the hypertrophy achieved. Athletes taking steroids have less contractile tissue per cross section than do those not on steroids. The amount of muscle glycogen, CP, and ATP increase. The increase in CP and ATP allows more repetitions near the one-repetition maximum. It is important to note, however, that the change in strength is not directly proportional to the increase in cross section, since other adaptations, as we have already discussed, are important in muscle strength.

Several theories have been advanced in an attempt to define critical stimulus for muscle growth. One theory is that the amount of tension involved causes an increase in protein synthesis and metabolic change. The more likely mechanism, however, is damage caused by forced contraction. Forced contraction, especially eccentric contraction, causes muscle damage with a temporary decrease of strength and power, suggesting a greater effect on the type II fibers. Hypertrophy is a repair response to this damage. This leads to the practical and theoretically-based observation that the greatest gains in strength come from heavy resistance activity carried out every 3 to 4 days. Lifting daily leads to decreased strength.

It is generally agreed that exercise at less than 60% of the one-repetition maximum yields no increased strength, though it increases endurance. Five to six repetitions at 90% of the one-repetition maximum will achieve increased strength and size. This number of repetitions is more effective than one to two repetitions.

MUSCLE SORENESS

Muscle soreness usually occurs 24 to 48 hours after activity and probably represents an overuse injury with excessive mechanical stress of the muscle and connective tissue. Eccentric contractions are noted to cause more soreness than concentric ones, probably because of the greater microtrauma involved in eccentric activity.

TYPES OF EXERCISE

Isometric exercises for strengthening are utilized initially during a period during which the joint is uncomfortable in a range of motion. This type of exercise helps maintain tone and a pattern of contraction. It is also used at times to strengthen a particular point in a range of motion that is weak. Isometrics is not, however, routinely utilized for strength training in other settings.

Most strength training is done with dynamic motion. Constant resistance is provided with free weight, the use of free weights being the technique of choice of most strength-based athletes and others attempting to build significant strength. A variation of the free weight theme is the use of machines that have cams. These variable cams allow more constant load, but this has not been proved superior to free weights as a method of strengthening, despite the claims of some of the manufacturers.

Eccentric exercises are quite effective in strengthening, but they do cause signficant muscle soreness at times. Such exercises are a necessary part of the use of free weights, as eccentric contraction occurs with such use. Eccentrics also come into effect with the use of plyometrics. Plyometrics involve a pre-stretch with an eccentric contraction followed by a concentric contraction of the same muscle, e.g., jumping on and off a bench. Injury is a potential danger with plyometric training.

Proprioceptive neuromuscular facilitation (PNF) is used at times, but it is primarily for rehabilitation. It combines isometrics with dynamic exercise in stretching.

The goal of all strengthening exercises is hypertrophy and the enhancement of recruitment and firing rates of the motor units. The principles of overload and specificity must be adhered to if strengthening is to be obtained. Additionally, adequate rest between sets is quite important. Most strength athletes use free weights with three or more sets of four to eight repetitions. Rest between sets allows full tension to be obtained with the next set. Large muscles are worked no more than twice a week. The periodicity—i.e., variation of the intensity of work and the type of work over weeks and months—alternates the volume, intensity, and duration of the exercise to avoid overstressing the musculoskeletal system. Theoretically this can increase strength and cause less injury, a type of approach that allows rapid biologic adaptation and maintenance of interest.

In outlining a typical program for strength training, principles of muscle physiology are followed. The initial phase for most untrained athletes can be referred to setting a "base." This involves highly repetitious exercise with endurance and muscle toning as a goal. Three sets of 10 to 12 repetitions can be done with weights that are easily handled. This allows the aquisition of adequate flexibility in addition to the building of endurance. The duration of this phase is normally 4 to 8 weeks.

The next phase in a typical strengthening program is the actual strength training. A wide variety of strategies are used by various trainers. Naturally, careful warm-up and stretch are necessary to avoid injury. This can easily be done with one to two sets of light weights through a full range of motion.

There are many strategies used by strength coaches and it is beyond the scope of this chapter to define them all. However, one technique of strengthening involves the use of three to five sets with the same weight. Another is a technique called pyramiding, which begins with lower weights and higher repetitions (12 to 15) for stretch, endurance, and warm-up and works through several more sets, each at higher weights with fewer repetitions (e.g., 8 to 10 and finally 4 to 6). Eccentric work with stress in the eccentric mode can also be employed, including a partner.

With the use of free weights, dumbbells can be used in lieu of a routine olympic bar or machines and will allow better isolation and development of symmetric strength and also greater development of coordination. Modification of weight type permits higher degrees of interest and motivation. The use of machines such as the Nautilus machine offers variety and, in some situations, safety, when partners are not available to spot particular exercises. Most frequently, workouts are organized by body parts to increase concentration and allow adequate rest on the 3- to 4-day cycle. Typical workouts might include back and chest on one day, arms and shoulders on another day, and legs still on another day. Abdominal muscles and calf muscles can be trained almost every day. Major compound moves such as the clean, that train more than body parts are also cycled in 3- to 4-day intervals. Maximum efforts are frequently reserved for every other workout, with the effort level at approximately 85% on the alternate workout.

During this phase of activity, the muscles that are to be strengthened are generally approached with two types of exercise. One is a compound exercise, which involves synergistic muscles; for instance, for lower limb strengthening, squats or leg presses can be performed, as they involve the use of the hamstrings, quadriceps and gluteals, among other muscles. Isolation exercise is generally added to the compound exercise. In terms of the lower limb, knee extensions again work the lower part of the quadriceps and, depending on the angle, the whole quadriceps upward to the hip. Exercises for some muscles should be done in different positions. For instance, the biceps and triceps work somewhat differently at different angles. Working the biceps with the arm at the side and out in front will work it in a different manner. Additionally, because of how the biceps works, it is susceptible to variation in hand position on the bar or on the dumbbell. The triceps can be worked down at the side, out straight ahead, or overhead, depending on the effect wanted or for variety in the training routine.

There is no set way to carry out strengthening activity. The principles of overload and specificity have to be kept in mind. Muscle must be stressed adequately to cause breakdown so that hypertrophy can occur. Additionally, muscles should be worked with their synergists so that better neural patterning and recruitment can occur. Muscles exercised in different positions train neural patterning. Finally, strengthening activities that mimic the motions or activities necessary in a particular sport should be included. This obviously implies a knowledge of the muscles used and the kinesiology involved in any particular sport activity or maneuver. For instance, jumping athletes can strengthen the muscles used in jumping by doing cleans. Throwers require isolated strengthening of the various muscles in the shoulder girdle, including those that control the scapula, and also patterned activities that strengthen the pattern of their throwing. The use of free weights, exercise machines, pulleys or elastic resistance exercises, such as rubber tubing, are all helpful in this regard. A key element in all of this is knowledge of sport-activity dynamics. Much of the art or the sport of strengthening assumes that the participant has a sense of feedback from his or her own body. One must learn when he or she has overworked and when modification of the training scheme is necessary. This comes only with time and experimentation.

Mention should be made of circuit training. It is generally done on machines requiring little or no setups so that it can be done quickly. Exaggerated claims have been made by some manufacturers regarding the aerobic benefits and strength gains possible on the circuit with brief intense exercise to multiple body parts. In fact, aerobic benefit is limited, and strength and endurance can be maintained. Little hypertrophy or strength beyond neural patterning will be achieved with very brief general circuit training.

CATEGORIES OF WEIGHT LIFTING

At this point, it is useful to review the various categories of weight lifting that exists in Western society.

Olympic Lifting

Olympic lifting is a competitive sport that in the past involved a variety of different defined lifts. At this time, however, it involves two lifts, the two-handed snatch and the two-handed clean and jerk. Training generally involves heavy weights and small numbers of repetition. These lifts involve much more than pure strength, as coordination, form and speed are quite important in their mechanics. Olympic lifting probably involves the highest degree of athleticism of the lifting sports. Most training techniques involve compound multiple muscle group exercises.

Power Lifting

Power lifting is a sport that involves three lifts—the squat, bench press and dead lift. Its governing body is different from that of Olympic lifting. Power lifters generally lift very heavy weights with low repetition and multiple sets.

Bodybuilding

It is important to realize that the purpose of bodybuilding is muscle hypertrophy, physical symmetry, and definition, rather than strength. Ideal parameters of physique are used in order to judge contestants. It is a highly competitive sport, which is growing in popularity. On a noncompetitive level, it is becoming more and more popular in the general population. Its most able practitioners are outstanding athletes who, at a professional level, train twice a day.

Though professional bodybuilders and many high-level amateurs use steroids as an adjunct, it is still true that success in bodybuilding requires a reasonable practicing knowledge of nutrition and strength training. Nutrition is important in order to reduce body fat to an absolute minimum, to maintain adequate energy storage for workouts, and to develop hypertrophied muscle. The greatest contribution bodybuilding can make to strength training is, however, the bodybuilder's exceptional knowledge of how to work, strengthen, and hypertrophy specific muscles or parts of muscle, that is, their knowledge of isolation exercises versus compound exercises. Bodybuilders have experimental knowledge of a variety of techniques and strategies for developing a particular body part. For instance, the anterior deltoid and rotator cuff can be worked on with 10 or 12 different exercises, any one of which can be used to circumvent either boredom or injury and still maintain a program of strengthening. Therefore, there is tremendous carryover from the experience of professional bodybuilding to strength training for general athletics and for post-injury and post-surgical rehabilitation.

Whether or not the bodybuilder is as "strong" per volume of muscle as the Olympic lifter or power lifter is a frivolous debate. The reality is that we have a lot to gain from the knowledge that has accumulated in bodybuilding. Olympic lifting is a sport, as specific as high jumping or shotputting. In the case of Olympic lifters, the competitors can train for specific moves. Bodybuilding, since it involves strengthening all body parts in order to gain hypertrophy, probably has more carryover into the general population. Certainly it has more carryover to aging athletes who are unable to safely carry out Olympic lifts and the intense maneuvers used to train for them.

I think it is also important to put to rest another myth about weight lifters and body builders and that is their alleged lack of flexibility. Certainly, while range of motion can be limited somewhat because of massive muscle hypertrophy, successful Olympic lifters and bodybuilders are flexible. These sports require working a muscle through its maximal range in order to gain strength. This sort of work is impossible if above-average flexibility is not present. Attention to the need for flexibility is very important in weight training for athletics in general. It becomes critically important for those entering the gym for the first time or after a prolonged layoff or at a relatively advanced age. It can take months before joint range is sufficient to carry out certain moves, for instance full squats, dumbbell flys, behind the neck military press, and many others. However, patience and attention to detail and the maintenance of flexibility will pay in the avoidance of joint overload and compression injuries, especially in the shoulder and elbow.

DIET

In the context of strength training, nutrition is of course important. The gain in muscle size is mostly from an increase in the volume of contractile protein within the muscle. There is significant synthesis of new capillaries and cellular elements such as mitochondria. Adequate protein intake is important. The standard recommendation is approximately 1 gram per kilogram per day; however, it has been found that, in the early phases of strength training, the requirement increases up 1.5 to 2 grams per kilogram per day. There is no benefit to added fat in the diet to facilitate strength training. Thus, lean poultry, fish and non-meat sources are preferred for dietary protein. It is possible that protein supplementation may be necessary during exhaustive training routines in highly competitive athletes. This is probably not necessary in the general population. Obviously an adequate intake of carbohydrates is necessary so that glycolytic metabolism can occur efficiently.

WEIGHT TRAINING FOR ATHLETICS

In general, programs designed for athletes by strength coaches at all levels involve a combination of the specificity of the bodybuilder's activity and the speed and coordination typical of Olympic lifters. This a mix of compound and isolation exercises. The exercises done by recreation athletes and post-therapy patients generally borrow heavily from bodybuilding techniques.

The critical underlying fact in the above discussion that has to be understood in applying any strength-training technique to the general population, as well as to subspecialized populations, are the concepts of overload and specificity. Strength and hypertrophy occur with strength overload. Endurance overload induces endurance and not strength. Additionally, the speed of activity may be improved by a function of velocity of the lift.

It is important to realize that persons outside the competitive arena rarely train for only speed, endurance or strength but rather have some combination in mind. They prioritize the type of training they do to achieve the gains necessary for their particular goal. As a practical matter, strength training cannot be isolated from endurance and speed in most activities. For instance, putting the shot is a power event; however, it requires particular coordination and speed, as do other power events such as the discus and hammer throw. A football player may train for strength, but he also has to have elements of aerobic endurance in order to stay fresh and function at the highest level throughout a contest. Strength training, therefore, should be rarely done in isolation, and certain aspects of muscular endurance have to be considered. In summary, understanding the physiologic basis of strength training allows a rational rehabilitation program to be designed. Trendy equipment and dangerous substances such as anabolic steroids have no place in the approach.

SELECTED READINGS

Physiology

Asterand and Rodahl: Work Physiology: Physiologic Basis of Exercise. New York, McGraw Hill Co., 1986.
Brooks and Fahey: Exercise Physiology: Human Bioenergetics and Its Applications. New York, John Wiley and Sons, 1984.
Brooks and Fahey: Fundamentals of Human Performance. New York, Macmillan Publishing Company, 1987.
Jones, McCartney and McComas (eds): Human Muscle Power. Champagne, Illinois, Human Kinetic Publishers, 1986.

Practical Training Manuals

Pearl and Moran: Weight Training For Men and Women: Getting Stronger. Bolinas, California, Shelter Publications, 1986.
Pirie and Reynolds: Getting Built. New York, Warner Books, 1984.
Schwarzenegger, A.: Encyclopedia of Modern Bodybuilding. New York, Simon and Schuster, 1985.

Periodicals

Strength Training and Coaching
Journal of the National Strength Coaches Association
Bodybuilding
Flex. Woodland Hills, California, Brut Enterprises.
Iron Man. Marina Del Rey, California, Iron Man Publishing.
Muscle and Fitness. Woodland Hills, California, Brut Enterprises.

JOEL S. SAAL, MD

AEROBIC AND ANAEROBIC TRAINING IN THE INJURED ATHLETE

Reprint requests to Joel S. Saal, M.D., Sports, Orthopedic and Rehabilitation Medicine Associates, 3250 Alpine Rd., Portola Valley, CA 94025.

Athletic competition presents a maximal challenge to the individual's ability to produce and utilize energy efficiently. The athlete's speed, power, and endurance depend upon a complex series of metabolic and circulatory events that represent energy production and delivery. It is from our knowledge of energy production on the cellular level that we have developed the prin-. ciples of athletic conditioning programs. Within the cell, there are three basic energy systems: alactic anaerobic, lactic anaerobic, and aerobic. The interaction of these cellular systems and the organism's circulatory system is the basis of an individual's overall energy-use capabilities. In the circumstance of the injured athlete, the ultimate goal of training is no different from that in the uninjured state—maximal efficiency in energy production and utilization. The focus is changed, however, from training to reach peak condition to training for minimizing loss of peak condition. The physiologic principles upon which training programs are designed are also unchanged in the injured athlete. However, the mechanism by which these goals are achieved requires some manipulation of those principles.

DEFINITION OF TERMS

Energy production is described in terms of quantity and quality. The major energy systems are the anaerobic (alactic and lactic acid) and aerobic. The anaerobic systems are divided into a system that produces lactic acid as a by-product and one that does not. Neither one of these has a requirement for oxygen for energy production. The aerobic system relies upon the use of oxidative metabolism (burning fuels in the presence of oxygen) for deriving energy.

The terms used to describe energy use include power, work, capacity, and endurance. Work is defined as the application of energy for performance of a task in physical terms. It is further defined as force × distance and is represented as foot-pounds, or kilogram-meters. Power is defined as the amount of work that can be performed per unit of time. It therefore represents the rate of energy production and utilization. It is expressed in terms of watts or joule-seconds. Capacity refers to the total quantity of energy available in a given system. In the aerobic system this is defined by the total amount of oxygen that is consumed (VO_{2max}) at maximal activity level.[2,74,96] There is, however, no single parameter to define this in the anaerobic system. Endurance refers to the ability for prolonged physical work (duration of energy production). This has components of both the aerobic and anaerobic systems.[19,27,53,55,58]

Fatigue refers to a state where the individual perceives a very low remaining energy capacity. This must be differentiated from exhaustion, which is a state of absolute lack of energy capacity. Fatigue is a relative state, with elements of subjective and objective lack of energy. Exhaustion is an objective state, where further work can not be performed even with the greatest individual motivation.

ENERGY SYSTEMS

Energy production is classically divided into endurance (aerobic) vs. sprint (anaerobic) systems (Table 1). The physiology of these systems will be discussed only as it directly relates to training on a practical level. Relative utilization of each system is dependent upon the intensity and duration of the task to be performed (Table 2). For a more detailed discussion, the interested reader is directed to any of the referenced books on work physiology.

At the onset of activity, initial energy is derived from stored oxygen in the form of myoglobin. The duration of useable stored oxygen in this form may be as long as 2–3 minutes at a very low activity level (i.e., less than ~40% maximal activity).[2,6,7] As the stored oxygen is depleted, energy is derived from the splitting of stored high-energy phosphate compounds (phosphocreatine and ATP, cumulatively referred to as phosphagen). These products are stored to a limited extent in the cytosol. This system is anaerobic (it has no requirement for utilization of oxygen). It runs out of fuel rapidly, requiring a shift to another system to meet the immediate energy needs. Phosphagen is replenished by rephosphorylation through oxidative metabolism. The process of rebuilding the phosphagen stores requires several minutes (approximately 50% recovery in 20 seconds, with complete recovery within 3 minutes).[11,26,52,70,71]

Anaerobic glycolysis follows in the sequence, the onset and degree of its use dependent upon the intensity level of exercise and the aerobic capacity of the individual. The lactate produced can be redistributed by venous blood back to liver or shuttled back into exercising muscle as fuel.[2,6,7,34] The process of lactate recovery (by conversion into pyruvate and subsequent oxidation) is enhanced by low-intensity-level activity during the recovery period rather than complete rest.[2,39,62] During a particular activity, limitations to further anaerobic glycolysis are due to intolerance of lactic acid produced as metabolic by-product. Perceived intolerance to lactate, lactate clearance, and inadequate skeletal muscle buffering capacity are all involved. Maximal anaerobic activity can only be supported for approximately 40 seconds.[71] For high-intensity-level activity for longer time periods, oxidative processes must take over. The aerobic system has a minimum time requirement to reach its maximal level of energy production (2 to 3 minutes).[2,33,84] This varies with the intensity of exercise and the relative state of aerobic fitness of the individual. The capacity of

TABLE 1. Characteristics of the Aerobic and Anaerobic Energy Systems in an Untrained Individual

Characteristic	Anaerobic System		Aerobic System
Subtype	Alactic	Lactic	
Other designations	ATP/PC, phosphagen	Glycolytic	Oxygen, oxidative phosphorylation
Fuel source	Stored ATP, PC	Stored muscle glycogen and glucose	Glycogen, glucose, fat, and protein
Enzyme system	Single enzyme	Single enzyme system	Multiple enzyme system
Metabolic by-products	ADP + P,C	Lactic acid	$CO_2 + H_2O$
Maximum rate of ATP production (moles/minute)	3.6	1.6	1.0
Time to maximal production rate	$\cong$ 1 sec	5–10 sec	2–3 min
Time limit for maximal production rate	6–10 sec	20–30 sec	3 min
Functional capacity (moles)	0.6	1.2	Theoretically unlimited
Time to exhaustion during *maximal* utilization	10 sec	30–40 sec	5–6 sec
Relative contribution (%) during *maximal* efforts of:			
10 sec	50	35	15
30 sec	15	65	20
2 min	4	46	50
10 min	1	9	90
Time for 50% recovery	20–30 sec	15–20 min	5–10 min
Time for 100% recovery	3 min	1–2 hours	30–60 min
Limiting factor(s)	Depletion of creatine phosphate stores	Lactic acid accumulation resulting from production exceeding buffering capacity	Depletion of carbohydrate, inability to supply adequate oxygen, cardiovascular drift, limitation of optimal carbohydrate supply

Based on the data of Fox EL: Orthop Clin North Am 1977; 8:534–548; and from Paterson DH: Coaching Theory Level III. Ottawa: Coaching Association of Canada, 1981.
Adapted from Plyley.[85]

the aerobic system is limited by a combination of central and peripheral factors. The central factors are circulatory (ability to raise cardiac output) and the peripheral factors refer to the fuel supply and utilization within the target organs.[2,6,7,85,86,92,96]

PHYSIOLOGIC ADAPTATIONS TO TRAINING

The efficiency and capacity of each of these systems have independent factors. The high-energy phosphate system is dependent upon the availability of high-energy phosphates and the limited ability for production via the enzyme myokinase. There is little difference between trained and untrained individuals in the efficiency of phosphate liberation.[2,6,7,11,12] Training of any type probably has only small effect on its concentration in muscle.[2,6,7,11,12,34] The absolute quantity of available phosphagen (ATP and phosphocreatine) will vary with programs that increase muscle mass,[2,36,66] but there has been no demonstrated change of its intracellular concentration following high-intensity training. However, this type of training has been

TABLE 2.   Physique and Maximal Aerobic Power of Male and Female Athletes

	VO$_2$ max (L/min)	
Sport	M	F
Alpine skiing	4.62	3.10
Baseball	4.47	–
Basketball	4.44	2.92
Canoeing/paddling	4.67	3.52
Cross country skiing	5.10	3.64
Cycling	5.13	3.13
Figure skating	3.49	2.38
Football	5.03	–
Gymnastics	3.84	2.30
Ice hockey	4.63	–
Orienterring	5.07	3.64
Raquetball/handball	4.78	–
Running	4.67	3.10
Rowing	5.84	4.10
Shotput/discus	4.84	–
Soccer	4.41	–
Speed skating	5.01	3.10
Swimming	4.52	2.54
Volleyball	4.78	–
Weight-lifting	3.84	–
Wrestling	4.49	–
Untrained	3.14	2.18

Based on the data of Wilmore JH, Am J Sports Med 1984; 12:120–127.
Adapted from Plyley.[85]

shown to decrease the rate of depletion of high energy phosphates for a given work level.[51]

The glycolytic system, however, does demonstrate a capability for adaptation with training. The overall ability to produce lactate[6,7,19,31,32,47] has been demonstrated in high-intensity trained individuals. Changes in the efficiency of the glycolysis itself is controversial. Conflicting results have been generated regarding changes in the concentration of glycolytic enzymes with training programs.[2,7,11] Whereas no significant differences have been demonstrated in enzyme activity with strength-training programs, increased levels of LDH (skeletal muscle type) and phosphofructokinase (a key glycolytic pathway enzyme) have been demonstrated by some investigators with intensive sprint-training programs.[11,12] There is uncertainty as to the significance of increased levels with training due to the very high levels of these enzymes already present in untrained muscles.[2,7,15] However, there is evidence that increased efficiency of glycogen transport and utilization can occur with training.[2,7,23] In addition to increased lactate production, the ability to withstand higher lactate levels also occurs as a result of high-intensity training. This is probably due to an increased skeletal muscle buffering capacity.[32,47,57,74,83,88,94] In part there is a component of desensitization to a given level of serum lactate, resulting in an increased perceptual threshold.

The initial physiologic adaptations to aerobic training that result in improved aerobic power and capacity are due primarily to circulatory factors. This includes an increase in cardiac output as a result of increased stroke volume (for the most part secondary to improved efficiency of cardiac contraction).[2,6,7,8,85,86,87,91,93,97] Aerobic training results in lower levels of serum lactate at a given level of submaximal exercise.[14,33,34,91,103] This is probably related to the circulatory adaptations. Increased concentrations of oxidative enzymes, a shift of muscle fiber characteristics[3,7,15,31,38,57,58,61] to slow oxidative types (a controversial issue), and increased peripheral utilization of fatty acids for fuel are later adaptations observed with prolonged training and increased capacity of the system.[33,34,50,52,54,73,74,76] Improved fat oxidation capacity and increased rate of clearance of lactate through the aerobic pathway probably result from a greater density of muscle mitochondria.[2,7,30] Enhanced glycogen storage is another late adaptation to aerobic training.[2,7,24,43]

ADAPTATIONS TO DECONDITIONING

Saltin[92] described in detail the physiologic effects of deconditioning on a group of healthy volunteers, some of whom were sedentary while others were aerobically trained. They were subjected to intensive physical training (both interval and continuous) following a 21-day period of bed rest. Parameters of aerobic capacity and power were evaluated. The rate of loss of aerobic capacity during the period of rest was similar for each group (approximately 1% of original level per day). Following the training period, the relative increase in aerobic capacity and power was greater for the previously sedentary subjects. The previously trained subjects were able to regain their pre bed-rest aerobic capacities. *However, they required thirty per cent (30%) longer to regain their aerobic capacity than they required to lose it (30–40 days vs. 21 days).* This study has served as the standard for assessment of physiologic adaptations to deconditioning. However, there is no similar "hard data" available for the response of the anaerobic system to the deconditioning process. The implications are clear regarding the rehabilitation of athletic injuries. Endurance, which is dependent upon high levels of oxidative enzymes and mitochondrial density, is lost more quickly than maximal aerobic power.[2,16,67] It is critical to avoid losses of aerobic capacity early in the rehabilitation process. Early attention to aerobic conditioning within the limits of the specific injury is essential.

MEASUREMENT

The aerobic system is easily available for evaluation, both in the laboratory in an exact manner and in the field by rough estimate. The quantity of expired oxygen can easily be collected and analyzed to determine the individual's VO_{2max}. As mentioned above, this is the gold standard of aerobic fitness.[2,7,87,97] It does have a significant limitation, however. In a highly trained endurance athlete, VO_{2max} itself does not correspond well to performance.[2,8,34,63,73,76,96,106] Beyond a certain level of fitness (competitive to elite athletes), changes in VO_{2max} are very small, with endurance performance differences probably secondary to mitochondrial density[7,30] and subsequent improvement in tissue respiratory capacity (especially the ability to burn fats as fuel in prolonged exercise). The change in resting heart rate after training[87,98] and the change in heart rate with submaximal and maximal exertion after training (decrease in heart rate for the same level of % maximal activity) are rough but fairly accurate and reproducible measures of aerobic capacity to be used in the field. On a more invasive level, muscle biopsy (most commonly from the vastus lateralis) with histochemical analysis of muscle fiber types and relative concentrations of both anaerobic and aerobic system enzymes is an accurate and reproducible method for determining physiologic adaptations to conditioning programs.

Anaerobic power and capacity, however, have no clear "gold standard" to compare with the aerobic system. There are multiple tests available (Wingate,

Douglas bag modification, maximal treadmill running, and various field tests utilizing specific athletic challenges).[9,10,12,18–21,25,58,59,75,84,100] None of these has clearly been shown to be superior to the others, each with specific limitations.[9,75,84,100] For example, a popular research method is the Wingate test. This determines the maximum power output in 30 seconds of bicycle ergometry. Due to the specificity of training phenomenon (see section on specificity of training), this may not be a very good indicator of anaerobic power in running or swimming athletes. Other difficulties include standardizing the resistance and differences in performance based on crank length (men vs. women vs. children).[9,75,84,100] It has not been demonstrated to correlate with sprint training programs that achieved improved anaerobic muscle enzyme levels measured by histochemical analysis.[11]

The anaerobic threshold is a misnomer, describing the transition of aerobic to anaerobic metabolism once exercise intensity has increased beyond the aerobic capacity (referred to as supramaximal). As work proceeds at a submaximal level, there is no detectable lactate in the blood in the normal individual. Once the activity exceeds 60% of VO_{2max}, lactate will begin to appear in the blood in a nonlinearly increasing manner. The point of inflection of the serum lactate concentration curve is referred to as the anaerobic threshold. There is often (but not always) a simultaneous inflection in the ventilatory rate. It has been argued that this serves as a marker for the shift of muscle metabolism to a primarily anaerobic activity.[69,82,101,103,104] There are, however, several problems with this assumption. Hagberg[35] demonstrated a ventilatory inflection in patients with McArdle's disease (genetic defect with the inability to produce lactate). The level of lactate in the blood can be affected by factors other than the mode of metabolism, such as nutritional state, blood flow, and body mass.[6,7] Although the concept of the anaerobic threshold is attractive, it does not have a simple direct correlate in ventilation but must be assessed by capillary lactic acid concentration and pH.

PRINCIPLES OF TRAINING

There are three central concepts regarding any endurance or sprint-training program: volume, intensity, and specificity. These are the variables that will determine the type and effectiveness of physiologic adaptations that occur with the training program.

Volume

In order to obtain the training effect in either of the energy systems, an overload of that system must occur. Therefore, a minimum volume (frequency × duration) of training must be performed above a threshold intensity. As the level of aerobic or anaerobic conditioning improves, the volume of training must be increased. The American College of Sports Medicine recommends that a minimum of three repetitions per week are required (lasting 20 minutes) for a significant increase in VO_{2max} to occur in a healthy untrained adult.[1] However, this may be inadequate for a recreational athlete when one considers the greater amount of condition lost with inactivity in trained athletes.[2,96] The volume necessary for a previously trained competitive athlete is higher, in the range of 35 to 45 minutes four to five times per week.[2,102] Further increases in the frequency of training will increase the effectiveness of the program but not in a linear manner (2 × frequency may only create 1.4 × the effect).[2] It is the overall volume of training (total work performed), not the frequency per se, that determines the effectiveness of the training program.[2,3,7]

In the case of the injured high-caliber athlete, the intensity of training required to minimize losses in the immediate post-injury period is high (i.e., 80–90% VO_{2max}). It will require a frequency of four to seven sessions per week (depending upon the specific athletic task), because of the high preinjury level of conditioning. There is less data available regarding the requirements of the anaerobic energy system. The rate of loss of aerobic capacity is well documented (as mentioned earlier in the Saltin study.[92]) It is not clear, however, at what rate anaerobic losses occur, in part due to the difficulty in measurement and definition of anaerobic condition and capacity. The phosphagen system relies on the total amount of stored high-energy phosphates, which is for the most part dependent upon muscle bulk. The rate of loss with immobility, therefore, probably follows the course of muscle atrophy and strength loss. Changes in the glycolytic system with disuse are not well documented. The glycolytic enzymes are not stored in large quantity and have a short half-life.[2,7] This has significant implications regarding the post-injury period, with a need to train this system by high-intensity activity within the restrictions placed by the injury.

Intensity

The intensity of training will determine which energy system is utilized. Intensity level is described in relation to VO_{2max}. Intensities higher than can be supported by aerobic processes alone are referred to as supramaximal. All other levels are described by relative % VO_{2max}. By definition, activity performed at supramaximal intensity is necessary for anaerobic training to take place. Just as the aerobic system must be overloaded in volume, so must the anaerobic system be challenged. This can be accomplished by repeated bouts of exercise at supramaximal intensity, such as sprint running (level or inclined surfaces to insure maximal output), with or without a combined program of strength training of the same muscle groups. To satisfy the overload principle, the training program must be continually adapted to aerobic conditioning gains by increasing the intensity of the activity to stay at an approximately 90% VO_{2max} in the well-trained athlete (70–90% may be acceptable in recreational athletes). For adequate anaerobic conditioning, the intensity must be continued at supramaximal levels (although further absolute increases in the intensity itself are small). As the anaerobic capacity increases, the activity may be simply carried out for a longer time period (increased total work).

Specificity

Aerobic and anaerobic training adaptations are specific to the training method employed. Sprint running is far superior to sprint swimming or cycling for training in the 100 meter dash run. Programs designed to enhance endurance require long duration overload with submaximal intensity exercise.[2,7,27,86,87] Sprint training has similar requirements for short duration maximal or supramaximal exertion. This has been demonstrated in several studies of minimal aerobic capacity improvement with sprint training alone, and lactate accumulation in endurance trained athletes in cross-over studies of sprint activity.[2,4,5,19,22,38,44,46,57,70,91] Upper extremity training produces improved aerobic capacity with arm exercise but only minimal improvements with lower extremity exercise (Saltin studies). However, leg training produces an almost equal improvement of aerobic capacity with arm and leg exercise.[14,57] This demonstrates the importance of peripheral as well as central adaptations to exercise training. The cross-over effect (improvement in upper extremity endurance after leg training) is due to the central adaptations (circulatory system changes). The observations of specificity-dependent-training effects are likely due to improved oxygen extraction capabilities in the exercised muscle groups. Additionally, simultaneous upper and lower extremity exercise can increase the overall intensity of aerobic challenge significantly.[2,7] This has important implications in rehabilitation programs.

Despite the multiple examples of the need for separation of training modalities, there is still a sound physiologic basis for the use of a balanced program for most athletes. The specific task to be performed and necessary skill requirements should highlight the portions of the training program to be reinforced. Even in those athletic events of short duration (100 meter sprint) that rely almost purely on anaerobic metabolism (although both alactic and lactic acid producing systems are involved), the recovery process is aerobic. In the setting of an individual event, and in the "meet" situation of multiple heats, training of the aerobic system is essential for maximum performance to optimize recovery.

There are further problems encountered when considering the specificity of training in athletes outside of "pure" track and field events. In football, wrestling, dance, tennis, and athletes who participate in multiple track events, there is a specific requirement for efficiency in both aerobic and anaerobic processes. There is evidence that training programs for strength and endurance are not only mutually exclusive but can interfere with each other's effectiveness.[22] In a program of strength and endurance training performed at high intensity in consecutive workouts, with mixture of concentration on each, one or the other suffered in efficiency of gains. In the athletes requiring both types of metabolic processes, this apparent double-bind can be overcome in a number of ways. This includes variations of seasonal components of training, with high intensity strength training preceding endurance training. A more effective method may be the use of interval training, as well as a newer concept, circuit-weight training.

TRAINING PROGRAM OPTIONS FOR REHABILITATION

Considering athletic injury, the specificity principle is essential to the establishment of the rehabilitation program. Limitations imposed by immobilization, pain, or joint instability often require utilization of alternative methods to the athlete's competitive event to accomplish training goals. To maintain the patient's strength; methods involving large muscle groups must be employed. This can be approached by upper, lower, or combined extremity exercise. In general, utilizing as many extremities as possible will generate the greatest central training effect.[2] In the presence of lower extremity injury requiring immobilization (or restricted weight bearing activity), upper extremity exercise in repetitive submaximal activity (UBE ergometer) can substitute well for the aerobic training needs of mixed endurance/anaerobic athletes. Although the specificity principle is not entirely satisfied, there is some crossover invoking a central training effect.[2,14,57,70,87,89,91,104]

Another very effective method is pool training, using a combination of upper and contralateral lower extremity resisted exercise. The unloading of joints with simultaneous large muscle group activity makes this a very useful alternative in lumbar spine injury of all types, lower extremity muscle contusions and tears, and ankle sprains in the early mobilization phases. A relatively high percentage of VO_{2max} is employed as a result of upper and lower extremity action, and a cross-training effect of the lower extremities also occurs to some degree. Anaerobic training can also be accomplished in the pool by performing high-step running in sprints while the athlete wears a weighted vest. Single-leg training by stationary bicycle has a limited role due to only fair improvement in VO_{2max}, and a poor cross-training effect for two-legged cycling. However, the addition of upper extremity repetitive exercise (Aerodyne ergometer) can invoke a significant central training effect. Additionally, a contralateral lower extremity training effect may also be accomplished to some degree in this manner. This can also be utilized in a sprint or interval mode for anaerobic training effect.

The use of a stationary bicycle or ergometry for a running or swimming endurance athlete may not be ideal due to the specificity requirements mentioned earlier regarding these activities. A significant central training effect does occur, however, making this an important albeit incomplete substitute for the specific competitive event. However, the cross-over result of swim training for treadmill running is limited. A group of recreational swimmers trained intensively at swimming demonstrated increased VO_{2max} for swimming but none for running on a treadmill.[70] This directly reflects the specificity principle. The reliance on upper extremity strength in swimming results in a lesser improvement in leg aerobic capacity, suggesting a correlation with peripheral factors in this type of training.

Therefore, substitution of a training method as similar as possible to the athletic activity is the training goal. This may be accomplished with substitution of upper-extremity activity and lower-extremity activity selectively (i.e., swimming with leg-use only or vice versa). Although it is more specific, the use of a swim bench may be as limited as swimming itself in the presence of recent shoulder surgery or other major upper-extremity injury. The use of a rowing machine can be very effective in this setting, due to the upper and lower extremity requirements, and the well-tolerated positioning of the arms (eliminating biceps tendon or rotator cuff impingement).[36,62,63]

Water training with use of a kickboard can help maintain specificity or training for the lower extremities. Cross-country ski machines (Nordic-Trac) are another alternative for combined upper and lower extremity training[2,90] in either an aerobic or mixed aerobic-anaerobic mode. Circuit-weight training can also be effective in this setting (theoretically) because of the central conditioning effect as well as the peripheral training effect in muscles frequently used in swimming.

Interval Training

Physical training can either be continuous or intermittent. There are advantages to each type. The total amount of work performed probably has the major influence on the effectiveness of a training program.[2,12,27,87,102] It is on this basis that interval training was developed. The total capacity for performing work is increased when periods of activity of varying intensity are interspersed with periods of rest. Initial studies of intermittent exercise disclosed that varying the intensity allowed for a greater overall energy expenditure and a subjective feeling of less exhaustion after completion of the task.[2,3,13] The training effect was as effective as continuous training for aerobic capacity.[2,3,13] The training effect obtained depends upon the intensity level and duration of the activity periods and the length of the rest periods compared to the activity periods. By manipulation of these parameters, the anaerobic system can be overloaded simultaneously or independently of the aerobic system. In addition, the specificity principle can also be satisfied by including the same relative intensity and muscle group involvement as in the target task.

An interval program that consists of submaximal intensity activity for periods of 3 minutes mixed with rest periods (here and below this refers to low intensity activity rather than complete rest) of equal duration can successfully challenge the aerobic system.[2,3,17,25,28,67] Interval programs with 45-second to one-minute supramaximal intensity exercise, mixed with three-minute rest periods (to allow for restoration of phosphagen stores and initial lactate clearance) will stress the anaerobic system. Very short duration exercise (15 seconds) with 45-second rest periods can theoretically maximally challenge the alactic (phosphagen) system. Decreasing the intensity slightly with an increase in the duration of the exercise bouts (1½ minutes) with similar change in rest periods theoretically can simultaneously train both systems.

Interval training can be a highly effective training method for several reasons. Maximal challenge to both types of energy systems is a major potential advantage. Additionally, it can satisfy the specificity principle by challenging these systems at a similar pace to the chosen athletic event. Since most ball sports are by definition interval exercise, this type of training may be highly specific.[2,29]

Circuit-Weight Training

The goal of including upper and lower extremity exercise can also be accomplished with circuit-weight training. Although presently offered as an alternative mostly for cardiac rehabilitation,[54,87] it has some advantages for athletic rehabilitation. Repetitive submaximal exertion, using a variety of upper and lower extremity weight-training stations (at approximately 70% of maximal weight) performed rapidly (30 sec) with short duration rest periods (15 to 30 seconds) is the general technique. This has also been combined with intervals of running or cycling (with modest additional improvement in VO_{2max}).[26,81] Circuit training has the advantage of increasing the endurance and strength of the exercised muscle groups.[2,29,54,87] However, the overall increases in VO_{2max} are small, with intensity levels during exercise reaching only 80% of VO_{2max}. Considering the specificity of training principle and the improvements in strength and endurance of exercised muscle groups, this can have utility as a rehabilitation option for athletes with upper extremity strength requirements in addition to aerobic needs (i.e., basketball, baseball, and football).

SUMMARY

Athletic rehabilitation requires attention to the aerobic and anaerobic condition of the athlete as well as the specific injury. The energy-producing systems of the body have a specific (although not completely understood) interaction that should influence the type of rehabilitation program employed. The principles of training the injured athlete are the same as those applying to the uninjured state. It is critical to minimize conditioning losses early in the post-injury period.

Maintenance of peak condition rather than reaching peak conditioning is the focus of athletic rehabilitation. The principles of volume, intensity, and specificity must be satisfied for each type of program. There are a number of conditioning methods available and a variety of modes in which they can be employed (interval vs. continuous vs. circuit vs. combined). There is no one formula that is correct in any given situation, but a number of options exist. The specific needs of the individual athlete and the limitations of the injury should define which methods and modes are chosen.

REFERENCES

1. American College of Sports Medicine. Position Statement on the Recommended Quantity and Quality of Exercise for Developing and Maintaining Fitness in Healthy Adults. Med Sci Sports 10:vii–x, 1978.
2. Astrand, Rodahl: Work Physiology: Physiologic Basis of Exercise. New York, McGraw-Hill Book Co., 1986.
3. Astrand I, Astrand PO, Christensen EH, Hedman R: Intermittent muscular work. Acta Physiol Scand 48:448–453, 1960.

4. Bar-Or O, Dotan R, Inbar O, et al: Anaerobic capacity and muscle fiber type distribution in man. Int J Sports Med 1:82–85, 1980.
5. Bouckaert J, Pannier J, Vrijens J: Cardiorespiratory response to bicycle and rowing ergometer exercise in oarsmen. Eur J Applied Physiol 51:51–59, 1983.
6. Brooks G, Fahey T: Exercise Physiology: Human Bioenergetics and Its Applications. Boston, John Wiley and Sons, 1984.
7. Brooks G, Fahey P-O: Fundamentals of Human Performance. New York, Macmillan Publishing Company, 1987.
8. Brown S, Wilkinson J: Characteristics of national, divisional, and club male Alpine ski racers. Med Sci Sports Exerc 15:491–495, 1983.
9. Bruyn-Prevost P, Sturbois X: physiological response of girls to aerobic and anaerobic endurance tests. J Sports Med 24:149–154, 1984.
10. Cellini M, Vitiello P, Ziglio P, et al: Noninvasive determination of the anaerobic threshold in swimming. Int J Sports Med 7:347–351, 1986.
11. Cheetham M, Boobis L, Williams C: Human muscle metabolism during sprint running. J Appl Physiol 61:54–60, 1986.
12. Cheetham M, Williams C, Lakomy H: A laboratory running test: Metabolic responses of sprint and endurance trained athletes. Br J Sports Med 3:81–84.
13. Christensen EH, Hedman R, Saltin B: Intermittent and continuous running. Acta Phys Scand 50:260–286, 1960.
14. Clausen J, Klausen K, Rasmussen B, Trap-Jensen J: Central and peripheral circulatory changes after training of the arms or legs. Am J Physiol 225:675–682, 1973.
15. Costill D, Daniels W, Evans W, et al: Skeletal muscle enzymes and fiber composition. J Appl Physiol 40:149–154, 1967.
16. Coyle EF, Martin WF, et al: Time course of loss of adaptations after stopping intense endurance training. J Appl Physiol 57:1857–1859, 1984.
17. Daniels J, Scardina N: Interval training and performance. Sports Medicine 1:327–334, 1984.
18. Davis H, Gass G: The anaerobic threshold as determined before and during lactic acidosis. Eur J Applied Physiol 47:141–149, 1981.
19. Davis J, Frank M, Whipp B, Wasserman K: Anaerobic threshold alterations caused by endurance training in middle-aged men. J Appl Physiol 46:1039–1046, 1979.
20. Davis J, Vodak P, Wilmore J, et al: Anaerobic threshold and maximal aerobic power for three modes of exercise. J Appl Physiol 41:544–550, 1976.
21. Droghetti P, Borsetto C, Casoni I, et al: Noninvasive determination of the anaerobic threshold in canoeing, cross-country skiing, cycling, roller and iceskating, rowing, and walking. Eur J Applied Physiol 53:299–303, 1985.
22. Dudley G, Fleck S: Strength and endurance training: Are they mutually exclusive? Sports Medicine 4:79–85, 1987.
23. Durnin J: Muscle in sports medicine—nutrition and muscular performance. Int J Sports Med 3:52–57, 1982.
24. Fielding R, Costill D, Fink W, et al: Effect of carbohydrate feeding frequencies and dosage on muscle glycogen use during exercise. Med Sci Sports Exerc 17:472–476, 1985.
25. Fleck S: Interval training: Physiological basis. NSCA Journal 40:October/November, 1983.
26. Fohrenbach R, Mader A, Hollmann W: Determination of endurance capacity and prediction of exercise intensities for training and competition in marathon runners. Int J Sports Med 8:11–18, 1987.
27. Fox E, Bartels R, Billings C, et al: Frequency and duration of interval training programs and changes in aerobic power. J Appl Physiol 38:481–484, 1975.
28. Gettman L, Ward P, Hagan R: A comparison of combined running and weight training with circuit weight training. Med Sci Sports Exerc 14:229–234, 1982.
29. Gillam G: Basketball:physiological basis. NSCA Journal 44:January 1985.
30. Gollnick PO, King DW: Effect of exercise and training on mitochondria. Am J Physiol Endocrino 224.
31. GreenH, Hughson R, Orr G, Ranney D: Anaerobic threshold, blood lactate, and muscle metabolites in progressive exercise. J Appl Physiol 54:1032–1038, 1983.
32. Green J, Jackman A: Peripheral limitations to exercise. Med Sci Sports Exerc 16:299–305, 1984.
33. Hagberg J, Hickson R, Ehsani A, Holloszy J: Faster adjustment to and recovery from submaximal exercise in the trained state. J Appl Physiol 48:218–224, 1980.
34. Hagberg J, Coyle E: Physiological determinants of endurance performance as studied in competitive racewalkers. Med Sci Sports Exerc 15:287–289, 1983.

35. Hagbert J, Coyle E, et al: Exercise hyperventilation in patients with McArdle's disease: respiration, environment, exercise, physiology. J Appl Physiol 52:991–994, 1982.
36. Hagerman F: Applied physiology of rowing. Sports Medicine 1:303–326, 1984.
37. Hakkinen K, Alen M, Komi P: Neuromuscular, anaerobic, and aerobic performance characteristics of elite power athletes. Eur J Applied Physiol 53:97–105, 1984.
38. Henriksson J, Reitman J: Time course of changes in human skeletal muscle succinate dehyrogenase and cytochrome oxidase activities and maximal oxygen uptake with physical activity and inactivity. Acta Physiol Scand 99:91–97, 1977.
39. Henriksson J: Training induced adaptation of skeletal muscle and metabolism during submaximal exercise. J Physiol 270:661–675, 1977.
40. Hermansen LS, Machlum ER, Pruett O, et al: Lactate Removal at Rest and Exercise in Metabolic Adaptation to Prolonged Physical Exercise. Basel, Switzerland, Birhaussen Verlag, pp. 101–105.
41. Hickson RC: Interference of strength development by simultaneously training for strength and endurance. Eur J Applied Physiol 45:255–263, 1980.
42. Holloszy JO: Adaptation of skeletal muscle to endurance exercise. Med Sci Sports 7:155–164, 1975.
43. Hollozy JO, Booth FW: Biomechanical adaptations to endurance exercise in muscle. Ann Rev Physiol 18:273, 1976.
44. Holmer I, Stein E, Saltin B, et al: Hemodynamic and respiratory responses compared in swimming and running. J Appl Physiol 37:49–54, 1974.
45. Holmer I: Oxygen uptake during swimming in man. J Appl Physiol 33:502–509, 1972.
46. Hoshizaki T: Relationships of muscular endurance among specific muscle groups for continuous and intermittent static contractions. Research Quarterly for Exercise and Sport 57:229, 1986.
47. Houston M, Thomson J: The response of endurance-adapted adults in intense anaerobic training. Eur J Applied Physiol 36:207–213, 1977.
48. Hultman E, Berstron J: Breakdown and resynthesis of physphocreatine and ATP in connection with muscular work in man. Scand J Clin Lab Invest 19:56–66.
49. Huston T, Puffer J, Rodney W: The athletic heart syndrome. N Engl J Med 313:24–32, 1985.
50. Ingjer F: Maximal aerobic power related to the capillary supply of the quadriceps femoris muscle in man. Acta Physiol Scand 104:238–240, 1978.
51. Jones N, Heigenhauser G, Kuksis A, et al: Fat metabolism in heavy exercise. Clinical Science 59:469–478, 1980.
52. Karlson J, Nordesjo W, et al: Muscle lactate, ATP and CP levels during exercise after physical training in man. J Appl Physiol 33:199–203, 1972.
53. Katch V, Weltman A: Interrelationship between anaerobic power output, anaerobic capacity and aerobic power. Ergonomics 22:325–332, 1979.
54. Keleman M, Stewart K: Circuit weight training: A new direction for cardiac weight training. Sports Medicine November/December, 1985.
55. Kindermann W, ßimon G, Keul J: The significance of aerobic-anaerobic transition for the determination of work load intensities during endurance training. Eur J Appl Physiol 42:25–34, 1979.
56. Kitamura K, Jorgensen C, Gobel F, et al: Hemodynamics correlates of myocardial oxygen consumption during upright exercises. J Appl Physiol 32:516–522, 1972.
57. Klausen K, Rasmussen B, Clausen J, Trap-Jensen J: Blood lactate from exercising extremities before and after arm or leg training. Am J Physiol 227:67–72, 1974.
58. Komi P, Rusko H, Vos J, Vihko V: Aerobic performance capacity in athletes. Acta Physiol Scand 100:107–114, 1977.
59. Komi P, Rusko H, Vos J, Vihko V: Anaerobic performance capacity in athletes. Acta Physiol Scand 100:107–114, 1977.
60. Komi P, Viitasalo J, Rauramaa R, Vihko V: Effect of isometric strength training on mechanical, electrical, and metabolic aspects of muscle function. Eur J Applied Physiol 40:45–55, 1978.
61. Komi P, Viitasalo T, Havu M, et al: Skeletal muscle fibres and muscle enzyme activities in monozygous and dizygous twins of both sexes. Acta Physiol Scand 100:385–392, 1977.
62. Koutedakis Y, Sharp N: Lactic acid removal and heart rate frequencies during recovery after strenuous rowing exercise. Br J Sports Med 19:199–202, 1985.
63. Lavoie J, Montpetit R: Applied physiology of swimming. Sports Medicine 3:165–189, 1986.
64. Lesmes G, Fox E, Stevens C, Otto R: Metabolic responses of females to high intensity interval training of different frequencies. Med Sci Sports Exerc 10(4):229–232, 1978.
65. Lusiani L, Ronsisvalle G, Bonanome A, et al: Echocardiographic evaluation of the dimensions and systolic properties of the left ventricle in freshman athletes during physical training. Eur Heart J 7:196–203, 1986.

66. MacDougall J, Ward G, Sale D, Sutton J: Biochemical adaptation of human skeletal muscle to heavy resistance training and immobilization. J Applied Physiol 43(4):700–703, 1977.
67. MacDougall J, Elder G, Sale D, et al: Effects of strength training and immobilization on human muscle fibres. Eur J Applied Physiol 43:25–28, 1980.
68. Mackova E, Melichna J, Vondra K, et al: The relationship between anaerobic performance and muscle metabolic capacity and fibre distribution. Eur J Applied Physiol 54:413–415, 1985.
69. Mader A, Heck H: A theory of the origin of "anaerobic threshold." Int J Sports Med Suppl 7:45–65, 1986.
70. Magel J, Foglia F, McArdle W, et al: Specificity of swim training on maximum oxygen uptake. J Appl Physiol 38:151–155, 1974.
71. Margaria A, Ceretelli PE, di Prampero CM, et al: Kinetics and mechanism of oxygen debt contraction in man. J Appl Physiol 18:371–377.
72. Margaria R, Cerretelli P, Mangili F: Balance and kinetics of anaerobic energy release during strenuous exercise in man. J Appl Physiol 19:623–628, 1964.
73. Margaria R, Aghemo P, Limas F: A simple relation between performance in running and maximal aerobic power. J Appl Physiol 38:351–352, 1975.
74. Martin B, Sparks K, Zwillich C, Weil J: Low exercise ventilation in endurance athletes. Med Sci Sports 11:181–185, 1979.
75. Maud P, Shultz B: Gender comparisons in anaerobic power and anaerobic capacity tests. Br J Sports Med 20:51–54, 1986.
76. Maughan R, Leiper J: Aerobic capacity and fractional utilisation of aerobic capacity in elite and non-elite male and female marathon runner. Eur J Applied Physiol 52:80–87, 1983.
77. Medbø, J, Sejersted O: Acid-base and electrolyte balance after exhausting exercise in endurance-trained and sprint-trained subjects. Acta Physiol Scand 125:97–109, 1985.
78. Moritani T: Critical power as a measure of physical work capacity and anaerobic threshold. Ergonomics 24:339–350, 1981.
79. Nikolic Z, Todorovic: Anaerobic threshold during arm and leg exercises and cardiorespiratory fitness tests in a group of male and female students. Int J Sports Med 5:330–335, 1984.
80. O'Donnell C, Smith D, O'Donnell T, Stacy R: Physical fitness of New Zealand Army personnel; correlation between field tests and direct laboratory assessments-anaerobic threshold and maximum oxygen uptake. NZ Med J 97:476–479, 1984.
81. O'Shea P: Interval weight training-a scientific approach to cross-training for athletic strength fitness. NSCA Journal 9:53–57, 1987.
82. Palka M, Rogozinski A: Standards and predicted values of anaerobic threshold. Eur J Applied Physiol 54:643–646, 1986.
83. Parkhouse W, McKenzie D: Possible contribution of skeletal muscle buffers to enhanced anaerobic performance: A brief review. Med Sci Sports Exerc 16:328–338, 1984.
84. Patton J, Duggan A: An evaluation of tests of anaerobic power. Aviat Space Environ Med 237–242, March 1987.
85. Plyley M: Cardiopulmonary Physiology. In Current Therapy in Sports Medicine. St. Louis, B.C. Decker Inc. and C.V. Mosby Co., 1985.
86. Pollock M, Cureton TK, Grenninger L: Effectsof training on working capacity, cardiovascular function and body composition in adult man. Med Sci Sports Exerc 1:70–74, 1969.
87. Pollock M, Wilmore J, Fox S: Exercise in Health and Disease. Philadelphia, W.B. Saunders Company, 1984.
88. Purvis J, Cureton K: Ratings of perceived exertion at the anaerobic threshold. Ergonomics 24:295–300, 1981.
89. Rusko H, Havu M, Karvinen E: Aerobic performance capacity in athletes. Eur J Applied Physiol 151–159, 1978.
90. Rusko H, Rahkila P, Karvinen E: Anaerobic threshold, skeletal muscle enzymes and fiber composition in young female cross-country skiers. Acta Physiol Scand 108:263–268, 1980.
91. Saltin B, et al: The nature of the training response: peripheral and central adaptations to one legged exercise. Acta Physiol Scand 96:289–297, 1967.
92. Saltin B, Blomquist G, Mitchell J, et al: Response to exercise after bed rest and after training. Circulation 38:1–55, 1968.
93. Shapiro L, Smith R: Effect of training on left ventricular structure and function: An echocardiographic study. Br Heart J 50:534–539, 1983.
94. Sharp L, Costill D, Fink W, King D: Effects of eight weeks of bicycle ergometer sprint training on human muscle buffer capacity. Int J Sports Med 7:13–17, 1986.
95. Shaver L: Maximum aerobic power and anaerobic work capacity prediction from various running performances of untrained college men. J Sports Med 15:147–150, 1975.

96. Shephard R, Godin G, Campbell R: Characteristics of sprint, medium and long-distance swimmers. Eur J Applied Physiol 32:99–116, 1974.
97. Snell P, Mitchell J: The role of maximal oxygen uptake in exercise performance. Clin Chest Med 5:51–62, 1984.
98. Tesch P, Larsson L: Muscle hypertrophy in bodybuilders. Eur J Applied Physiol 49:301–306, 1982.
99. Thorland W, Johnson G, Cisar C, et al: Strength and anaerobic responses of elite young female sprint and distance runners. Med Sci Sports Exerc 19:56–61, 1987.
100. Vandewaille H, Peres G, et al: Standard anaerobic tests. Sportsmed 56–61, 1987.
101. Wasserman K, Whipp B, Koyal S, Beaver W: Anaerobic threshold and respiratory gas exchange during exercise. J Appl Physiol 35:236–243, 1973.
102. Wenger H, Bell G: The interactions of intensity, frequency and duration of exercise training in altering cardiorespiratory fitness. Sports Medicine 3:346–356, 1986.
103. Withers R: Anaerobic work at submaximal relative workloads in subjects of high and medium fitness. J Sports Med 17:17–24, 1977.
104. Withers R, Sherman W, Miller J, Costill D: Specificity of the anaerobic threshold in endurance trained cyclists and runners. Eur J Applied Physiol 47:93–104, 1981.
105. Wood P, Terry R, Haskell W: Metabolism of substrates: diet, lipoprotein metabolism, and exercise. Fed Proc 44:358–363, 1985.
106. Wyndham C, Strydom N, Van Rensburg A, Benade A: Physiological requirements for world-class performances in endurance running. South African Medical Journal 996–1002, 1969.
107. Yoshida T, Nagata A, Muro M, et al: The validity of anaerobic threshold determination by a Douglas bag method compared with arterial blood lactate concentration. Eur J Applied Physiol 46:423–430, 1981.

JERYL J. WIENS, MD
JEFFREY A. SAAL, MD

REHABILITATION OF CERVICAL SPINE AND BRACHIAL PLEXUS INJURIES

Reprint requests to Jeryl J. Wiens, M.D., Sports, Orthopedic and Rehabilitation Medicine Associates, 3250 Alpine Rd., Portola Valley, CA 94025.

This chapter briefly reviews relevant anatomy, biomechanics and mechanisms of insult to (primarily) soft tissues of the cervical spine and brachial plexus. Combined with a working knowledge of the principles of rehabilitation, one is then equipped to direct a specific and aggressive rehabilitation program. The purpose of rehabilitation is not just early return to activity but also prevention of recurring injury and patient education. The scope of rehabilitation does not begin after injury but should include prehabilitation. Just as the internist/cardiologist must constantly follow his cardiac patient with updated history, physical exams, and serial diagnostic studies, so must the rehabilitation specialist be continuously re-evaluating the injured athlete with questions, examinations and repeated studies (anatomic and physiologic). This is required to avoid anticipated pitfalls and complications that occur during a rehabilitation program and to enable accurate prognostic information.

CERVICAL SPINE

Anatomy and Biomechanics

An understanding of functional anatomy, biomechanics and pathophysiology of injury forms the basis for cervical spine and brachial plexus injury rehabilitation.

The cervical spine serves to protect the spinal cord while allowing combined motions in three dimensions. The bony structures surround and protect the spinal cord and its enveloping membranes. Supporting ligaments are also important structural elements. The C1–2 complex is designated as the upper cervical segment with the C3–7 levels forming the middle and lower cervical segments. The occipito atlanto axoid complex forms a combination of bony structures that enables unique motions to occur. Nodding motion of the head occurs primarily at the atlanto-occipital joints. The atlas-axis complex, with the ondontoid process, allows for approximately 50% of the cervical spine rotation. Available rotation totals approximately 80 degrees in each direction. Total cervical flexion and extension approximates 100 degrees. Flexion increases foraminal size but tightens nerve roots. Extensional decreases foraminal size. The third cervical vertebrae is the first to have a true vertebral body and intervertebral disk.

The shape of the vertebral bodies positions the uncovertebral joint, or joints of Luschka, in a position of potential danger to the neural tissue, especially with the development of chronic degenerative changes. The vertebral bodies are thought to act as shock absorbers during axial loading via a hydraulic type mechanism. The cervicovertebral disk, with its annulus fibrosis and nucleus pulposus, transmits forces to the vertebral bodies of the cervical spine. The disks play a significant role in cervical biomechanics. They additionally play a particularly important role in potential injury to the neural axis via degenerative changes and/or acute discopathy. The planar orientation of the facet joints allows for flexion, extension and rotational motions. To a lesser extent, lateral bending motions are allowed, although this is a combined motion pattern that includes rotation occurring in the mid-cervical segments.

The spinal ligaments form a complex network of supporting structures and restraints. From the base of the skull, the tectorial membrane extends inferiorly to form the posterior longitudinal ligament. This ligament runs along the posterior aspect of the vertebral bodies, providing longitudinal support as well as an element of protection from postero-central disk herniations encroaching upon the spinal canal and theca. The anterior longitudinal ligament runs along the anterior aspect of the vertebral bodies, providing resistance to hyperextension movements. The ligamentum flavum lies posteriorly in the neural arches and adds stability when the cervical spine is hyperflexed.

The capsule of the uncovertebral joint has less laxity than the ligaments and capsules of the facet joints. The facet joint and neural arch combined with the ligamentous supporting tissue provide posterior stability.

Deep muscles of the cervical spine, including the interspinalis, semispinalis, splenius, and erector spinae, along with suboccipital muscles, are susceptible to strains. The levator scapulae, rhomboids and trapezius muscles are also prone to soft tissue failure.

An understanding of the neurologic components of the cervical spine and their anatomic relationships as they exit via the foramen is important in understanding the injury mechanism. As the nerve root exits the intervertebral foramen, the dural sleeve, with its accompanying cerebrospinal fluid, terminates. The epineurium that surrounds the nerve fibers serves to anchor the spinal nerves to the periosteum of the transverse processes in the lower cervical vertebrae. This has significance when analyzing the pathomechanics of brachial plexus and cervical root injuries.

Mechanism of Injuries to the Cervical Spine

The biomechanics and classification of cervical spine injury and recovery have been well studied by a multitude of authors.[4,6,12,13,14,18,20,21,22,25,32,34] Important injury mechanisms include axial loading or compression, flexion, extension, lateral bending, horizontal shear forces, rotational forces or a combination. The cervical spine is relatively stable in each plane of motion mentioned, unless a rotational force component is present. This can lead to a variety of subluxations, dislocations, fractures and fracture dislocations.[1] The treatment of fractures will not be discussed in this chapter, but it can be reviewed in the available literature. Epidemiologic, cinematographic, and other experimental studies have demonstrated that axial loading or compression injuries are responsible for a significant percentage of cervical spine and spinal cord injuries in sports.[5] This is especially so if the head is positioned in a slightly forward flexed posture forming a column with absence of the normal cervical lordosis.

Flexion injuries occur in most collision sports, including football, rugby and ice hockey.[28] If the forces cause hyperflexion, without compression, segmental distraction with or without disruption of the supraspinous and interspinous ligaments and facet capsule ligaments can occur. Flexion with compression forces leads to compression wedge fractures or comminuted vertebral body fractures. Extension injuries will potentially lead to disruption of the anterior ligamentous complex, and if they are combined with compressive forces, dislocations as well as dislocations and fractures may ensue.[10]

SOFT TISSUE INJURY

Disks

The natural history of a cervical spine degenerative process from repetitive injuries (not necessarily related to sporting activities) leads to a degenerative cascade, elucidated by Kirkaldy-Willis.[3] With an accumulation of disruptive forces to the annulus fibrosis over a period of time, there is initially dysfunction of the diskovertebral joint. This then can lead to subsequent degenerative changes in the facet joints, leading to capsular laxity, with further instability and progressive disk disruption. With eventual progression of the degenerative process and enlargement of the articular process, osteophytes will be forming in the adjoining vertebral bodies, uncovertebral joints and facet joints.

As evidenced by the remarkable degenerative process noted in the relatively young population of professional athletes involved in collision sports, one assumes that the repetitive trauma to the cervical spine may play a significant role in the advancement of the degenerative process. It is also felt that repetitive trauma, with resultant accumulation of redundant fibrous tissue and ligamentous hypertrophy, may also lead to soft tissue stenosis and a predisposition for neurologic injury. This mechanism could eventually contribute to a radiculopathy. Acute cervical disk herniation can occur with or without myelopathy or radiculopathy.

Cervical Sprain

This diagnosis has a tendency to be used with minimal precision. The definition of a sprain is "an injury to a joint, with possible rupture of some of the ligaments or tendons, but without dislocation or fracture." In this phenomenon, the patient will have a marked restriction in his cervical spine range of motion, often with a compressive mechanism of injury and patient complaints of a "jammed neck." No neurologic abnormalities are noted on physical examination. To facilitate appropriate, accurate and aggressive rehabilitation in a precise manner, a careful physical exam with accurate localization of segments involved is necessary.

Cervical Strain

This diagnosis also tends to be overused in a less than precise manner. Cervical strain, by definition, refers to an injury to the musculotendinous unit. In the cervical spine, it can occur to the muscles that were previously listed in the anatomic section. Additionally, the scalene and sternocleidomastoid muscles can be affected. Again, there is no neurologic deficit associated with the strain. Pain is reproduced by employing resistive motion testing utilizing the involved muscle. Passive motion of the bony ligamentous complex should not reproduce the pain in this injury unless significant soft tissue contracture has occurred.

Primary soft tissue injuries can lead to secondary as well as tertiary problems. They may include substitution patterns for previously established engrams, interference of normal joint kinetics, muscle strength imbalance, sclerotomal-referred pain, and trigger-point sensitivity.

Predisposing factors for development of these injury types include poor flexibility, strength, endurance and power; improper training techniques; and soft tissue contractures. Additionally, genetics may play a role in those individuals with congenital spinal canal stenosis or predisposition to acquired stenosis. Scoliosis, "long neck," and other structural variations, may impose a relative risk to the patient participating in collision or contact sport. These issues are currently very controversial and remain to be elucidated by carefully controlled studies.

PATIENT EVALUATION

The cervical spine plane of motion involved in the injury mechanism and the forces involved are important in reconstructing the insult. The immediate symptoms, i.e., a history of transient quadraparesis versus quadraparesthesia, are important to assess. In assessing potential spinal cord involvement, a history of upper and/or lower extremity involvement is important. Also, questioning regarding motions that exacerbate the symptoms; quality, quantity, and location of paresthesias; dysesthesias; and pain radiation are important components in assessing the significance, type and location of potential injury.

Examination

Postural evaluation, such as observing for a wry neck, can give valuable clues to location and type of injury. For example, in an acute posterolateral disk protrusion or herniation, the patient will have a natural tendency to enlarge the foramen on the involved side and thereby list away from the injury. Active as well as passive range of motion should be tested to assess the potential structures involved in the injury. With cervical spine palpation, which is often times done best in the supine position, one can be relatively accurate in localizing areas of greatest tenderness with posterior/anterior excursion of the respective spinous processes and lateral masses.

A neurologic exam including careful sensory testing of light touch and pin prick 2-point discrimination, proprioception, deep tendon reflexes, as well as motor strength testing of upper and lower extremities, is necessary. This can yield information regarding location and extent of the lesion. A search for pathologic reflexes, such as Hoffmann's, Babinski's sign, and hyperflexia, is also important.

The initial x-ray evaluation should include a cervical spine series including AP, lateral, bilateral obliques and odontoid views. Flexion and extension views are necessary if suspicion of instability exists. Once the acute post-injury phase is resolved, one must consider the necessity for flexion/extension views in order to rule out potential delayed instability. Should there be a question of radicular versus non-radicular referred pain, electrodiagnostic studies are helpful. This is an important diagnostic point that will effect treatment. This also serves to provide information regarding the presence of neurologic involvement and to assist in grading the lesions, and prognostication.

When indicated, computerized tomography (CT) yields extremely valuable information in assessing bony structures.[6] In our experience, CT scanning has identified a subtle facet fracture not well appreciated on plane roentgenograms. The clinical suspicion of the injury drove the physician to order the test. Magnetic resonance imaging scans (MRI) also are beginning to accurately complement CT studies to further identify injured structures. Its forte is in the evaluation of the soft tissue. It remains a matter of controversy which imaging technique is best utilized to assess spinal canal diameter.

REHABILITLATION PROGRAM

Principles of rehabilitation initially involve the control of the inflammatory process. This is facilitated by specifically prescribing relative rest and anti-inflammatory medicines, usually of the nonsteroidal type. Judicious use of oral corticosteroid medications can be very useful. Rarely an injection of corticosteroid is indicated in an involved and specifically identified cervical spine or ligamentous structure. Acupuncture has also been reported to assist in reducing pain and inflammation. A soft cervical collar can improve comfort level, assuming no cervical spine instability exists. Should this be of concern, a Philadelphia collar is initially employed. Traction techniques are useful in cases of diskogenic radiculopathy but can exacerbate pain in stenotic radiculopathy.

Once the acute phase passes gentle range of motion (ROM) can be begun. Spinal motion can be inhibited by neural mechanisms. Spinal manipulative therapy may also be helpful during the pain control phase and useful to improve segmental motion. There are reported mechanical neurophysiologic, as well as psychological, effects from manual treatment.[23]

The neurophysiologic techniques, such as oscillation, can be beneficial in recently injured joints. The cervical spine is notorious for referring pain to large and diffuse areas of the trunk, interscapular region, and extremity.[35] Stretch manipulation, intermittently, either mechanically or manually, can be beneficial to help break a pain cycle.[15,26,38]

The next phase in the overall rehabilitation process is restoration and maintenance of joint ROM and soft tissue extensibility. The physical examination should yield information whether or not the restriction in ROM is secondary to articular or soft tissue processes. If the process is articular in nature, then specific joint mobilization and manipulation techniques can be of benefit.[23,1] There are specific as well as general contraindications to manipulation of which one needs to be aware. Specific contraindications include acute fractures, significant degenerative spondylolysis as well as instability. More general contraindications include an exacerbation of inflammatory joint disease, osteopenia, bleeding dyscrasias, and cerebrospinal vascular disease, as well as obvious diseases of the spine, such as an infection or metastatic disease. If the primary limiting factor in the joint range of motion limitation is soft tissue in nature, then a soft tissue extensibility program is appropriate.[3] Myofascial trigger point syndromes may be observed secondary to joint, disk, or nerve-root irritation. Shortened muscles will lead to joint dysfunction, which can set up a continuous and difficult cycle that necessitates specific intervention.[7,24,26,29]

Numerous modalities may be used in these situations, but spray and stretch, and trigger point injection technique can be quite effective. Once the soft tissue extensibility is improved, specifically directed manual resistive exercises can be pursued. The ROM exercises should be in each of the six directions, i.e., flexion-extension, bilateral rotational, and bilateral-lateral bending.

THERAPEUTIC EXERCISES/TRAINING

Once the patient's pain is under control and ROM is improving, therapeutic strengthening exercises are appropriate. Initially, isometric exercises in the neutral position are usually the first exercises the patient is able to tolerate. Of great importance in the overall cervical spine rehabilitation program is shoulder girdle stabilizer strength. This includes the scapular protractors and retractors, as well as truncal/torso stabilizers. These are important in order be able to maintain appropriate postural ergonomics by eliminating the head-forward posture associated with a "stooped shoulder" alignment.

Position of the head and shoulder girdle in a somewhat "chest out" posture requires muscular strength and endurance as well as body-position awareness. If this is not obtained, the recovery will be less than satisfactory. Following the initial cervical isometric exercises, progression to total upper-body isotonic and/or iso-kinetic programs will improve the strength and stability of the entire upper torso. The upper trapezius is a specific area of attention. Postural thoracic outlet symptoms are a potential complication of cervical spine injuries and brachial plexus problems, secondary to poor muscle balance and flexibility. The reinforcement of good postural ergonomics specifically including cervicothoracic and pectoral-girdle posture mechanics is imperative.

Developing specific sports-related biomechanical skill patterns is the next phase. In the case of a pitcher or racket sport participant who has sustained an insult to the soft tissues surrounding the cervical spine, with referral to the dominant upper extremity, there may be substitution pattern development that can lead to a host of complications, including an impingement syndrome and elbow injuries. It is not until the pain, ROM and strength are returned to the normal state that biomechanics of the throwing motion can be practiced. Specific PNF exercises for the lower extremities, pelvis, torso, and shoulder girdle can be implemented in a serial progression until the appropriate and full biomechanical skill is obtained.

Video-taping of the actual motion can be instructive in identifying faulty techniques or substitution patterns. This educational tool and feedback mechanism can be used as a rehabilitative as well as preventive educational assist. In our experience the patients can be made acutely aware of the different phases of the sports-specific related activity with this method.

RETURN TO PLAY DECISIONS

Multiple factors go into the complex decision concerning return to play. They are covered in greater detail in a separate chapter of this book. However, the subjective and objective guidelines that are customarily used include full and pain-free ROM of the involved structures, with no evidence of neuromuscular deficit. It is important to note that muscular strength, power and endurance must be conditioned and must be up to the anticipated task. Social, parental or peer factors can not affect appropriate medical decision making.

BRACHIAL PLEXUS

Anatomy

The brachial plexus is derived from the anterior rami of the lower four cervical and first thoracic nerves. C5 and 6 join to form the upper trunk. The middle trunk

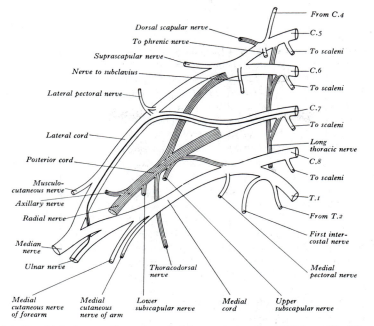

FIGURE 1 Brachial plexus. (Reproduced with permission from Williams PL, Warwick R: Gray's Anatomy, 36th ed. Edinburgh, Churchill Livingstone, 1980, p. 1095.)

is an extension of the C7 root. The C8 and T1 combine to form the lower trunk. Each trunk then divides to contribute to the anterior and posterior division. The lateral cord is formed by the anterior division of the superior and middle trunk. The medial cord is formed mainly from the anterior division of the inferior trunk, with the posterior cord being formed by the posterior division of the superior, middle and inferior trunk.

The primary terminal branch of the lateral cord is the musculocutaneous nerve. The median nerve is the primary terminal branch formed from the lateral and medial cords. The ulnar nerve is the terminal branch extension of the medial cord. The radial nerve is the terminal branch of the posterior cord. There are important branches above the clavicle, including the dorsal scapular, long thoracic, suprascapular and subclavical nerves. Below the clavicle, nerves from each of the cords include the lateral pectoral nerve from the lateral cord; the subscapular and thoracodorsal nerve from the posterior cord, and, from the medial cord, the medial pectoral nerve, medial brachial cutaneous and medial anti-brachial cutaneous nerves. Lesion localization is dependent upon knowledge of the composition of the trunks, cords and terminal branches of the plexus, from the cervical root level to the periphery (Figure 1). Correct localization has a major bearing in prognosis and treatment.

Mechanism of Injury

The major types of injuries to the brachial plexus include (1) penetrating trauma, (2) traction and (3) compression.[2,5,30] Penetrating injuries are rare in sports and therefore will not be discussed. Previously the most common mechanism producing brachial plexus injury in collision sports, particularly football, was thought to be due to cervical spine lateral flexion to the contralateral side, with ipsilateral shoulder depression. More recent reports, however, indicate a common mechanism of injury is associated with cervical spine extension, compression and rotation to the involved side.[37] This has significant implications for diagnosis and prevention.

With the arm in a relaxed position, the C5 and 6 roots are under a greater degree of tension than are the lower roots. This may predispose them to an increased frequency of injury. If the upper plexus is pulled in an anterior and inferior manner, the C5 and C6 roots are placed on traction around the anterior tubercle of the transverse process. If they are pulled in a posterior-inferior manner, they are put on traction around the posterior tubercle. The attachment of the nerve root to the spinal root is the weak link in the chain of the central-peripheral neuroaxis, thereby lending itself to injury at the root level not plexus level.

Nerve root avulsion can result from an extravertebral traction injury as well as from displacement of the spinal cord. The anatomical basis for traction injuries resides in the lattice network arrangement of the spinal nerves proximally and the cord more laterally. The rate of deformation, attachment of the sheaths of the C5–7 spinal nerves at the transverse process, plexiform structure elasticity, and strength of the funiculi are all factors contributing to the complex and often incomplete picture of "brachial plexus injuries." On the basis of this patho-anatomic construct, "stingers" are not plexus injuries but rather root level injuries, from either traction or foraminal compression.

PATIENT ASSESSMENT

History

When obtaining the patient history in the case of possible brachial plexus injury, understanding the injury mechanism is a critical factor. Various reports indicate a variety of mechanisms may be at work. These include cervical spine extension, extension with ipsilateral or contralateral rotation, lateral bending of the cervical spine with and/or without depression of the ipsilateral shoulder (i.e., an increase in the acromiomastoid distance), and hyperabduction of the involved extremity. Location, description and chronology of pain onset, sensation, paresthesias and dysesthesias are also important. The common names in athletic circles for these types of injuries are "burners" and "stingers." The name is derived from the description the athlete often details. Pre-existent conditions such as shoulder dislocations or separations, disk injuries, known spinal stenosis, or previous similar "stingers" are important factors in the history.

Physical Examination

As soon as practical, an immediate physical exam should involve sensory as well as motor testing. Oftentimes the deficits involve the entire upper extremity. However, as time passes, whether this is minutes, hours, or days, depending upon the grade or severity of injury, the remaining deficits will be localized to the areas of greatest involvement. Pre-existent conditions and lesions are important factors in the history.

Cervical spine range-of-motion testing, including Spurling's maneuver (a test for cervical foraminal nerve encroachment; compression of the head with extension of the neck causes radicular pain in the upper extremities) and Lhermitte's sign (defined as the development of sudden, transient, electric-like shocks spreading down the body when the patient flexes the head forward; seen in compression and other disorders of the cervical cord) are important. Segmental mobility should be assessed with attention towards the mid-cervical segments and areas of hypomobility. Paying particular attention to the glenohumeral scapulothoracic rhythm of motion is important. Palpation of the supra- or infraclavicular region of the plexus, while trying to elicit pain reproduction or paresthesias, can be useful in localization. Trigger-point palpation can yield information regarding secondary myofascial pain sources. Palpation of the ribs, clavicle, acromioclavicular joint and sternoclavicular joint to assess related injury is imperative. We have seen a case of posterior sternoclavicular joint dislocation resulting in a plexus injury in a rugby player.

On inspection, look for anatomic asymmetry, i.e., abnormal position of scapula and scapular winging. Thoracic and cervical postural alignment should also be noted. The presence of a head forward posture and a thoracic kyphosis have implications in the formulation of the treatment plan. Cervical and thoracic scoliosis should also be noted. Dynamic postural mechanisms must be highlighted in the rehabilitation program. Fixed skeletal deformities should be noted and worked around.

Manual muscle testing will reveal information on the function of the levator scapulae, rhomboid and serratus anterior muscles. This will help localize a proximal root lesion that may carry with it a poorer prognosis. The remaining major muscle groups of the upper extremity should be carefully assessed for weakness, fatigue, atrophy and contracture. Sensory examination is also helpful to distinguish root, trunk, cord and/or peripheral nerve injury distribution in the upper extremity. Deep tendon reflex testing and assessment of pathologic reflex patterns are a portion of a complete examination.

The usual case presents with an incomplete nerve injury (versus complete injury), making specific localization of the injury more challenging. Other physical examination findings, such as Horner's syndrome and vasomotor changes in the distal upper extremity, are additional factors to look for. These findings will also help establish the prognostic conclusion.

Electrodiagnostic studies, including electromyography and nerve conduction studies, are very valuable aids in defining and grading the lesion.[8,17] Electrodiagnostic testing is also helpful to establish a prognosis. Serial exams are often necessary for this purpose. Deciding between pre- and post-ganglionic lesions is facilitated with sensory nerve studies. Within a few days of a significant postganglionic lesion that is associated with sensation loss, the SNAP (sensory nerve action potential) in the governing cutaneous sensory branch will be unobtainable. In a complete preganglionic lesion at the C6 level, with resultant anesthesia in the C6 dermatome, the superficial radial sensory nerve action potential will still be present.

F-wave studies of an ulnar innervated muscle can be helpful in assessing a lower trunk plexus injury. Compound motor action potential (CMAP) analysis of the muscles suspected to be involved in the process should be analyzed and followed. Finally, progressive CMAP diminution is a poor prognostic sign. On the contrary, short-term (3-week) diminution, with a steady rise in CMAP amplitude over the ensuing weeks, is consistent with a neuropractic injury and a better prognosis. Conduction studies with brachial plexus stimulation are therefore necessary in the assessment of these injuries.

Findings of spontaneous activity can be detected within a 1–3 week period in deinnervated muscles. Thus, recruitment abnormalities can be noted on day one as can F-wave latency asymmetry.

The mapping of involved muscles yields the necessary information to localize the lesion. Serial changes in MUAP recruitment are important to follow the reinnervation process. Combining this data with CMAP changes and the disappearance of spontaneous activity will establish the basis for prognosis. A plateau in reinnervation before the predicted interval based upon severity of the initial injuries and the length of the nerve segment involved is a poor prognostic sign. The rate of reinnervation should be quite predictable and should follow a predictable pattern. Matching manual muscle test findings with electrodiagnostic studies sharpens the examiner's impression and allows a better understanding of nerve lesions.

Diagnostic Studies

Cervical spine x-rays, including flexion-extension views, looking for fractures, instability, stenosis, degenerative disease or deformity, are necessary in any case where the neurologic deficit persists for longer than a few hours. Individuals with pre-existent degenerative disease at the involved segment have a less favorable outlook for a quick symptom-free recovery.

Somatosensory evoked potentials may be helpful to determine the presence of root avulsion.[31] Cervical myelography with water-soluble agents has been shown in numerous studies to be helpful in demonstrating nerve root avulsions via a meningeal diverticulum. Computed tomography scans with and without dye appear to be more sensitive and specific at the C5 and 6 levels.[19] This corresponds well with the areas of plexus injury most often observed.

Axonal reflex testing has been performed in the past, but it has its limitations. Magnetic resonance imaging shows promise for improved diagnostic accuracy and localization of lesions in a noninvasive manner. Currently MRI can demonstrate disk displacement and central canal narrowing. It is a poor indicator of foraminal stenosis.

Timing of Diagnostic Testing

(1) *Electrodiagnostic studies*: within the first week for cases of persistent weakness, then every month for 3 months, and then every 3–6 months until recovery. (2) *Cervical spine x-rays*: within 24 hours for a persistent lesion or within a few days of a recurrent injury. (3) *CT scanning with dye*: as soon as possible following an injury associated with suspected root avulsion. (4) *MRI scanning*: within the first few weeks of a persisting neurologic lesion, to rule out a disk displacement or significant stenosis.

Treatment and Rehabilitation

To simply refer a patient to a physical therapist with a diagnosis of "brachial plexus injury with shoulder weakness" is inappropriate. The greater the precision in evaluating the deficits present, the earlier, more appropriate and anticipatory the rehabilitation program can be.

In our experience we have noted a variety of neurologic injuries in the brachial plexus region, with varying patterns of involvement and recovery. These patterns include initial weakness in shoulder abduction, and wrist and thumb extension, with the latter being the last to resolve. Other patterns have manifested suprascapular innervated muscle weakness as the last to resolve. This may be due to concomitant suprascapular nerve injury or to a selected axon disruption of the axons that supply the suprascapular nerve. The same pattern has been noted with the long thoracic nerve and the serratus anterior muscle.

The rehabilitation approach includes control of the inflammatory process, control of pain, restoring and maintaining joint range of motion and soft tissue extensibility, improving muscular strength, improving muscular endurance, developing specific sports-related biomechanical skill patterns, and improving general cardiovascular endurance. The specifics of the overall rehabilitation program are governed by the pathophysiology of the injury, which establishes the rational for rehabilitation.

The inflammatory control component is accomplished by a variety of cryotherapy techniques to diminish edema and to assist in pain control. The family of nonsteroidal anti-inflammatory medications is useful as well as the judicious use of steroidal anti-inflammatory medications.

Functional electrical stimulation of specific weak muscles may be helpful, though cumbersome and poorly tolerated. The pain-control phase includes the use of nonsteroidal anti-inflammatories, transcutaneous nerve stimulation, movement of specific joints, and occasionally acupuncture. Restoration of cervical and upper extremity range of motion by employing active as well as passive techniques in combination with above mentioned modalities can prevent soft tissue contractures and their attendant complications (see chapter on flexibility).

Specific strengthening exercises should be designed for the individual muscles involved in the injury. For example, in a C5/C6 root level injury, the spinatae, deltoid and bicep muscles are often most involved. The information derived from the electrodiagnostic studies helps determine which muscles are trainable and at what intensity.

For the spinatae muscles, isolating the supraspinatus via the supraspinatus isolation position, as well as external rotation for the infraspinatus muscle, is appropriate while the arm is both abducted and adducted.

Resistance exercises including abduction, flexion, and extension for the anterior and posterior portions of the deltoid are indicated. Strength training for the biceps brachii muscle should include flexion exercises of the forearm, as well as forearm supination (see strength training chapter).

While performance of strengthening exercises for the individual deficits is important, one cannot neglect other muscles and functions of the shoulder girdle and upper extremity. The specifically directed exercises will not, of course, rehabilitate the nerve per se, nor speed up its recovery process, but will allow for maintenance of the existing functional components of the neuromuscular axis. During this process it is also important to avoid imbalance of muscles, i.e., undue strengthening of functional muscles not affected by the injury, thereby leading to an increased imbalance of strength, which in itself can lead to complications.

Injuries to other parts of the brachial plexus or root levels with identified deficits are treated in a similar manner, using an appropriate combination of isometrics, isotonic, and isokinetic therapeutic exercises. The concept of specificity of exercise, as well as the use of such techniques as PNF to facilitate patterns of movement, is important. Muscular endurance must be improved as well as the training of sports-related biomechanical skill patterns.

During the rehabilitation process, maintaining cardiovascular endurance is important. This can be accomplished by bicycling, cross-country ski machines, and similar methods.

PREVENTATIVE MEASURES

Technique training in football, rugby, and other collision sports is imperative. Learning proper tackling techniques and proper equipment fit and design are absolute necessities. Proper fitting of football shoulder pads, for example, should allow for appropriate shock absorption and protection of the shoulders. They should be fitted snugly to the chest and fix the mid-cervical spine to the trunk. These features can be accomplished by having a long and rigid front and back panel fitted securely around the entire chest. Lateral build-ups can play an important role in prevention of cervical spine root and plexus injuries.

RETURN TO PLAY DECISION

Return to play decisions are based upon the patient having full and painfree range of motion of the involved joints. Patients should also have a normal neurologic exam, including normal muscle strength, power, and endurance. Normal sensation and symmetrical and normal deep tendon reflexes are also necessary.

Sideline decision making regarding return to play necessitates a thorough evaluation, as previously detailed. No player can return to play until the criteria elaborated above are complete. Pressure from family members, other players and coaches should not affect the appropriate medical decision. Additional factors that go into the return to play decision include the frequency of recurrence of injuries, the level of competition, age of the patient, goals of the participant, and future aspirations.

REFERENCES

1. Babcock J: Cervical spine injuries. Arch Surg 111:646–651, 1976.
2. Bateman J: Nerve lesions about the shoulder. Orthop Clin North Am 11:307–326, 1980.
3. Chamberlain G: Cyriax's friction massage: A review. JOSPT 4:16–22, 1982.
4. Chesire DJE: The stability of the cervical spine following the conservative treatment of fractures and fracture-dislocations. Paraplegia pp. 193–203.
5. Clancy WG Jr, Brand RL, Bergfeld JA: Upper trunk brachial plexus injuries in contact sports. AM J Sports Med 5:209, 1977.
6. Daffner R, Deeb Z, Rothfus W: "Fingerprints" of vertebral trauma—a unifying concept based on mechanisms. Skeletal Radiol 15:518–525, 1986.
7. Delacerda F: A comparative study of three methods of treatment for shoulder girdle myofascial syndrome. JOSPT 4:51, 54, 1982.
8. Di Benedetto M, Markey K: Electrodiagnostic localization of traumatic upper trunk brachial plexopathy. Arch Phys Med Rehabil 65:15–17, 1984.
9 Fielding J, Cochran G, Lawsing J III, Hohl M: Tears of the transverse ligament of the atlas. J Bone Joint Surg 56A:1683–1691, 1974.
10. Forsyth H: Extension injuries of the cervical spine. J Bone Joint Surg 46A:1792–1797, 1964.
11. Grieve GP: Modern Manual Therapy Of The Vertebral Column. New York, Churchill-Livingstone, 1986.
12. Harris J, Edeiken-Monroe B, Kopaniky D: A practical classification of acute cervical spine injuries. Orthop Clin North Am 17:15–30, 1986.
13. Holdsworth F: Review article: Fractures, dislocations, and fracture-dislocations of the spine. J Bone Joint Surg 52A:1534–1551, 1970.
14. Heulke D, Nusholtz G: Cervical spine biomechanics: A review of the literature. J Orthop Res 4:232–245, 1986.
15. Kekosz V, Hilbert L, Tepperman P: Cervical and lumbopelvic traction. Postgrad Med 80:187–194, 1986.
16. Kirkaldz-Willis: Managing Low Back Pain. New York, Churchill-Livingstone, 1983.
17. Liveson J: Nerve lesions associated with shoulder dislocation; an electrodiagnostic study of 11 cases. J Neurol Neurosurg Psychiat 47:742–744, 1984.
18. Lysell E: Motion in the Cervical Spine. Acta Orthop Scand Supplement 123, 1969.
19. Marshall R, De Silva R: Computerised axial tomography in traction injuries of the brachial plexus. J Bone Joint Surg 68B:734–738, 1986.
20. Paley D, Gillespie R: Chronic repetitive unrecognized flexion injury of the cervical spine (high jumper's neck). Am J Sports Med 14:92–95, 1986.
21. Panjabi M, Summers D, Pelker R, et al: Three-dimensional load-displacement curves due to forces on the cervical spine. J Orthop Res 4:152–161, 1986.
22. Panjabi M, White A III, Johnson R: Cervical spine mechanics as a function of transection of components. J Biomechanics 8:327–336, 1975.
23. Paris S: Spinal manipulative therapy. Clin Orthop Rel Res 179:55–61, 1983.
24. Reynolds M: Myofascial trigger point syndromes in the practice of rheumatology. Arch Phys Med Rehabil 62:111–113, 1981.
25. Roaf R: A study of the mechanics of spinal injuries. J Bone Joint Surg 42B:810–823, 1960.
26. Rothman S: Computed tomography of the spine in older children and teenagers. Clin Sports Med 5:1986.

27. Saunders H: Use of spinal traction in the treatment of neck and back conditions. Clin Orthop Rel Res 179:31–38, 1983.
28. Schneider R: The treatment of the athlete with neck, cervical spine, and spinal cord trauma. In Schneider RC (ed): Sports Injuries: Mechanisms, Prevention, and Treatment. Baltimore, Williams and Wilkins, 1985.
29. Simons D: Myofascial trigger points: A need for understanding. Arch Phys Med Rehabil 62:97–99, 1981.
30. Stanwood J, Kraft G: Diagnosis and management of brachial plexus injuries. Arch Phys Med Rehab Feb. 1971, pp. 52–60.
31. Sugioka H: Evoked potentials in the investigation of traumatic lesions of the peripheral nerve and the brachial plexus. Clin Orthop Rel Res 184:85–92, 1984.
32. Sunderland S: Nerves and Nerve Injuries, 2nd ed., New York, Churchill-Livingstone, 1978.
33. Taylor A: Fracture dislocation of the cervical spine. Ann Surg 90:321–340, 1929.
34. Thompson R: Current concepts in management of cervical spine fractures and dislocations. J Sports Med 3:159–167, 1975.
35. Travell J: Myofascial Pain and Dysfunction: The Trigger Point Manual, Baltimore, Williams and Wilkins, 1983.
36. Torg J: Management guidelines for athletic injuries to the cervical spine. Clin Sports Med 6 :1987.
37. Watkins R: Neck injuries in football players. Clin Sports Med 5:1986.
38. Zylbergod R, Piper M: A comparison of three types of traction. Cervical Spine Disorders Spine 10:867–871, 1985.

JEFFREY A. SAAL, MD

REHABILITATION OF THROWING AND TENNIS-RELATED SHOULDER INJURIES

Reprint requests to Jeffrey A. Saal, M.D., Sports, Orthopedic and Rehabilitation Medicine Associates, 3250 Alpine Rd., Portola Valley, CA 94025.

The intricacy and interplay of total body motion and functional anatomy combine to yield the throwing motion. An analysis of this phenomenon is necessary to establish the rationale for physiologically sound rehabilitation. The cardinal sin of the analytic process is a tunnel vision view of the shoulder rather than a panoramic one of the entire fluidity of body motion. Motion is accomplished by a delicately balanced feedback system of neurophysiologic messages interpreted and converted into mechanical action by musculoskeletal action. Joint geometry and stability coupled with the musculotendinous and skeletal lever arm determine the physical requirements to accomplish the motion task.

The neurophysiologic component of motion production involves a pre-programmed encoded and compartmentalized engram of detailed and specific information that is transmitted from the "brain computerbank" through a relay system of central nervous system feedback and feedforward circuit loops to lower centers.[16] At the spinal level the signal is further modulated and transmitted via lower motor neuron pathways to the periphery. The peripheral nerve axons ultimately transmit the individual signal sequence to the effector muscle unit. Proprioceptive feedback loops from the musculotendinous units and joints act as a servomechanism to carefully modulate the output signal.

A refined encoded engram will provide greater efficiency and economy of motion and energy. Engram transmission by the central nervous system center should be accomplished without volitional modulation. Avoiding volitional input "purifies" the motion sequence and eliminates central nervous irradiation. Irradiation will cause

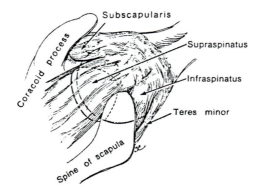

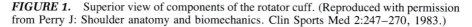

FIGURE 1.   Superior view of components of the rotator cuff. (Reproduced with permission from Perry J: Shoulder anatomy and biomechanics. Clin Sports Med 2:247–270, 1983.)

spread into substitution and accessory movement pathways not contained in the compartmentalized engram.[16,35] Motion repetition that includes "imperfect" substitution and accessory patterns eventually lead to inclusion of imprecise information into the encoded engram. Therefore, carefully controlled repetition is absolutely necessary to attain the program form. Form should always precede speed to eliminate imprecise patterning that can be difficult to "unlearn."

Injury leads to abnormal joint kinematics and muscular effort. Caution must therefore be exercised to ensure against the encoding of substitution program data into the "central computer" that will carry over after the injury is long gone. Rehabilitation programs must therefore be carefully designed and monitored.

PATHOANATOMICAL CONSIDERATIONS

Scapulothoracic motion is a key element in the shoulder mechanism. When the arm is abducted 150 degrees, 60 degrees is accounted for by the lateral rotation of the inferior angle of the scapula. The first 90 degrees of arm abduction is accomplished by 30 degrees of scapular motion.[12,14,17] See Figures 1–3 for anatomic diagrams.

The clavicle acts as a balancing beam that supports the shoulder. Fifty degrees of clavicular rotation is necessary to accomplish 180 degrees of abduction.[25] Therefore the acromioclavicular joint is stressed continually during arm motions. The humeral head is 45 ± 10 mm in diameter[23] and is retroverted 32 degrees.[11] Forty-five degrees of medial angulation also exists in relation to the humeral shaft.[17] These relationships place lateral structures such as the greater tuberosity of the humerus in a relatively anterior position, thereby making them more prone to impingement against the anterior acromial edge during the throwing motion. The glenoid fossa is pear-shaped with an average size of 41 by 25 mm. It is retroverted 7 degrees[27] and inferiorly angulated approximately 5 degrees.[21] Therefore inferior support of the humeral head can be attained only with the help of scapular rotation to elevate the angle of the fossa. The bone to bone acromiohumeral interval has been measured to be 7–14 mm with a mean of 9 ± 1.7 mm.[23] The glenoid labrum increases the depth of glenoid fossa to 75% of humeral head diameter as opposed to 25% without it.[27] The shoulder capsule measures 2 × the surface area of the humeral head.[21,26] The capsule has a distal recess measuring 5–15 mm, which lies opposite the subscapularis tendon.[17]

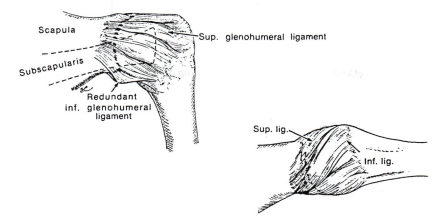

FIGURE 2. The shoulder capsule with wringing associated with abduction and external rotation. (Reproduced with permission from Perry J: Shoulder anatomy and biomechanics. Clin Sports Med 2:247–270, 1983.)

The inferior glenohumeral ligament exists as a local thickening of the shoulder capsule and is the most important static anterior inferior stabilizer of humeral head motion.[27] The subscapularis tendon loses its ability to restrain forward motion when the arm is abducted above 90 degrees due to its positional shift to a more superior location when the arm is in that position.[21] Therefore, passive static stability of the glenohumeral joint is quite poor and dynamic forces must be relied upon to supply the necessary environment to maintain joint integrity.

Nine muscles cross the shoulder joint and influence its function. The *deltoid muscle*, with its three parts each having a different angle of pull, is the most

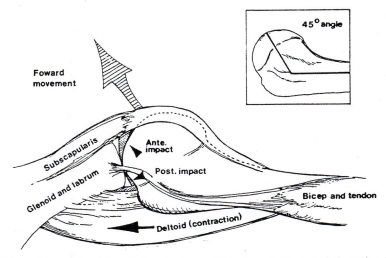

FIGURE 3. The mechanism of injury during cocking phase is illustrated. Posterior deltoid extensor force pulls the humeral head against the glenoid rim. Anterior shear force is created with continued contraction. (Reproduced with permission from Perry J: Shoulder anatomy and biomechanics. Clin Sports Med 2:247–270, 1983.)

superficial of the muscle groups. The *anterior deltoid* is the major forward elevator of the arm, while the *posterior deltoid* with its extension capabilities acts as a balancer of anterior shear forces. The *middle deltoid* is the major abductor and possesses a vertical vector of pull that must be counterbalanced by supraspinatus muscle contraction to maintain joint compression.[8,9,17,18] The clavicular head of the *pectoralis major* assists the anterior deltoid in forward elevation with some assistance from the *biceps brachii* and the *coracobrachialis*. The *latissimus dorsi* supplies an extension force when the arm is elevated and therefore acts as a shoulder depressor. The *teres major* assists in extension.[28,29] The rotator cuff muscles—the *subscapularis, teres minor, infraspinatus* and *supraspinatus*—possess a confluence of tendons that make up the rotator cuff. The supraspinatus is categorized as an abductor of the humerus, the infraspinatus as an external rotator, the teres minor as an extensor, and the subscapularis as an internal rotator.[8,9,10,17,28,29] The center of rotation of the glenohumeral joint is maintained within a 1-mm locus.[10] The muscular control to eliminate greater tuberosity impaction into the acromion while maintaining this instantaneous center of rotation when the arm is forcefully accelerated from external to internal rotation must be considered. The paramount function of the rotator cuff musculature appears to be the maintenance of this instantaneous center of rotation. Their precise role in the throwing motion will be elaborated later in this chapter. The *serratus anterior* protracts the scapula to allow the scapular inferior angle to externally rotate. The scapular retractors, composed of the *middle trapezius* and the *major and minor rhomboid* muscles, balance scapular rotation by maintaining the proper scapulothoracic angular relationship.[12,14] The scapulothoracic joint may indeed be the key in shoulder motion. Inferior scapular abduction serves three major functions:[12,14,21,23]

1. It advances the deltoid origin to maintain the length of its lever arm.
2. It rotates the greater tuberosity away from acromion.
3. It enhances joint stability by elevating the inferiorly oriented glenoid fossa.

Poor scapulothoracic motion has serious consequences, attention to which, in my opinion, is poor or absent in most unsuccessful shoulder rehabilitation programs. By its neuromuscular inhibitory nature, pain causes scapular fixation in an elevated adducted position, leading to continued anterior impingement as well as "new" posterior myofascial pain. Release of myofascial pain sources that have led to weakened and shortened tissue must be incorporated in the rehabilitation program. The upper trapezius, the rhomboids, the teres major, the levator scapulae, and the thoracic paraspinal musculature are the major culprits in this regard. Eight bursae have been identified about the shoulder joint,[21] the most important being the subacromial bursa. The frictionless plane it is supposed to promote is negated by the onset of superior rotator cuff inflammation. The bursa can be quickly converted into a mass of adhesions that limit motion and create pain. It may also act as the conduit for spread of inflammation to the inferior aspect of the acromioclavicular joint.[25] Special mention should be made of the biceps tendon. It is not a portion of the rotator cuff but rather arises from the superior glenoid rim to rest in the intertubercular groove invested in its own synovial-lined sheath. Other than with external rotation, the biceps tendon is angulated around the medial wall of the bicipital groove.[17,21,23] Therefore the tendon is at constant risk of impaction, traction and shear forces.

The cervical spine must be considered in the shoulder model. Obviously the cervical spine acts as the exit point for the lower motor neuron function to drive the shoulder system. Muscle substitution patterns and scapular dysrhythmic motion can cause altered cervical biomechanics, leading to facet pain and cervical radicular injury. The cervical radicular injury can be subtle and chronic. Repetitive traction and compression forces on the normally fixated exiting cervical nerve roots can lead to injury.[6]

Considering that the shoulder girdle musculature receives the vast majority of its nerve supply from the fifth and sixth nerve root levels and that these are the most commonly affected motion segments leads to some interesting interrelationships. Chronic radiculopathy can result in weakness and fatigue of the rotator cuff musculature, leading to altered joint kinematics secondary to loss of axis of rotation maintenance and thereby to the development of impingement syndrome. The pain sources therefore may be a combination of the inflamed rotator cuff and/or bicipital tendon, the subacromial bursa, scapular-related myofascial components and the cervical nerve root. This must be adequately recognized to plan successful rehabilitation programs.

In 1980, while working with injured baseball pitchers and tennis players, this interrelationship became evident to me. I had the opportunity to evaluate and treat a large number of athletes who had "failed" conservative care. A number of the failures fell into the neck-shoulder syndrome category. It is often difficult to be certain which problem occurred first. In a baseball player with a herniated C5–6 disc, clearly the rotator cuff injury was a result of neurologically weakened musculature. After successful nonoperative treatment of the disc herniation, the rotator cuff injury was easily rehabilitated. Examples such as this should serve as notice to be aware of this interplay. Similarly, brachial plexus injuries and isolated peripheral nerve lesions must be recognized.

Axillary nerve entrapment in the quadralateral space and long thoracic nerve injury cause pain and changes in function in the deltoid and serratus anterior, respectively.[6,19] Serratus anterior muscle paralysis in particular causes severe impingement due to lack of scapular rotation with arm elevation.[10,12,14]

Suprascapular nerve injury causing weakness of the supraspinatus nerve and/or the infraspinatus muscle (dependent upon location of the nerve injury) could change shoulder function dramatically.[7] However, I know of two major league baseball pitchers with infraspinatus paralysis secondary to suprascapular nerve injury who continue to perform at a successful level, which points out the dependency on muscle lever arm orientation to accomplish function. Due to its angle of pull, the suprascapular is the key muscle in the maintenance of both joint compression forces and the instantaneous center of rotation.[31] The infraspinatus with its oblique orientation would have only to balance the posterior deltoid in its extension force but it is helped by the teres minor to limit anterior shear forces in this regard and therefore may be able to be substituted for.

Pain causes significant alteration in motion biomechanics. Control of pain and working within the confines of pain are important principles in the rehabilitation process. Intact peripheral nerve axons are necessary to relay the message sequence to the working muscle and to transmit proprioceptive feedback to the feedback loops. Nerve injury, even subtle, can hamper this delicate process.

THROWING MECHANICS AND NEUROMUSCULAR REQUIREMENTS

The throwing motion is classically divided into four phases: windup, cocking, acceleration, and follow through.[5,30] The *windup phase* is preparatory in nature and does not involve significant rotator cuff function but rather uses quadriceps, gluteus medius, gluteus maximus, abdominals, and latissimus dorsi function. The importance of this phase is often ignored. Optimally the windup positions the legs and trunk to serve as chief accelerators of the arm.

The *cocking phase* positions the arm in its extremes of external rotation and abduction prior to the initiation forward acceleration. The supraspinatus and infraspinatus simultaneously work to maintain optimal instantaneous axis or rotation, whereas the deltoid with its vertical axis abducts the arm. The internal rotators fire at the end of the cocking phase to counteract the external rotation of the humerus and decelerate the cocking motion. The anterior shoulder capsule is maximally ''wound-up'' at this point, and potential energy is stored in the elasticity of the (wound-up) capsule and internal rotator tendons.[16] The legs and trunk are now poised and optimally positioned to utilize their combined force to accelerate the readied arm. The leg drive requires strong lower extremity musculature, including the quadriceps, gluteus medius and maximus, gastroc-soleus complex, tibialis anterior, and peroneus longus. Iliopsoas musculotendinous flexibility is also important in maintaining optimal trunk positioning. Due to its origin on the spine and its insertion on the lesser trochanter of the femur, it controls lumbar lordosis and lumbar lateral flexion counterbalancing.[15]

As the *acceleration phase* begins, the rotator cuff musculature fires minimally, it major function being to maintain rotation axis of the glenohumeral joint.[18] The anterior capsule unwinds, and the internal rotator tendons convert potential energy into kinetic energy. The latissimus and pectoralis exert internal rotation and shoulder depressor force that must be balanced by the external rotators to limit glenohumeral shear.[25] The rapid transition from external to internal rotation can lead to greater tuberosity impingement if motion is not well controlled.[23]

The *prime accelerators* of the arm should be the trunk and the legs.[2,3] The legs must also maintain the body's center of gravity as low as possible and not allow it to rise too quickly during the motion. Optimal force generation and efficiency of motion are closely correlated with maintenance of the center of gravity.[2,3,35] A ratcheted center of gravity force vector dissipates energy and necessitates poorly time-phased muscular effort. The center must be kept ahead of the rotating trunk and must itself be accelerated in the same vector line as the object, i.e., the ball or racquet. Lumbar spine biomechanics are optimized in this model as well.

Deceleration naturally follows the rapid acceleration phase. The deceleration forces are tremendous (greater than 300 pounds per square inch) and place extraordinary stress on the shoulder girdle.[25] Deceleration moment causes traction on the capsule and posteriorly attached musculature. The throwing of breaking pitches, (i.e., curve ball and slider) requires greater deceleration effort,[31,32] and thereby places greater stress on the posterior capsule. Theoretically the same may be true for the spin tennis serve.

Follow-through smooths out the deceleration forces and positions the player to field a hit ball or rush the net. The trunk and legs should be efficiently utilized to accomplish this function.

The tennis motion is basically the same as the baseball throw, except that the axis of trunk windup and acceleration, and center of gravity acceleration are more compact. The long lever arm presented by the tennis racquet relieves the force placed upon the shoulder complex. The latissimus dorsi and triceps are probably more active in the tennis motion in order to serve as an accelerator and decelerator to counteract the long lever-arm effect.[1,25,33]

Throughout all phases of motion, the scapulothoracic joint must be efficient

TABLE 1. Posterior Shoulder Subset

1. Posterior capsular strain
2. Teres minor "syndrome"
3. Scapulothoracic myofascial syndromes
4. Posterior glenoid labrum tear
5. Posterior subluxation

in its service to optimal glenohumeral positioning. Obviously strength and flexibility must be coupled and balanced to attain this complicated motion.

REHABILITATION PROGRAMS

The diagnostic subsets that require rehabilitation are presented in the following Tables 1–3. For convenience, the pathologic entities have been divided into *anterior, posterior* and *neurogenic* to permit an understanding of the types of problems that develop in the various phases of motion and of the anatomic structures involved.

The *anterior* injuries are sustained during the cocking and acceleration phases, whereas the *posterior* subsets occur during the deceleration and follow-through phase. The *neurogenic* phases must be further subdivided into those elements that are tractioned versus those that are compressed during the throwing motion. The cervical nerve roots are potentially compressed in a narrow neuro-foramen during the cocking phase, especially in the tennis motion, whereas the brachial plexus elements and the fixated cervical nerve roots are tractioned during deceleration. The posterior cord of the plexus can be compressed in the quadralateral space during cocking and be tractioned during deceleration. The same can be said for the musculocutaneous nerve and anteriorly placed structures. The treatment program can be followed by the phases discussed in the chapter on General Rehabilitation Principles. The first treatment stage for each of the subsets requires anti-inflammatory and pain control actions. An anti-inflammatory program and pain control program may include the following:

1. Rest
2. Ice
3. Nonsteroidal anti-inflammatory drugs
4. Oral corticosteroids
5. Injection of corticosteroids
   Intrabursal
   Intra-articular (acromioclavicular joint, glenohumeral joint)
   Bicipital groove
6. Iontophoresis, phonophoresis
7. Pulsed galvanic muscle stimulation
8. Transcutaneous nerve stimulation

TABLE 2. Anterior Shoulder Subset

1. Impingement syndrome
2. Biceps tendonitis
3. Acromioclavicular joint synovitis
4. Anterior glenoid labrum tear
5. Anterior subluxation

TABLE 3. Neurogenic Shoulder Pain Subset

1. Cervical radicular injury
2. Thoracic outlet syndrome
3. Axillary nerve entrapment
4. Posterior brachial plexus cord entrapment
5. Suprascapular nerve entrapment
6. Long thoracic nerve injury
7. Dorsal scapular nerve injury
8. Accessory nerve injury
9. Musculocutaneous nerve injury
10. Forearm nerve entrapments with proximal pain referral

9. Acupuncture
10. Trigger point injection

The degree and duration of the inflammation and pain determine how quickly one may advance through the program. Injections are useful to instill medication into the subacromial bursa, the glenohumeral joint, the acromioclavicular joint, or into the biceps tendon sheath.[4] Direct intratendinous injection of cortisone is to be avoided.[20] Fluoroscopic localization is often necessary to ensure proper placement of medication intraarticularly. Acupuncture and trigger point injections can be useful to reduce pain and facilitate substitution free motion re-education.

Ultrasound, by virtue of its biophysical properties, enhances soft tissue flexibility and decreases pain perception but has no inherent anti-inflammatory action.[22] Modalities such as pulsed electrical stimulation and transcutaneous nerve stimulation can be helpful to reduce pain and thereby enhance range of motion programs.[13,24] The efficacy of phonophoresis and iontophoresis is not scientifically established but has been empirically noted to be effective by many practitioners.

After the pain and inflammation are reduced, the program is advanced to regain lost range of motion (ROM). Passive ROM exercises directed to the specific tissues that have become inflexible is combined with active and active-assistive programs. Pre-stretching after ultrasound application followed by post-stretch icing with or without pulsed galvanic stimulation is utilized. The athlete is encouraged to practice ROM exercises at least twice daily. The athlete is taught pre-stretch heating and post-stretch icing.

The athlete must be instructed to develop a sense of feel of the tissues that are being stretched. Discomfort without significantly prolonged post-exercise pain is felt with proper exercise performance. Totally ''painfree'' stretching is not stretching the tissue in the range necessary and undue post-exercise pain is indicative of overzealous stretching. Stretching for all portions of the shoulder capsule and rotator cuff are encouraged, with the exception of the subluxation subsets, in which stretching the already-attenuated involved (either anterior or posterior) tissues must be avoided.

Flexibility programs are necessary to allow proper arm positioning during the motion and to allow the elasticity of the capsule and the tendons to act as potential energy converters to accelerate the arm. The specific areas of inflexibility must be highlighted on the physical examination and throughout the rehabilitation process.

Flexibility is an absolute component of the maintenance and prevention program for all throwing athletes. Tissue flexibility is necessary not only in the upper extremity but in the lower extremity as well. Specific note should be made of the hip flexors and quadriceps musculature. Thoracic trunk mobility is also an important component. The hip flexors and quadriceps participate in proper trunk positioning

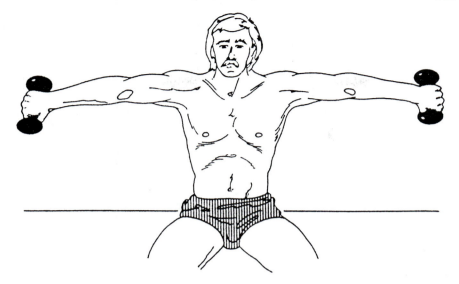

FIGURE 4. Supraspinatus isolation strengthening. (Reproduced with permission from Moynes DR: Prevention of injury to the shoulder through exercise and therapy. Clin Sports Med 2:413–422, 1983.)

for acceleration and deceleration. The trunk must be able to whip the arm without being itself injured.

In impingement syndrome the specific areas of concern are the anterior capsular tissues, the biceps tendon, the superior rotator cuff, and the scapulothoracic attachments. In the posterior capsular strain and the teres minor syndrome, the posterior tissues are concentrated upon but anterior inflexibility is usually noted as well. Specific vigorous stretching is necessary in the teres minor syndrome. Local injection into the muscle is often necessary to facilitate this goal. The appropriate exercises are demonstrated in Figures 4–11.

The scapular stabilizers and movers are an often-neglected portion of the flexibility program. The rational for not forsaking the scapulothoracic joint was discussed earlier. As ligamentous and musculotendinous tissues are stretched, so is neural tissue. The neural tissue has the same need for range of motion and extensibility; if ignored, it can become fixated and thereby potentially symptomatic.

Strength programs advance from the isometric state, which is used when joint ROM is limited and when pain accompanies isotonic and isokinetic full ROM workouts. Muscle weakness and fatigability are pinpointed during the physical examination and concentrated upon in the rehabilitation process. Isokinetic testing is also beneficial in this regard. Strength through a full ROM and endurance are the goals. Supraspinatus strength and endurance have been noted to be key factors in impingement syndrome rehabilitation. Balanced strength is important, thus no muscle should be ignored. The scapulothoracic musculature must be trained with scapular retraction and protraction exercises. The truncal muscles, namely the latissimus dorsi, pectoralis major clavicular head, and oblique abdominals, must be strengthened. The triceps, a potent decelerator, must not be ignored, especially the proximal portion. Quadriceps strength will allow strong leg drive and maintenance

FIGURE 5. External rotator strengthening. (Reproduced with permission from Moynes DR: Prevention of injury to the shoulder through exercise and therapy. Clin Sports Med 2:413–422, 1983.)

of center of gravity. Gastroc-soleus strength as well as tibialis anterior and peroneus longus strength will promote good footing and propulsion.

Manual resistance with no joint motion, i.e., isometric patterns, is used in the initial stages following injury. Later, manual resistance is applied throughout the full ROM program. Finally isotonic isolation techniques using dumbbells are instituted. Isokinetic programs can also be used during this stage; by virtue of their smooth action, they enhance full ROM muscle contractions. Maintenance programs are designed for specific muscle groups. Upper extremity strengthening exercises using dumbbells, pulleys, tennis ball cans filled with sand, or surgical tubing for resistance are encouraged and monitored. My preference is to use pulley systems, because of their smooth action and the ability to isolate each muscle group in the appropriate angle and position. Inverted leg press assists quadriceps muscle strength-

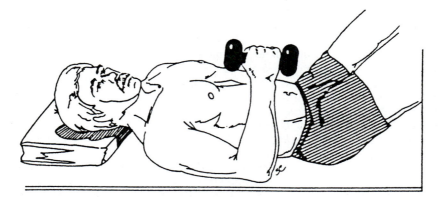

FIGURE 6. Internal rotator strengthening. (Reproduced with permission from Moynes DR: Prevention of injury to the shoulder through exercise and therapy. Clin Sports Med 2: 413–422, 1983.)

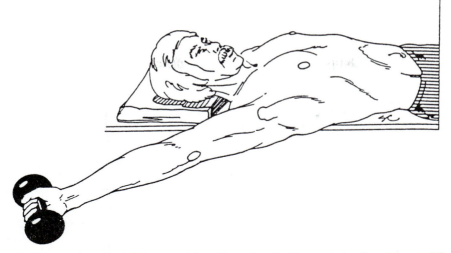

FIGURE 7. Anterior-inferior stretching. (Reproduced with permission from Moynes DR: Prevention of injury to the shoulder through exercise and therapy. Clin Sports Med 2:413–422, 1983.)

ening while using weighted calf raises and pulley-resisted ankle dorsiflexion and eversion are utilized. Leg extension machines and free bar squats are also effective for quadriceps strengthening, but inverted leg press is safer on the back and allows knee angle alteration to decrease patellofemoral loading.

Strengthening of posterior musculature is highlighted during the rehabilitation of the posterior subsets, whereas the internal rotators and the supraspinatus are the targets in anterior subluxation. Balanced strength must be stressed in all cases, but areas of specific attention may take precedence during the early phase of an individual program. Strength of the decelerators must never be forgotten. Even though they contract eccentrically, it is not clear whether eccentric strength training programs for these muscles, although theoretically attractive, enhance the outcome.

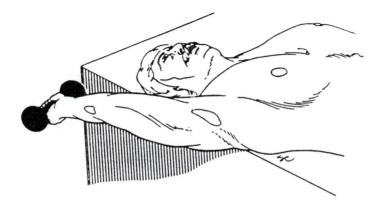

FIGURE 8. Inferior stretching. (Reproduced with permission from Moynes DR: Prevention of injury to the shoulder through exercise and therapy. Clin Sports Med 2:413–422, 1983.)

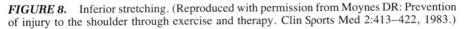

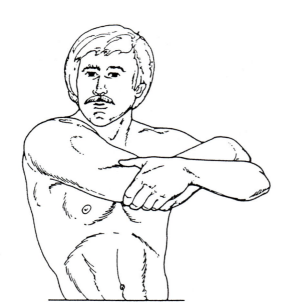

FIGURE 9. Posterior stretching. (Reproduced with permission from Moynes DR: Prevention of injury to the shoulder through exercise and therapy. Clin Sports Med 2:413–422, 1983.)

After full ROM and strength are attained, the challenging task of *movement retraining* begins. The intricacies of the throwing motion and movement program were discussed earlier. Emphasis was placed on elimination of substitution patterns.

The *return to throwing program* concentrates first on form training (Table 4). After appropriate pre-throwing stretching and deep heating, the thrower begins the

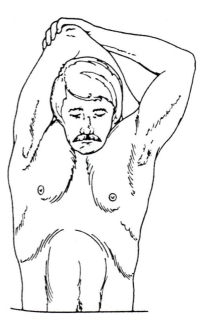

FIGURE 10. Posteroinferior stretching. (Reproduced with permission from Moynes DR: Prevention of injury to the shoulder through exercise and therapy. Clin Sports Med 2:413–422, 1983.)

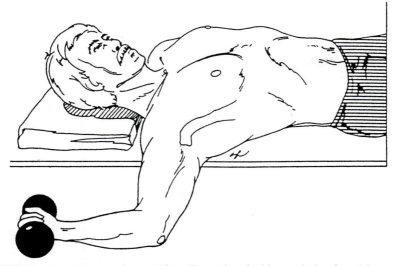

FIGURE 11.   Anterior capsule stretching. (Reproduced with permission from Moynes DR: Prevention of injury to the shoulder through exercise and therapy. Clin Sports Med 2:413–422, 1983.)

program with long tosses. Form is monitored and velocity is minimized. Four to five minutes of throwing is undertaken. After two to three days of this sequence, a twice-daily program of long toss is instituted. Two days of throwing and one day of rest is initially recommended. After approximately five successful workouts, short toss at half-speed is added. Long toss is done for five minutes and short toss for five minutes. The long toss program is then discarded and the short toss is advanced to 60 feet and then to 90 feet. Velocity is added slowly and is the last ingredient. Post-throwing stretch and icing are also employed.[34]

For tennis players the long toss portion of the program includes serving to an area deep to the service box with minimal velocity (Table 5). The program is advanced to serving into the deeper portions of the service box. Higher velocities are added only after form is perfected and pain is not experienced. The pre-exercise and post-exercise stretching described in the throwing program is also utilized here.

In some athletes this program may take six weeks, in others only one to two weeks. The amount of layoff time and the postoperative course for some patients will by necessity prolong the program.

Maintenance programs with pre- and post-exercise stretching as well as strength training are necessary. Injury prevention appears to hing heavily upon these is-

TABLE 4.   Progressive Return to Tennis Serving

1. Low-velocity serving 5–10 feet past service box once daily
2. Advance to twice-daily program
3. Low-velocity serving deep into service box
4. Gradually increase velocity
5. Flat serves only
6. Normal serve depth
7. Spin serves
8. Full unrestricted serving

TABLE 5.   Progressive Return to Throwing Program

1. Long toss, minimal velocity 4–5 minutes once daily
2. Long toss, gradually adding velocity
3. Long toss routine, twice daily
4. Short toss, 60 foot distance once daily, with long toss once daily
5. Short toss, twice daily
6. Short toss, advancing distance to 90 feet
7. Increase velocity incrementally
8. Full windup, flat fastballs
9. Full windup, breaking balls
10. Fastball throwing from stretch position
11. Curve ball throwing from stretch position
12. Full unrestricted throwing

sues.[4,31,32] Remember that athletes often begin a season in good physical condition but gradually decondition as the season progresses. Off-season conditioning and throwing are necessary to maintain adequate fitness of the shoulder mechanism.[32] Five days of throwing at half-speed with two days of rest are encouraged.

An algorithm for the treatment of shoulder impingement is presented in Figure 12. This algorithm outlines the program presented in this chapter. All programs must be individualized for the athlete; therefore caution not to follow the guidelines too rigidly must be exercised.

SUMMARY

The shoulder is an unstable joint, and the throwing motion places tremendous stresses upon it. Thus rehabilitation of shoulder injuries is a complex endeavor. A thorough understanding of the relevant anatomy, biomechanics, muscular physiology, pathologic entities, and the scientific rationale for rehabilitation procedures is necessary to succeed.

REFERENCES

1. Anderson M: Comparison of muscle patterning in the overarm throw and tennis serve. Res Q 50:541–553, 1979.
2. Ariel G: Biomechanical analysis of shotputting. Track Field Q Rev 79:27, 1980.
3. Ariel G: Biomechanical analysis of the hammer throw. Track Field Q Rev 80:41, 1980.
4. Aronen JG: Shoulder rehabilitation. Clin Sports Med 4:xxx–xxx, July 1985.
5. Atwater A: Biomechanics of overarm throwing movement and of throwing injuries. Exer Sport Sci Rev 7:43–85, 1979.
6. Bateman J: Nerve injuries about the shoulder in sports. J Bone and Joint Surg 49:785–792, 1967.
7. Clein LJ: Suprascapular entrapment neuropathy. J Neurosurg 43:337–342, 1975.
8. Colachis S, Strohm B, Brecher V: Effects of axillary nerve block on muscle force in the upper extremity. Arch Phys Med Rehabil 50:647–654, 1969.
9. Colachis S, Strohm B: Effects of suprascapular and axillary nerve blocks on muscle force in upper extremity. Arch Phys Med Rehabil 52:22–29, 1971.
10. deLuca C, Forrest W: Force analysis of individual muscles acting simultaneously in the shoulder joint during isometric abduction. J Biomech 6:385–393, 1973.
11. Distefano V: Functional anatomy and biomechanics of the shoulder joints. Athl Training 12:141–144, 1977.
12. Doody S, Freedman L, Waterland J: Shoulder movements during abduction in the scapular plane. Arch Phys Med Rehabil 51:595–604, 1970.
13. Fox EJ, Melzack R: Transcutaneous electrical stimulation and acupuncture: comparison of treatment for low-back pain. Pain 141–148, 1976.
14. Freedman L, Munro R: Abduction of the arm in the scapular plane: scapular and glenohumeral movements. J Bone Joint Surg 48A:1503–1510, 1966.
15. Gracovetsky S, Farfan H: The optimum spine. Spine 11:xxx–xxx, 1986.

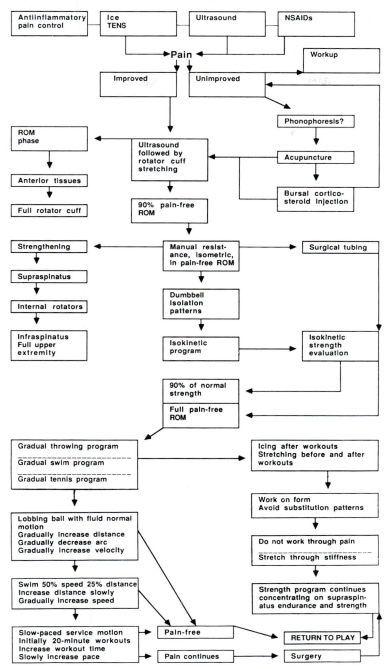

FIGURE 12. Shoulder Impingement Rehabilitation Algorithm. (Reproduced with permission from Saal JA: Rehabilitation of the injured athlete. In DeLisa J: Principles and Practice of Physical Medicine and Rehabilitation. Philadelphia, J.B. Lippincott, 1988, in press).

16. Harris, FA: Facilitation techniques and technological adjuncts in therapeutic exercise. In Basmajian JV (ed): Therapeutic Exercise, 9th ed. Baltimore, Williams and Wilkins, 1984.

17. Inman V, Saunders J, Abbott L: Observations on the function of the shoulder joint. J Bone Joint Surg 26:1–30, 1944.

18. Jobe F, Tibone J, Perry J, et al: An EMG analysis of the shoulder in throwing and pitching. Am J Sports Med 11:3–5, 1983.

19. Johnson J, Kendall H: Isolated paralysis of the serratus anterior muscle. J Bone Joint Surg 3:567–574, 1955.

20. Kennedy JC, Baxter-Willis R: The effects of local steroid injections on tendons: A biochemical and microscopic correlative study. Am J Sports Med 4:11–18, 1976.

21. Kent B: Functional anatomy of the shoulder complex. Phys Ther 51:867–887, 1971.

22. Lehman JF, DeLateur BJ: Therapeutic heat. In Lehman JF (ed): Therapeutic Heat and Cold, 3rd ed. Baltimore, Williams and Wilkins, 1982, p. 531.

23. Lucas D: Biomechanics of the shoulder joint. Arch Surg 107:425–432, 1973.

24. Mannheimer JS, Lampe GN: Clinical Transcutaneous Electrical Nerve Stimulation. Philadelphia, F.A. Davis, 1984, pp. 210–212.

24a. Moynes DR: Prevention of injury to the shoulder through exercise and therapy. Clin Sports Med 2:413–422, 1983.

25. Perry J: Anatomy and biomechanics of the shoulder in throwing, swimming, gymnastics, and tennis. Clin Sports Med 2:247–270, 1983.

26. Reeves B: Experiments on the tensile strength of the anterior capsular structures of the shoulder in man. J Bone Joint Surg 50B:858–865, 1968.

27. Saha AK: Anterior recurrent dislocation of the shoulder. Acta Orthop Scand 68:479–493, 1967.

28. Shevlin M, Lehmann J, Lucci J: Electromyographic study of the function of some muscles crossing the glenohumeral joint. Arch Phys Med Rehabil 50:264–270, 1969.

29. Sugahara R: Electromyographic study of shoulder movements. Jpn J Rehab 11:41–52, 1974.

30. Tullos H, King J: Throwing mechanism in sports. Orthop Clin North Am 4:709–720, 1973.

31. Van Linge B, Mulder J: Function of the supraspinatus muscle and its relation to the supraspinatus syndrome. J Bone Joint Surg 45B:750–754, 1963.

32. Zarins B, Andrews J, Carson W (eds): Injuries to the Throwing Arm. Blackburn T: The off-season program for the throwing arm. Philadelphia, W.B. Saunders Co., 1985, pp. 277–292.

33. Zarins B, Andrews J, Carson W (eds): Injuries to the Throwing Arm. Leach R: Tennis serving compared with baseball pitching. Philadelphia, W.B. Saunders Co., 1985, pp. 307–310.

34. Zarins B, Andrews J, Carson W (eds): Injuries to the Throwing Arm. Fauls D: General training techniques to warm up and cool down the throwing arm. Philadelphia, W.B. Saunders Co., 1985, pp. 266–276.

35. Zarins B, Andrews J, Carson W: Injuries to the throwing arm. In Ariel G (ed): Body Mechanics. Philadelphia, W.B. Saunders Co., 1985, pp. 3–21

JEFFREY A. SAAL, MD

REHABILITATION OF SPORTS-RELATED LUMBAR SPINE INJURIES

Reprint requests to Jeffrey A. Saal, M.D., Sports Orthopedic and Rehabilitation Medicine Associates, 3250 Alpine Rd., Portola Valley, CA 94025.

The rehabilitation of an athelete with a lumbar spine injury presents a significant challenge to the sports medicine physician. The true incidence of lumbar spine injuries is not available but in our busy sports medicine practice it accounts for approximately 20% of injured athletes evaluated. Sports activities involve repetitive flexion, extension, and torsional stresses to the lumbar motion segments, which predispose the lumbar spine to injury. The sports most commonly associated with lumbar spine injuries are gymnastics, weight lifting, football, dance, rowing and wrestling.[37,40,41,60,82] It has been reported that 30% of collegiate football players will at some time have complaints and missed playing time secondary to a lumbar spine complaint.[21,58] A recent seven-year survey of NFL injuries noted a 12% incidence of spine injuries necessitating time loss from play.[72]

Once the athlete has sustained an injury to the lumbar spine and presents for medical attention, a number of considerations become important. Number one is the establishment of an accurate diagnosis. This can be accomplished only with a thorough understanding of the biomechanics of the specific sport coupled with an indepth understanding of the pathomechanics and anatomy of the lumbar spine. Treatment and rehabilitation follow the diagnostic phase. The treatment and rehabilitation phase can be subdivided into the pain control phase and the training phase. The training phase can be further subdivided into beginning and advanced stages.

The purpose of this chapter is to formulate the rationale for the rehabilitation of lumbar spine disorders in the injured athlete. Treatment programs will be outlined that advance from initial

TABLE 1. Classificaton of Lumbar Spine Injuries by Diagnostic Category

	Pain Location			Physical Examination			
Diagnostic Subsets	back	buttock	leg	SLR	Flexion	Ext.	Neuro
Disc Subsets							
Annular tear	+	+	−	Bp	+	−	−
Herniation							
a. with nerve root irritation and no neurologic deficit	+	+	+	Lp	+	−	−
b. with neurologic deficit	+	+	+	Lp	+	−	+
c. with no nerve root irritation	+	+	+/−	Lp	+	−	−
Degenerative disc, exacerbation (repeat annular tears)	+	+	−	Bp	+	−	−
Internal disc disruption syndrome	+	+	+/−	Bp	+	−	−
Posterior Element Subsets							
Facet pain syndrome	+	+	+/−	Bp	−	+	−
Spondylosis (with and without olisthesis without nerve irritation)	+	+	+/−	Bp	−	+	−
Spondylolisthesis							
a. with nerve root irritation and no neurologic deficit	+	+	+	Lp	+	+	−
b. with nerve root irritation and neurologic deficit	+	+	+	Lp	+	+	+
Stenosis Subsets							
Central canal	+	+	+	Lp	−	+	+/−
Lateral recess	+	+	+	Lp	−	+	+/−
Foraminal	+	+	+	Lp	+	+	+/−
Extra-foraminal	+	+	+	Lp	+/−	+/−	+/−
Segmental Instability							
a. without nerve root irritation	+	+	−	Bp	+/−	+	−
b. with nerve root irritation	+	+	+	+/−	+/−	+	+/−
Soft Tissue Subsets	+/−	+/−	+/−	−	+ to −	−	−

Bp = back pain; Lp = leg pain; +/− = may be present, or positive; + to − = initially painful turning to painless; + = present, pain increased by or positive finding; and − = absent, pain not changed by or negative finding.

acute treatment to refined programs for specific injuries and sport types.

TYPES OF INJURY

Lumbar spine injuries can be classified by diagnostic category as well as by sports-related categories. The diagnostic categories are listed in Tables 1 and 2. The anatomic sites of injury have been separated into discogenic, posterior element, and soft tissue subsets. The diagnostic information necessary to establish these diagnoses is also presented in the tables.

In my experience 70% of sports-related lumbar spine injuries involve the posterior elements. The intervertebral disc can be implicated as the pain source in 25% of cases, although the majority of these cases are uncomplicated annular tears in which pain resolution occurs within two to six weeks. The remaining 5% encompass a melange of inflammatory spondyloarthropathies, neoplasms, sacroilac joint syndromes, spinous and transverse process fractures, vertebral body compression fractures, direct contusions, and viscerogenic and vascular syndromes.

The classification of lumbar spine injury by sport is somewhat arbitrary and

TABLE 2.   Findings of Diagnostic Studies in Lumbar Spine Injuries

Diagnostic Subsets	Diagnostic Study Findings			
	CT	MRI	EMG/SSEP	Injections
Disc Subsets				
Annular tear	−	−	−	epidural +/−*
Herniation				
a. with nerve root irritation and no neurologic deficit	+	+	+/−*	epidural + snrb +
b. with neurologic deficit	+	+	+	epidural + snrb +
c. with no nerve root irritation	+	+	−	epidural −
Degenerative disc, exacerbation (repeat annular tears)	+**	+**	chronic +	epidural +/−
Internal disc disruption syndrome	+	−	chronic +	discogram +
Posterior Element Subsets				
Facet pain syndrome	−	−	−	facet +
Spondylosis (with and without olisthesis without nerve irritation)	+	+/−*	−	pars +***
Spondylolisthesis	+	+/−*	+	
a. with nerve root irritation and no neurologic deficit				
b. with nerve root irritation and neurologic deficit	+	+/−*	+	snrb +
Stenosis Subsets				
Central canal	+	+	+	epidural + snrb +
Lateral recess	+	+/−*	+	epidural + snrb +
Foraminal	+	−	+	epidural +/− snrb +
Extra-foraminal	+	−	+	epidural + snrb +
Soft Tissue Pain Subsets	−	−	−	epidural − snrb − facet −
Segmental Instability				
a. without nerve root irritation	−	−	−	facet + epidural −
b. with nerve root irritation	?	?	+	facet + epidural + snrb +

* = may be positive; ** = bulge or + = present, pain increased by or positive finding; + = positive finding, or alleviation of pain with injection; − = negative finding, no change in pain with injection; snrb = selective nerve root block; ? = stenosis may be noted, coupled with facet degenerative changes; chronic + : chronic finding; pars = injection of the defect.

involves an understanding of the biomechanics of the sport to fully appreciate the loads that are placed upon the lumbar spine and to extrapolate which lumbar spine structure is at greatest jeopardy (Table 3).

DIAGNOSTIC PRINCIPLES

The first and most important task is to establish a diagnosis. Without an accurate and timely diagnosis, it is virtually impossible to plan a specific treatment and

TABLE 3. Sport-Specific Lumbar Injury Subsets

Sport	Type of Stress
1. Gymnastics	Posterior element loading
2. Dance	Posterior element loading
3. Rowing	Torsional disc loading
4. Football Lineman	Posterior element loading
5. Equestrian	Axial disc loading
6. Diving	Axial disc loading
7. Jumping sports	Posterior element loading, axial and torsional disc loading
8. Raquet sports	Torsional disc and posterior element loading
9. Baseball	Torsional disc loading, posterior element loading
10. Weight lifting	Axial and torsional disc loading, posterior element loading

rehabilitation program to enable the athlete to return to competition. Localization of the pain generator is paramount in spinal pain diagnostics. Indeed, the structure that appears to be most involved on a CT scan or other imaging study may not be the structure that is generating the disabling pain. Therefore, careful correlation of the history, mechanism of injury, physical examination, and diagnostic studies is imperative to establish the location of the pain generator(s). An adequate understanding of referral pain and potential pain generators is necessary for this undertaking.

Anatomic studies have demonstated the presence of nociceptive nerve endings in the annulus fibrosis of the lumbar intervertebral disc.[8] Annular tears can, therefore, cause pain referral of purely discogenic origin into the low back, buttock, sacroiliac region, and lower extremity, even in the absence of neural compression. Neural compression caused by an annular tear that has progressed to become a protruded disc can be an obvious source of pain. Disc protrusion without neural compression can precipitate an inflammatory response with secondary radiculitis, raising the possibility of chemically induced inflammatory neural pain.[55,64,71] The lumbar zygapophyseal joints, i.e., facet joints, are well innervated structures and thus are potent potential pain generators. Facet arthropathy can cause low back pain as well as referral pain into the buttock and lower extremity.[62] Mixed spinal nerve root compression or irritation in the intervertebral foramen secondary to facet synovitis can refer pain along the ventral primary ramus into the buttock and lower extremity.[51] The sensory fibers by virtue of their proximity to the facet capsule will be the first to become irritated by an inflammatory process, which manifests as back pain coupled with paresthesias in the lower extremity. The medial branch of the dorsal primary ramus, which supplies sensory innervation to the facet capsule as well as to the motor branch of the multifidus, theoretically can be entrapped in the fibro-osseous tunnel as it courses around the superior articular process to the root of the transverse process.[22] This may present as lower back pain with referral pain to the buttock and lower extremity.

The dorsal nerves have a larger diameter than the ventral nerve roots, which some feel may explain the greater susceptibility of the sensory axons to compressive forces. The S1 nerve roots are approximately 170 mm long, whereas the L1 nerve roots are 60 mm long.[85] The greater length of the lower lumbosacral roots may explain their precarious predisposition to injury. Spinal nerve roots lack the connective tissue protection that sheaths peripheral nerves. This sheathing has considerable mechanical strength and possesses properties to form a barrier to diffusion of certain molecules. The spinal nerve roots, therefore, are at a disadvantage mechanically and possibly biochemically. The nerve roots are surrounded, however, by cerebrospinal fluid which, together with the dura, gives the spinal nerve roots an element of mechanical protection. The dura of the spinal nerve root appears to be continuous with the epineurium of the peripheral nerve. It should be remembered that the nerve root complex must be extraordinarily mobile. We must think of the nerve root complex as we do other soft tissue structures that necessarily adapt to dynamic change of spinal position. Nerve roots must change length depending upon the degree of flexion, extension, lateral bending, and rotation of the lumbar spine. Limitation of nerve root motion by fibrosis of either intraspinal or extraspinal origin creates traction upon the nerve root complex, causing ischemia and secondary neural dysfunction. Intraneural blood flow is markedly affected when the nerve root is stretched about 8% over the original length. Complete cessation of all intraneural blood flow is seen at 15% elongation.[74] Suspensory ligaments within the dura as well as at the level of the intervertebral foramen limit spinal nerve root excursion.[81] Instability with or without fibrosis or stenosis may cause significant traction upon the spinal nerve root, potentially causing dysfunction. Compression significantly compromises internal blood flow as well. The interruption of intraneural blood flow causes secondary increase in capillary permeability with the consequent development of intraneural edema. If intraneural edema is allowed to remain, intraneural fibrosis may develop. Dorsal root ganglion (DRG) stimulation may potentially explain primary discogenic pain syndromes and other nondescript pain referral syndromes.[38] Vibration, mechanical distortion and neurotransmitters such as substance P have all been demonstrated to cause repetitive firing of DRG.[92] Posterior element injuries likewise cause DRG stimulation and manifest not only as back pain but as concomitant referral zone pain to the buttocks and lower extremity.

Repetitive torsional loads to the lumbar spine have been noted to cause annular injury that leads to disc degeneration.[18,20] Recently these same torsional stresses have been shown to cause leakage of synovial fluid from the lumbar facet joints, which may lead to early progression of facet arthropathy.[52] The motion segments at risk for torsional injury lie above the intercrestal line, i.e., usually the L4-5 interspace coupled with the L3-4 interspace. The L5-S1 motion segment is reportedly more susceptible to axial compression injury than the segments above.[18,20] In the skeletally immature athlete, the vertebral endplate is at risk for intraosseous disc herniation, probably as a direct consequence of an axial loading injury.[57] Schmorl's node formation is caused by intraosseus disc herniation into the vertebral end plate.[75] Repetitive extension and loading of the posterior elements of the lumbar spine have been associated with fatigue fractures of the neural arch, i.e., spondylolysis.[11,39,41] The incidence of spondylolysis in the gymnastic population has been cited to be as high as 22%.[40] An incidence of 21% has been reported in a survey of 677 male high school and university athletes.[37] A recent study of collegiate football players reported an incidence of lumbar spondylolysis of 15.2%, which did not significantly increase during their collegiate years.[58] Reports indicate that the higher incidence of spondylolysis in interior linemen is probably related to repetitive loading of the posterior elements when rising from the stance position to blocking posture while maintaining lumbar lordosis.

Due to the high incidence of posterior element injuries in the sporting population, an adequate understanding of the biomechanics of the posterior elements is necessary. The lumbar facet joints are exposed to increased articular cartilage loading pressures during extension and in torsional maneuvers.[2,3] Repetitive extension maneuvers can cause facet synovitis and lead to facet arthropathy. A degenerative segment has decreased resistance to torsional stress.[44] Changes in foraminal size have been demonstrated in the degenerative segment with postural movement.[69] An appreciation of this phenomenon is important to understanding the potential cause of foraminal nerve root injury in the presence of only a mildly narrowed neuroforamen. Facet tropism leads to transfer of asymmetric loads to the facet articular surfaces and to the annulus.[10] Facet tropism may predispose to the development of facet pain syndromes in athletes but this needs to be elucidated in controlled research studies.

The hallmark work of Kirkaldy-Willis in outlining the stages of the degenerative process form the foundation for understanding lumbar spine injuries.[94] The sporting population spans all ages. Rehabilitation of the lumbar spine therefore emcompasses degenerative processes as well as pure injuries. The finding of a degenerative segment in the collegiate athlete is neither rare nor surprising if one considers the loads placed on the spinal structures not only in athletic training and competition but in daily life as well.

A final note on the diagnostic phase deserves mention. Diagnostic studies that examine only structural changes are unable to establish the cause of persistent pain when used in isolation. This has been demonstrated repeatedly in studies attempting to correlate structural changes seen on lumbar x-rays, myelograms, and CT scans with a patient's pain complaints. The competent diagnostician has the ability to sort out the clinical information derived from the history, the mechanism of injury, a careful physical examination, electrophysiologic studies (i.e., EMG, SSEP), imaging studies, results of treatment, and the social factors surrounding the pain process to arrive at a diagnosis.

REHABILITATION PROGRAMS

Pain Control Phase

The pain control phase is the earliest phase of treatment, corresponding to phases 1–3 in the general principles of athletic rehabilitation (see the chapter on General Principles). The pain control phase should be instituted as early and efficiently as possible. It is important not to get stuck in the pain control phase but rather to advance as rapidly as possible to the training phases of treatment. As outlined in General Principles, pain control involves reducing inflammatory response and improving range of motion.

The initial step, *back first aid*, involves the application of ice,[17] resting in a position of comfort, and basic instruction in body mechanics to facilitate pain-free movement while getting in and out of chairs, cars, bathtubs, etc. The patient is taught to control pain and muscle spasm by these methods. The use of medications should be kept to a minimum. The type of injury sustained (anterior structures versus posterior structures) determines the position of comfort. During this initial phase, rest is also specifically prescribed. The use of bedrest is the most abused and overprescribed treatment in lumbar spine care. Bedrest need only be utilized to control pain in the early days following the injury. There is absolutely no evidence to support total and absolute bed rest after any injury to the lumbar spine.[14] Excessive bed rest leads to hypomobile lumbar motion segments, tightened soft tissues, loss of muscle strength, blunting of motivation, and loss of mineral matrix from bone.[12] To equate conservative care with three weeks of bedrest and to threaten surgery if this initial treatment is unsuccessful is ludicrous, uninformed, and barbaric.

Pain-relieving modalities such as transcutaneous nerve stimulation[26] and pulsed galvanic stimulation along with ice may be used to reduce acute pain.[46,80] *Extension exercises* are valuable to reduce pain in discogenic injury subsets.[53] The principle of extension exercises may well be explained by a reduction in neural tension rather than by nuclear migration as initially proposed.[76] When extension exercises cause centralization of low back pain without exacerbating or peripheralizing the lower extremity, i.e., radicular pain, they can be utilized. Peripheralization of pain is a contraindication to the use of extension exercises and may indicate stenosis, far lateral disc protrusion, or posterior element pathology. The correction of a lumbar shift is necessary before beginning extension exercises. If the exercises are attempted while the patient is still listed, exacerbation of pain may occur, which may lead to an erroneous decision to abandon the extension exercise program. The overuse of extension exercises, even in a pure discogenic injury subset, can lead to facet pain and must be watched for. No individual should remain on one particular type of exercise regimen during the entire treatment phase, but should advance through all treatment phases. No one should remain purely on an extension program.

Flexion exercises are most useful in posterior element injury subsets. Flexion has been noted to cause a reduction in articular, weight-bearing stress to the facet joints.[2] Flexion exercises have an additional benefit of stretching the dorsolumbar fascia.[7]

Spinal immobilization is rarely necessary in athletic spine injuries. There are proponents of immobilization for an acute pars interarticularis stress fracture.[84] Studies fail to report compelling evidence that stress fracture healing occurs to any greater degree with or without immobilization. In my experience this type of immobilization is rarely necessary, and the abstinence from athletic competition along with adequate pain control therapy will alleviate the symptoms and seem to make no additional difference in the potential healing of the stress fracture. Symptomatic segmental instability caused by spondylolisthesis, previous surgery or a degenerative segment may benefit from immobilization with a molded body jacket. The symptoms of internal disc disruption can sometimes be controlled by the same technique. In all of these cases the use of immobilizing apparatus *may* yield important information regarding potential candidacy for surgical fusion. The use of a unilateral hip spica incorporated into a lumbar cast is necessary if one truly wishes to obtain lumbar segmental immobilization.[47] Equestrians with lumbar injuries presents one of the few circumstances in which the use of a brace or corset can be effectively utilized during athletic competition. Neoprene lumbar corsets have been useful to maintain warmth and to enhance flexibility in a variety of athletes but are useless in controlling instability.

The use of *mobilization* techniques can be extraordinarily useful to attain articular and soft tissue range of motion.[89] Stiffened segments should be mobilized and tight soft tissues must be adequately stretched. Ultrasound application is useful to facilitate soft tissue extensibility in order to allow adequate articular and soft tissue mobilization.[49] Caution must be exercised in the use of ultrasound in the presence of a "hot" radiculopathy, owing to possible post-treatment exacerbation of radicular symptoms probably related to neural swelling. A specific area of attention in mobilization is the thoracolumbar junctional segments, which often become hypomobile and can indeed be pain generators in their own right, often masquerading as lumbar pain syndromes.[54] Overvigorous mobilization can be harmful in all types of injuries and should be carefully graded and timed in the treatment program. For instance, the use of mobilization techniques in an individual with a painful spondylolysis or spondylolisthesis would be contraindicated at the local lumbar level of the defect but may be beneficial when carried out at the upper lumbar segments. Forceful manipulations that present torsional stress on the lower motion segments may further disrupt annular tears and potentially turn a simple annular tear into a frank disc herniation. Manipulation of a displaced facet meniscal process probably explains the dramatic response that patients sometimes experience to these techniques.[6,77] In the more advanced degenerative segment, the pain process derives from other factors, and therefore the response to manipulative techniques is not nearly as dramatic.

Traction may be useful to obtain symptomatic relief in the treatment of discogenic injury subtypes. There are proponents of gravity inversion,[66,68] gravity lumbar reduction,[83] autotraction,[28] and pelvic traction.[35] Depending on the size of the patient, the type of equipment available, and the type of disc pathology, all of these traction modalities may be useful to provide symptomatic relief. Although many studies report subjective symptom improvement, there is no scientific evidence to support the contention that any of the traction techniques actually facilitate nuclear migration. There is also no direct correlation with disc contour changes before and after traction.[35] Autotraction possesses a special advantage in its ability to be poly-axial and patient-controlled.[48] Gravity inversion traction can be used at home and on an ongoing basis as long as hypertension or retinal problems do not contraindicate its use.[34,45] A force equal to approximately 26% of the body weight is required to overcome just the surface resistance of the lower half of the body.[42,43] Bed traction, therefore, is unable either to overcome this enormous resistance factor or to facilitate any separation of the vertebral elements, and can only serve to restrain the patient. By the use of a split table to reduce frictional forces, a weight equaling 50 pounds of intermittent force for 15 minutes has been reported to cause posterior interbody separation, although no residual separation has been noted 30 minutes after traction.[9] It is therefore unclear by what mechanism traction reduces symptoms. Theoretically pain relief may be mediated by a neurophysiologic mechanism that reduces the transmission of the pain message rather than by direct mechanical forces upon the disc.

One of the most powerful tools in the pain control phase armamentarium is the use of *selective injections*. The list of selective injections include epidural cortisone injection from the tanslumbar or sacral approach, intraarticular facet injections, lumbar selective nerve root blocks, trigger point injections, and acupuncture techniques.

It is counterproductive to prolong the pain control phase of treatment. The use of an *epidural cortisone injection* for lumbar radiculopathy caused by disc injury or stenosis can provide dramatic relief.[13,93] Early aggressive use of epidural cortisone injections in this clinical setting can be of tremendous benefit in the rehabilitation program. Injections are used purely as combined facilitators and are not treatment in their own right. They must be combined with a therapeutic exercise program and the other principles of treatment outlined. Fluoroscopic localization of proper epidural positioning is important to eliminate technical injection failures. The caudal approach is preferable in the majority of circumstances, especially in young athletes, in whom the L4-5 and L5-S1 disc spaces are the most commonly involved. If the L3-4 disc space is the site of the pain generator, then a translumbar epidural is necessary. Epidural cortisone is most beneficial for patients with more leg pain than back pain and who manifest dural tension signs on physical examination.

Intraarticular *lumbar facet injections* under fluoroscopic guidance are useful to place corticosteroids into inflamed facet capsules.[51] Actual injection of spondylitic defects has also been shown to provide symptomatic relief, probably due to the spreading of the medication onto an inflamed exiting nerve root subjacent to the lytic defect.

The use of medial branch dorsal ramus blocks may have a place in the treatment of pure discogenic pain syndromes and is currently under investigation. A rhizotomy of this medial branch can be used to denervate the facet joint,[13,78] but in my experience has never been necessary or indicated in the athletic population.

Lumbar selective nerve root block is useful to instill medication around an inflamed nerve root that is principally entrapped within the foramen or entrapped by a large lateral disc fragment that has migrated foraminally.[87] Extraforaminal nerve entrapment by an enlarged transverse process at the L5-S1 level is also another circumstance in which this technique is useful. The combination of epidural injection and selective nerve root block is often necessary in a very large disc herniation with or without foraminal stenosis. The retirement-age recreational golfer with walking intolerance due to neurogenic claudication associated with degenerative spinal stenosis can be helped by coupling epidural and foraminal cortisone injections.

Triggerpoint injections with local anesthetic should be used only to reduce painful muscle spasm associated with persistent trigger zones identified in the offending muscles.[88] There is no physiologic basis for the addition of corticosteroids into this type of injection.[50] Although attempts have been made to explain these triggerpoints on the basis of inflammatory focus, this has never been satisfactorily described. Triggerpoint injections followed by soft tissue stretching and mobilization programs can result in improvement in range of motion and reduction of pain. Often the soft tissue component of pain is the principal disabling pain factor even in the presence of a structural diagnosis of discogenic pathology. It has been reported that every known triggerpoint injection in the Western literature corresponds to a known *acupuncture* point.[59] It has also been reported that dry needling a triggerpoint is just as effective as injecting the triggerpoint with local anesthetic solution alone, saline alone, or local anesthetics solution plus corticosteroid alone.[27,50] Endorphin release following acupuncture treatment has also been scientifically demonstrated.[79,80,86,91] Cerebrospinal fluid (CSF) from cats pretreated with acupuncture, which is then transferred into donor cats, reduces pain responses in the donor cats.[86] Treatment with naloxone blocks the endorphin release and can blunt acupuncture analgesia.[56] This has been demonstrated to eliminate analgesia in the donor cats when the pretreated cats were given naloxone prior to transfer of their CSF to the donor cats. Numerous well-controlled scientific studies demonstrate the usefulness of *acupuncture* as a pain-relieving modality.[73] However, acupuncture and the other injection procedures described above are purely facilitators of treatment and should be considered as adjunctive therapy only. They are useful in the pain control phase and should be employed in a framework and clinical context to enhance rehabilitation rather than as treatment ends in themselves.

The use of *anti-inflammatory medication* in the early phases of treatment may be appropriate. The analgesic effect of the nonsteroidal anti-inflammatory agents and their ability to act as prostaglandin synthetase inhibitors have a role in the treatment of lumbar pain syndromes. The prescribing of "so-called" muscle relaxants has no physiologic basis. All currently marketed muscle relaxants are central nervous system depressants and not peripherally-acting muscle relaxants. I would, therefore, caution against their use on this basis as well as on the basis of their potential addictive nature.[30] Opiate analgesics are occasionally necessary in the initial week of treatment of lumbar pain syndromes but are rarely needed beyond that time. The proper use of positioning, rest, ice, transcutaneous nerve stimulation, extension and/or flexion exercises, and the selective injections procedures described above usually obviate the need for opiate analgesics.

Oral corticosteroids can be useful in the treatment of acute radiculopathy. Caution must be exercised in young athletes, specifically in regard to seizure activation potential, gastric distress, disorientation, and flaring of acne vulgaris. The flaring of acne may be the most disturbing side effect to the young athlete. The use of anabolic steroids or male hormone supplements has no place in the treatment of the injured athlete.

An understanding of the degenerative cascade as initially described by Kirkaldy-Willis is absolutely imperative.[94] The degenerative cascade can be greatly accelerated in the athlete and will be encountered in all levels and ages of athletic competitors. Adjacent motion segments within the lumbar spine are often at different stages along this cascade. Therefore when planning a rehabilitation program, a thorough understanding of the pathomechanics of the entire lumbar spine is necessary.

Training Phase

The primary goal of the training phase is to attain adequate musculoligamentous control of lumbar spine forces to eliminate repetitive injury to the intervertebral discs, facet joints, and related structures. If the program were not advanced after the pain control phase, the individual would be at risk for suffering a repeat injury, further limiting his or her activity. It is important to identify why the individual injured himself or herself, and the injury risk factors. The athlete needs to be aware of these factors so that preventive measures can be taken. Once injured, a lumbar motion segment is at risk for re-injury. Numerous studies point out the recidivism rate in low back pain patients.[63] Studies have demonstrated the benefits of prevention programs in the industrial work place.[61] These same principles can be applied to the athletic population. Applying the principles of "back school" to the athletic population requires the participation of the physician, the physical therapist, and the coaching staff. It is well recognized that recreational athletes are not full-time athletes but rather are working persons who injure themselves in their leisure time. The back school approach enables instruction that transcends athletics and relates to normal daily function. It is my supposition that the majority of athletic injuries to the lumbar spine actually result from repetitive microtrauma that is sustained during nonathletic events and then is summated during an athletic contest. Pain may be initially experienced at the time of the athletic endeavor but should not be thought of as a result of one incident. This concept is exceedingly important in the understanding of lumbar injuries. Studies have demonstrated the effect of fatigue on the lumbar intervertebral disc and the progressive development of gradual disc prolapse.[4] This demonstrates the biomechanical construct of repetitive injuries to the intervertebral disc, leading to progressive pathology. It also should make us aware of how a "simple" annular tear may, with subsequent annular injury, progress to a full-blown disc protrusion or herniation. Therefore, early identification of an annular tear by placing the individual in a back school program help to eliminate future injury. Our role in delivering care to the injured athlete is not simply to supply "band-aid" treatment. Our goal is not simply to make the athlete painfree enough so he or she can return to competition only to sustain a similar injury and potentially a more severe injury. Programs to prevent further injury is imperative in our rehabilitation regimen.

The concept of patient responsibility for care is important as well. All lumbar spine patients, athletes included, must participate in their own care. It is well recognized that physicians rarely "cure" any condition but rather diagnose, ameliorate symptoms, and educate. The athlete with a lumbar intervertebral disc injury should not be looking for a "quick fix" to alleviate pain. Health care professionals should foster patient responsibility and long-term management.

TABLE 4. Lumbar Spine: General Risk Factor Identification

1. Age
2. Gender
3. Posture; general
4. Scoliosis
5. Kyphosis
6. Lower extremity alignment
7. Segmental mobility
8. Osteoporosis
9. Abdominal strength
10. Quadriceps strength/flexibility
11. Hamstring flexibility
12. Iliopsoas flexibility
13. Sport type, position
14. Competition level
15. "Coachability"
16. Goals; short and long term

In planning the training program, the first step is the identification of potential risk factors. These are presented in Table 4. Postural abnormalities must be identified. The presence of fixed scoliotic and kyphotic deformities, leg-length discrepancies, and lower extremity biomechanical malalignments (such as excessive pes planus or torsional malalignment of the tibia and/or femur) should be noted. The identification of segmental mobility abnormalities such as hypermobility secondary to a spondylolisthesis or hypomobility secondary to a fixed scoliotic curve or a degenerative segment is important. Optimal positioning of the spine for activity is one of the principal elements of spine training. If there are specific postural abnormalities that can be corrected, then specific muscle strengthening and flexibility programs should be implemented. If fixed deformities are noted, then compensatory mechanical mechanisms must be designed. Losses of segmental mobility can be often alleviated by appropriate articular mobilization techniques, and the identification of hypermobile segments is important to plan a strengthening program to balance out the increased mobility of that segment.

One of the key factors in risk identification is abdominal strength. There has been much discussion regarding the role of the abdominal muscles in preventing intervertebral disc injuries. Initial thoughts revolved around the increase in intraabdominal pressure as a direct way of relieving intradiscal pressure.[67] Recent studies have not demonstrated a direct correlation between increased intraabdominal pressure, decreased intradiscal pressure, or decreased myoelectric activity in the lumbar paraspinal musculature.[32,36] Exquisitely detailed biomechanical studies by Gracovetsky and Farfan describe the abdominal mechanism.[31] It is their view that the abdominal mechanism works in conjunction with the thoracolumbar fascia and the midline ligaments of the spine to act as a lumbar corset that stabilizes torque and shear stress on the lower lumbar segments. In order to evoke this response a slight correction in lumbar lordosis to tighten the midline ligament is necessary. This translates to a slight kyphotic posturing of the lumbar spine from its habitual lordotic position into what has become known as the "neutral spine concept." A more detailed discussion appears in a subsequent section on stabilization concepts. Abdominal strength, therefore, is an important risk factor to be identified in both injured and noninjured individuals. Numerous testing devices have been described to test abdominal strength, none of which has been shown to be superior to fatigue testing and timed situp testing.[65]

Quadriceps strength and flexibility play an important role in lumbar spine rehabilitation. The quadriceps allow balanced knee flexion to occur so that squatting can replace bending. In the sporting population strong quadriceps not only substitute squatting for the straight-knee-bending posture but also lower the center of gravity during all athletic activities. This is facilitated by knee flexion coupled with anterior pelvic tilting, reducing lumbar lordosis, thereby allowing trunk rotation to occur with a combined shoulder and hip movement rather than a torsional movement purely from the lumbar spine. The lordotic posture increases rotational movement of the lumbar intervertebral segments. Slight kyphotic posturing not only pulls in the midline ligament and sets up the abdominal mechanism but also reduces the intervertebral rotary translation. Flexibility of the quadriceps and hip flexors balanced with flexibility of the hamstrings is important to eliminate asymmetrical forces on the pelvis. The position of the pelvis determines the posturing of the lower lumbar spine. An individual with tightened hip flexors, quadriceps, and hamstrings will have a difficult time correcting a hyperlordotic posture. Biomechanical abnormalities in the lower extremity may also lead to placement of asymmetrical loads on the lumbar spine. This fact should not be overstated or give license to the inappropriate prescription of podiatric appliances to correct all forms of back pain. Rather it is meant to serve as a notice that lower extremity abnormalities must be considered in lumbar spine rehabilitation. The flexibility factors previously mentioned along with orthotic correction of pes planus and symmetrical muscle strengthening of lower extremity groups should be incorporated.

The specific sport, the level of competition, the specific position in the sport type and the age and gender of the patient are important factors in designing rehabilitation programs. For instance, interosseous disc herniation occurs in younger age groups, whereas foraminal stenosis and instability secondary to a degenerative disc is encountered in older populations.

Identification of individuals who smoke and of those who either have or are at potential risk for developing osteoporosis is important in designing prevention programs. "Coachability" may be the most important factor in determining success in a training program. If an individual is willing to accept responsibility for his or her problem and participate in a program and make appropriate changes that are necessary, this individual will be successful. The individual who displays false bravado or is unwilling accept the consequences of injury most likely will not be successful in maintaining a painfree lumbar state.

STABILIZATION CONCEPTS

Repetitive torsional stress to the lumbar intervertebral discs and facet joints leads to advanced degenerative changes.[18,20] The concept of gradual disc prolapse secondary to fatiguing of annular fibers is important in understanding repetitive microtrauma to the lumbar segments.[4] The stabilization concept supports elimination of repetitive microtrauma, thereby limiting the injury and allowing healing to occur. The concept also holds that the "natural history" of degenerative processes can be altered by eliminating repetitive microtrauma to the spine.

The concept of the muscle fusion involves the co-contraction of the abdominal muscles to maintain a "corseting" effect on the lumbar spine by using the midline ligament and thoracolumbar fascia, combined with proper pelvic positioning (Fig. 1). The use of the spinal extensor muscles to reduce translational stress to the intervertebral segments is important during activity, and these muscles need to be trained to balance off shear stress to the intervertebral segments. The multifidus muscle appears to be the most active in this regard and is also the most difficult

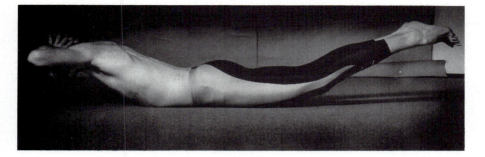

FIGURE 1. Prone extension: co-contraction of the gluteus maximus, hamstrings, spinal extensors, and lower rectus abdominis to train synergistic patterns of balance and strength.

to strengthen because of its short segmental nature. The gluteus maximus may indeed be the most important extensor muscle controlling lumbar spine lifting power.[19]

In the biomechanical and pathophysiologic construct, the hypothesis is that, for its own protection, the intervertebral joint reacts to internal stress to control the force exerted upon it by an applied load. Furthermore, a feedback mechanism monitoring the stress at the intervertebral joint can modify muscular activity in such a way as to minimize stress at the joint and therefore reduce the risk of injury. Muscular activity controls stress and the ligaments by its capacity modify spinal geometry. The stress induced by these muscles and their activities can also be monitored and controlled by a potential feedback mechanism. By lowering the level of equalized stress to a minimum, the potential of risk of injury to the lumbar spine can be reduced. A well-developed network of nervous fibers that is extensively distributed and has connecting receptor systems located in areas such as periosteum has been identified. This system is important in pain transmission and perhaps in kinesthetic feedback for joint positioning.[31]

Due to the changes in axial rotation that occur at the intervertebral segments at different degrees of lordosis, control of lordosis in flexion/extension is extremely important. The psoas is a prime candidate for the control of lumbar lordosis during these movements. Alternating lateral bending of the spine, such as occurs with running, is associated with axial rotation of the lumbar spine. Normal gait allows lateral bending of the spine in the order of 7° for the entire spine. Potentially the contralateral psoas muscle can derotate the spine by literally pulling it back from its lateral bending and axial rotation position to the contralateral side, thereby correcting the lumbar spine curve. This derotation activity allows rotation to occur in the opposite direction, once again facilitating locomotion. These mechanisms can lead to an understanding of balanced muscular function and flexibility, which control stresses applied to the lumbar intervertebral segments. The annulus of the intervertebral disc appears to be entirely responsible for load transmission of the intervertebral segment. Removal of the nucleus reportedly does not greatly affect the joint response. Therefore, repetitive loads applied to the lumbar intervertebral joint by necessity fall upon the outer fibers of the annulus, leading to progressive tearing, progressive fatigue, and potentially progressive disc prolapse.

It is simpler to understand load transmission to the facet joints by repetitive extension maneuvers. It has been well demonstrated that narrowing of the intervertebral disc increases load transmission to the facet joints.[15] The combination of a degenerative segment and repetitive extension and rotation loads to the lumbar intervertebral joints can lead to joint failure. The principle of neutral spine positioning can be applied to this portion of the motion segment as well.

The concept of spinal stabilization in neutral must be advanced to the dynamic model. Therefore, specific training in movement is imperative. In the nonathletic population this is applied to the activities of daily living such as emptying a dishwasher, getting into and out of the car, and putting an infant in a car seat. In the sporting population this is applied to the tennis serve, the pitching motion, running, and swimming.

As an historical note, Chinese martial arts training 5,000 years ago centered upon ''maintaining one's center.'' An analysis of this concept demonstrates that reduction in lumbar lordosis and pelvic tilting were used to maintain a neutral spine. Strong quadriceps muscles helped to lower the center of gravity while balancing either on one or both legs. Lumbar spine torque was eliminated by a combination of hip and shoulder movement girdle movement. Flexible hip supporting musculature and ligaments are necessary for this task. The Chinese martial arts concept of balance and symmetry can be validated by biomechanical modeling systems. In deed we may be not discovering any new thought processes in these concepts but rather coming to grips with the understanding of some very old and well-thought-out body training mechanisms.

In order to apply the muscle fusion concept, adequate flexibility and spinal range of motion must be attained.

Adams et al., who investigated diurinal variations and stresses on the lumbar spine, found changes in lumbar disc and ligament extensibility as the day progressed.[1] This is based upon creep of the soft tissue structures, leading to increased range of motion. They pointed out that bending and lifting activities, when applied to nonextensible ligamentous and annulus fibers, cause the disc to damage more easily early in the morning than later in the day. This concept can be applied to the need for flexibility of the structures to eliminate repetitive fatigue stress to the intervertebral joint.

We should think of the muscles that attach to the pelvis as ''guy wires'' that can effectively change the position and symmetry of the pelvis. Considering that the pelvis is the platform upon which the lumbar spine rests, pelvic positioning is the key to postural control of the lumbar spine. Therefore, adequate hamstring, quadriceps, iliopsoas, gastroc-soleus, hip rotator, ITB, and ITB flexibility is important, as are flexible neural elements. The nerve roots are held by suspensory ligaments[81] and can potentially be confined in a stenotic foramen, limiting their mobility. The concept of nerve root flexibility becomes even more important after intervention, such as lumbar surgery or disc injuries, which may lead to inflammation in the epidural space or nerve root adhesions that must be freed by dural stretching programs. These programs can be facilitated by the use of epidural cortisone injections and selective nerve root blocks if necessary.

The flexibility of the upper extremities and thoracic spine must also be considered in the rehabilitation program. For instance, a tennis player with poor rotator cuff flexibility may compensate for this by excessive thoracolumbar lordosis during the windup phase of the tennis serve. In the case of poor thoracolumbar junction motion, the stresses are applied to the lower lumbar spine, which is inadequate to accept rotational stress due to the inherent anatomical restrictions governed by facet orientation in the lower lumbar regions. Sports-specific flexibility patterns must be applied in the treatment program of every athlete.

TABLE 5. Basic Stabilization Routines

1. Hamstring stretching
2. Quadriceps stretching
3. Hip flexor stretching
4. Hip rotator stretching
5. Gastroc-soleus stretching
6. Abdominal curls; basic program
7. Pelvic bracing
8. Prone neutral spine positioning
9. Prone leg raises
10. Sidelying leg raises
11. Bridging
12. Advanced bridging
13. Bridging with stepping
14. Ball-balanced bridging
15. Quadraped
16. Kneeling stabilization
17. Squat strengthening; wall slides, counter squats
18. Position transition; with and without weight

STABILIZATION TRAINING ROUTINES

Stabilization training routines may be basic or advanced. The basic level exercises are listed in Table 5. The basic level program has been classified by some as a neurodevelopmental stage of postural control, starting from the most primitive postural positions of supine and prone lying, advancing to kneeling, standing, and position transition movements. The precise observation of meticulous technique is imperative in these exercises. A skilled and experienced physical therapist must work with the patient in a painstaking manner. Initially the exercises are carried out with one-on-one instruction and then in a class situation after the basic stages are satisfactorily completed. Each of the exercises is designed to develop isolated and co-contraction muscle patterns to stabilize the lumbar spine in "neutral position" (Figs.2–4). Neutral position must be defined for each individual. Neutral spine *does not* necessarily mean zero degrees of lordosis but rather the most comfortable position for the individual based upon the biomechanical principles discussed earlier in this chapter. The therapist utilizes hands-on technique to demonstrate optimal positioning while the patient tries to maintain this spinal positioning when carrying out the exercises in each level of the program. Care must be taken to ensure proper form and slow exercise repetition speed. The neurophysiologic principle of central pathway irradiation secondary to increased amplitude of effort must be kept in mind.[33] Engram programming is the goal; therefore, careful repetition with precision of movement is imperative.

Once the individual has graduated from the basic level and is able to demonstrate proper form and technique, the same principles apply to the weight training portion of the program. The athlete is taught how to get on and off weight training equipment while adhering to stabilization principles. Care must be exercised while changing the weight stack resistance pin on the machines and while lifting and racking free weights. The athlete is then taught how to use resistance equipment, including free weights, pulleys, and single station weight machines using co-contraction of the lower abdominal musculature to maintain optimal anteverted pelvic positioning while flattening the lower back against a back support and maintaining a stabilized neutral spine. The specific strengthening program for the athlete is

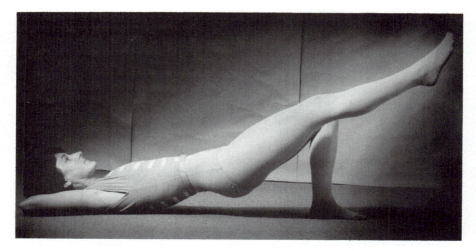

FIGURE 2. Advanced bridging: lower rectus abdominis contraction is balanced by stabilizing leg co-contraction of the gluteus maximus and quadriceps muscles to train proprioceptive balance and strength. Careful attention to ''neutral spine'' positioning is imperative.

tailored to the individual sport and deficits of the injured athlete. Therefore, the weight training program is not greared purely to the truncal musculature but is taken a step further to a total fitness program. Incorporated in this total fitness program is aerobic and anaerobic training. Teaching the individual to stabilize the spine while riding a stationary bicycle, while running on the treadmill, and while swimming become integral portions of the training program. One-on-one instruction to demonstrate proper spinal positioning while carrying out each one of these activities is mandatory. Athletes are advanced from treadmill walking to treadmill running,

FIGURE 3. Quadraped: this position requires balance and strength in the spinal extensors and gluteus maximus. Proprioceptive skill is necessary to maintain ''neutral spine'' position with alternate arm and leg motions.

FIGURE 4. Iliopsoas stretch: this position trains flexibility of the soft tissues that cross anterior to the hip joint in the extended leg. Balance is trained to maintain "neutral spine" while stretching.

and finally to supervised running on a track. Each activity is further advanced to the point where the individual is ready to begin the recoordination phase for the individual sport. The recoordination phase requires specific instruction in sporting technique coupled with stabilization principles. The most energy-efficient form in any sport incorporates control of one's center of gravity.[5]

Tennis players are taught how to move on the court while maintaining optimal spinal positioning, which necessitates strong quadricep muscle contraction to maintain a deep knee-bend position. Flexible hamstrings and iliopsoas musculotendinous groups and strong abdominal muscles, especially lower abdominals and oblique muscles, enable the player to dip low for balls while maintaining spinal posturing and thereby decreasing rotational stresses to the lower lumbar spine. Weight trans-

TABLE 6. Advanced Stabilization Routines

1. Advanced abdominal program
2. Weight training program
3. Stationary bike riding
4. Treadmill running
5. Cross-country ski machine
6. Swimming
7. Sport-specific "neutral spine" training

ference to facilitate proper pelvic and upper body rotation while eliminating lumbar torque is instructed.

A specific program has also been developed for baseball pitchers. In this particular program, the pitching motion is broken down into its individual components and during each phase careful attention is paid to pelvic, lumbar and shoulder position. The basic formula is strong abdominal musculature, strong quadricep musculature, and flexible hip flexor and hamstring musculotendinous units. Rotator cuff flexibility and elimination of idiosyncratic motions of accessory upper extremity are important as well. The pitcher is taught how to use the trunk to accelerate the throwing arm while carefully controlling the center of gravity and pelvic rotation. The pitcher is taught not to excessively extend the lumbar spine or rotate at the thoracolumbar junction to attain motion. Attention to the degree of leading leg and knee flexion is important to eliminate excessive torque on the thoracolumbar spine. Arm throwing is discouraged and the use of truncal acceleration to minimize lumbar torsion is encouraged. The training program for football linemen incorporates the same principles. In this particular program the tasks of the lineman are broken down into individual components. This includes stance positioning, back pedaling while pass blocking, and "pulling" and dive positions for run play blocking. Stress is placed on adequate knee flexion and strong abdominal muscles that co-contract with the gluteus maximus to attain the forward pelvic tilt, thereby eliminating excessive lordosis of the lumbar spine during axial loading. The player is taught how to take a blow and use contraction of the abdominal muscles to stabilize the spine. The player is also taught how to fall and roll with abdominal contraction. The motivated football player finds this type of positioning both comfortable, efficient, and powerful. One-on-one drills are designed to reinforce stabilization principles while being pushed and pulled.

Jumping athletes such as volleyball players and basketball players are taught by jumping drills how to control spinal movement with takeoff and landing. By repetition of the exercise routine, the athlete can attain a "reflex" status of balanced muscle control that will come into play during athletic endeavors without the necessity for voluntary control.

In the gymnasts and dancers, neutralization of the lumbar lordosis is necessary to eliminate stress fractures of the pars interarticularis. Careful coaching to eliminate hyperlordosis during dismount has been reported to be successful in reducing injury rates in young gymnasts.[60]

The nature of many sports involves torque to the lumbar spine. It is impossible to totally eliminate rotational stresses. The goal is to minimize and control stress in those situations in which control can be exercised. The majority of athletic lumbar spine injuries actually occur in the weight room and occur secondary to repetitive microtrauma before the athlete sets foot on the playing field or gymnasium floor.

During the sports-specific training programs, the athlete advances from basic exercises, to advanced training, to the sports-specific training. The sports-specific training begins with one-on-one mat work, advancing from isolated to compound movements. In a baseball pitcher, anterior pelvic rotation to facilitate trunk acceleration is initially taught along with manually applied resistance exercises with the athlete supine, kneeling position, and finally in standing position, before the upper extremity is used (Fig. 5). Once these exercises can be mastered and initial control of one's "center" is attained, the upper and lower extremities can be incorporated into the motion (Fig. 6). Each phase of the motion is added separately, layer on layer, making sure to maintain one's balance point. It is not until all the layers can be added that the individual can begin to practice this technique in an athletic

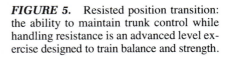

FIGURE 5. Resisted position transition: the ability to maintain trunk control while handling resistance is an advanced level exercise designed to train balance and strength.

setting. The use of videotaped exercise sessions and videotaping the performance of specific athletic techniques are a valuable coaching and training aid. The principles mentioned regarding athletic spine training may be applied to virtually all sports. Working carefully with the individual coaches is imperative prior to designing any training programs. The team approach must be applied in rehabilitation of these complicated problems.

STRENGTHENING PROGRAMS

Throughout this chapter, strength has been mentioned as a primary element of lumbar spine rehabilitation. The specific techniques for strengthening key muscles are now addressed.

The *abdominal muscles* play a key role in lumbar spine stabilization. Many exercises to strengthen the abdominal muscles have been advocated and taught, although a careful review of the scientific literature on this subject is quite revealing. The iliacus is the major muscle involved in the phase of the situp exercise from 45° degrees to vertical sitting.[16] The exercise that requires the least effort of the

FIGURE 6. Dumbbell kneeling: this exercise trains arm movements against resistance with the ability to maintain trunk balance by the previously trained synergistic contraction of lower rectus abdominis, internal oblique, and gluteus maximus muscles.

abdominal muscles are full situps and abdominal curlups after the initial 30% percent of motion.[23] The total concentric phase revealed a greater percentage of activity in the abdominal muscles than during the total eccentric phase.[25]

The oblique musculature and the rectus abdominus are most active during the initial head and shoulder phases of abdominal situps. The force of contraction can be increased by adding resistance, either by slantboard inversion, manual resistance, or cross-chest weight holding.[25] The magnitude of muscle recruitment for the lower section of the rectus was greatly increased when the feet were supported in a hook lying position.[25] Nonsupported feet during this exercise favored greater contraction of the upper section of the rectus. Raising both legs while supporting the trunk, such as in an elevated chair position or hanging from a bar or rings, caused the greatest degree of muscle recruitment than any other exercise.[25] The trunk curl with only raising the head and scapula off the surface with the knees flexed at 45 degrees, with or without the feet supported accompanied by a body twist, caused greater muscle recruitment in all portions of the rectus abdominus and oblique musculature than symmetrical exercises.[25] This curlup position with only the scapula and head raised off the surface have also

TABLE 7.   Abdominal Program: Basic to Advanced Progression

1. Curl ups, symmetric and rotational
2. Incline curl ups, symmetric and rotational
3. Leg raises supine
4. Bent-knee leg raises in upright trunk-supported position
5. Incline curl ups adding weight or manual resistance
6. Straight leg raises in upright trunk-supported position.

been demonstrated to cause the least amount of movement of the lumbar spine.[29] Leg circling is accomplished in supine lying with the knees flexed on the chest as the starting position. The knees are dropped to the left and the legs make a low circle around to the right where the knees are flexed and brought to the starting position on the chest. The legs are then dropped to the opposite side and the movement performed in reverse. This is one of the few exercises that is performed mainly by the external oblique muscles.[90]

The internal obliques participate in any activity involving tilt to the pelvis.[69] Trunk rotation is performed largely by the internal obliques. The rectus abdominis does not function as a trunk flexor but rather only shows a firing pattern when the spine has attained almost full flexion.[70,90] A recent report of the use of electrical stimulation combined with exercises to strengthen the abdominal musculature has been reported. The group that utilized electrical stimulation only without exercise had minimal if any improvement when compared to a nonexercise group. The group that utilized combined electrical stimulation and volitional exercise had the greatest gains in isometric strength but no significant gain in endurance. The training period in these groups was four weeks, which is quite, short and the number of participants in the study was only eight per group. Despite these limitations, this study suggests that use of electrical stimulation combined with volitional exercise training may be valuable in a sedentary patient subset but is probably not applicable to the athletic population. Women athletes who have undergone abdominal surgical procedures may potentially benefit from this type of training program in the early phases of treatment. I have noted a high incidence of lumbar spine injuries in postpartum mothers upon their return to activity, especially those who have undergone cesarean section. Abdominal muscle weakness is probably the key risk factor in this group.

It would appear that the curlup exercise, with the feet either supported or unsupported while only raising the head and scapula off the ground using both a symmetrical contraction pattern and a rotated diagonal pattern, is an appropriate beginning exercise for abdominal strengthening. There is no need to do a "complete" situp. The abdominal muscles do not work in the second 45 degrees of the motion but rather the iliacus and rectus femoris muscles do all the work. In a complete type of situp, greater stress is placed on the lumbar spine. From a exercise physiology and biomechanical point of view, the full situp exercise should not be carried out even in an individual without a lumbar spine problem. Remember that many lumbar spine injuries are caused by improper abdominal strengthening technique. Combining fast and isometric repetitions involves all of the muscle fibers and will train endurance and absolute isometric strength of the abdominal musculature. It would seem prudent to use the foot-supported position for the situp activity with the knees bent at 45 degrees to allow for maximal contraction of the lower rectus and oblique muscles, due to their importance in pelvic tilting; performing

FIGURE 7. Roman chair spinal extensions: lumbar spine posture is controlled by co-contraction of the gluteus maximus, hamstrings, spinal extensors, and lower abdominal muscles. Repetitions in an arc from 30 degrees of flexion to 15 degrees of extension are practiced. Isometric holds at 0 degrees then follow. The set is finished with rapid repetitions in an arc of motion from 5 degrees of flexion to 5 degrees of extension.

some repetitions unsupported enables more isolated upper rectus strength to be developed.

Advanced abdominal exercises can be carried out with bilateral straight-leg-raising while supporting oneself in an elevated chair, with meticulous control of pelvic tilt to eliminate repetitive ''swaying'' of the lumbar spine during performance of this exercise. Slowly raising and lowering the legs ensures lower abdominal isolation and eliminates cheating movements associated with leg swinging. A more advanced program also includes the use of curlups on an incline board both in symmetric and diagonal patterns. Adding manual resistance by a workout partner or holding a weight plate securely across one's chest can provide gains in abdominal strength. Side-lying trunk raises theoretically cause excessive axial rotation of the lumbar spine. This type of exercise can probably be carried out in a very controlled fashion in individuals who have no lumbar disc disease and by individuals who have been totally rehabilitated from previous lumbar spine problems. It is unclear whether these exercises have any significant benefit in a strength training program, although it has advocates in the coaching population. This exercise is currently not recommended as a portion of our abdominal training program. Highly advanced abdominal training in the elite power athlete, i.e., word class discus thrower, shotputters, and javelin throwers when carried out properly are apparently quite valuable. In this exercise the individual is supine upon a Roman chair with the arms held straight above, holding a heavy weight or medicine ball. The trunk is then rotated 30 to 45 degrees in either direction while the athlete supports himself in this elevated position.

Quadriceps strengthening is accomplished by wallslide exercises, single-legged squats with or without weights held in the hands, and inverted leg press at 45 degrees. Seated leg press is an alternative to inverted leg press if unavailable, and seated knee extensions can be utilized if seated leg press is unavailable. Extreme caution must be exercised in spinal positioning during any of these exercises, with co-contraction of the lower abdominals to ensure pelvic tilting.

Gluteus maximus strengthening can be attained by prone leg raises, prone leg flutter kicks, prone or standing pulley hip extensions, and a standing hip resistance machine. Lunges and the inverted leg press can be utilized in advanced programs. Free bar squats are discouraged and are replaced with the above mentioned techniques. The use of the pulleys and the standing machine require very careful control of balance and should be carried out only in the advanced stages. The pulleys can be utilized with the patient lying on a bench in the prone position, which will make it easier to stabilize the spine.

Gluteus medius strengthening can be accomplished with side-lying leg raises with or without ankle weights, the standing hip machine, and with pulleys. The same precautions apply as for the gluteus maximus workout.

The *latissimus dorsi* is a key muscle utilized in spinal stabilization. It inserts via the dorsal lumbar fascia to the L3 spinous process and can thereby control thoracolumbar motion.[1] The use of ''lat pull'' exercises can successfully strengthen these muscles and specific isolation techniques can be utilized for the upper, mid, and lower latissimus.

The *spinal extensor muscles* are strengthened by prone trunk raises, which progress from the flat position to an incline board and finally to a Roman chair apparatus (Fig. 7). The Roman chair routine includes midrange slow repetitions followed by a series of isometric contractions and fast minimum range repetitions. This exercise has the potential to improve strength of all aspects of the paraspinal musculature while specifically training the short arc muscles, i.e., the multifidus, to contract rapidly in a rhythmic stabilization pattern. Single station weight machines for spinal extensor strengthening may be useful but may add greater risk of lumbar injury and supply no greater benefit than the program described. Currently available isokinetic trunk strengthening equipment has been advocated for this purpose but due to poor pelvic control and excessive trunk sway, extensor isolation is not achieved and injury potential is present. A note of caution is in order regarding equipment that necessitates trunk rotation in the sitting position. This type of exercise is contrary to the construct of training and teaching pelvic-shoulder rotation as a unit to eliminate lumbar spine rotational stress.

Pulley systems for strengthening upper and lower extremities in co-contraction patterns can be useful to train spine stabilization with dynamic motion. Specifically, training the scapular protractors and retractors enhances cervicothoracic postural control, which is necessary to maintain optimal lumbar spine positioning. The injured athlete advances from a supervised gymnastic program to a group program, then finally to an unsupervised gymnastic program.

When the athlete is released to full competition, a maintenance program is designed. The maintenance program encompasses basic stabilization exercises, advanced stabilization exercises, and strengthening and gym programs. The athlete must be counselled that continuation of the training program is important to maintain his or her long-term ability to participate in sports. Depending upon the social profile of the athlete (the sport, age and gender of participant, level of competition, and goals within the sport), this program can be tailored to the individual.

REFERENCES

1. Adams MA, Dolan P, Hutton WC: Diurnal variations in the stresses on the lumbar spine. Spine 12:130–137, 1987.
2. Adams MA, Hutton WC: The mechanical function of the lumbar apophyseal joints. Spine 8(3):1983.
3. Adams MA, Hutton WC: The relevance of torsion to the mechanical derangement of the lumbar spine. Spine 6(3):May/June 1981.
4. Adams MA, Hutton WC: Gradual disc prolapse. Spine 10(6):1985.
5. Ariel G: In Zarins, Andrews, Carson: Injuries to the throwing arm. Philadelphia: W.B. Saunders, 1985, pp. 3–14.
6. Bogduk N, Engel R: The menisci of the lumbar zygapophyseal joints: a review of their anatomy and clinical significance. Spine 9:454–460, 1984.
7. Bogduk N, MacIntosh JE: The applied anatomy of the thoracolumbar fascia. Spine 9(2):1984.
8. Bogduk N, Tyran W, Wilson A: The innervation of the human lumbar intervertebral disc. J Anat 132:39–56, 1981.
9. Colachis SC, Strohm BR: Effects of intermittent traction on separation of lumbar vertebrae. Arch Phys Med Rehab 50:251, 1969.
10. Cyron BM, Hutton WC: Articular tropism and stability of the lumbar spine. Spine 5(2):March/April 1980.
11. Cyron BM, Hutton WC: The fatigue strength of the lumbar neural arch in spondylolysis. J Bone Joint Surg, 60B(2):May 1978.
12. Dehne K, Kriz FK: Rationale of immediate immobilization and the restoration of joint function. J Bone Joint Surg, 49A:1235, 1967.
13. Derby R: Diagnostic block procedure. Spine: State of the Art Reviews 1:47, 1986.
14. Deyo RA, Diehl AK, Rosenthal M: How many days of bed rest for acute low back pain? A randomized clinical trail. N Engl J Med 315(17):Oct. 1986.
15. Dunlop RB, Adams MA, Hutton WC: Disc space narrowing and the lumbar facet joints. J Bone Joint Surg, 66B(5):Nov. 1984.
16. Ekholm J, Arborelius U, Fahlcrantz A, et al: Activation of the abdominal muscles during some physiotherapeutic exercises. Scand J Rehab Med 11:75–84, 1979.
17. Eldred E, Lindsky DF, Buchwald JS: The effect of cooling on mammalian muscle spindles. Exp Neurol 2:144–157, 1960.
18. Farfan HF: Effects of torsion on the intervertebral joints. Can J Surg 12:336, 1969.
19. Farfan HF: Muscular mechanism of the lumbar spine and the position of power and efficiency. Orthop. Clin. North Am, 6:135–144, 1975.
20. Farfan HF, Cossette B, Robertson GH, et al: The effects of torsion on the lumbar intervertebral joints: the role of torsion in the production of disc degeneration. J Bone Joint Surg, 52A:468–497, 1970.
21. Ferguson RJ, McMaster JH, Stanitski CL: Low back pain in college football linemen. J Phys Sportsmed 2:63–69, 1974.
22. Fischer MA, Kaur D, Hauchins J: Electrodiagnostic exam, back pain, and entrapment post rami. Clin Neurophysiol 25:183–189, 1985.
23. Flint M: Abdominal muscle involvement during the performance of various forms of sit-up exercise: an EMG study. Am J Phys Med Rehab 44:1965.
24. Flint M: An EMG comparison of the function of the ilacus and the rectus abdominus muscles. J Am Phys Ther Assoc, 45:248–253, 1965.
25. Floyd WF, Silver P: EMG study of activity of the anterior abdominal muscles in man. J Anat 84:132–145, 1950.
26. Fox EJ, Melzack R: Transcutaneous electrical stimulation and acupuncture: comparison of treatment for low-back pain. Pain 141–148, 1976.
27. Frost FA, Jessen B, Siggaard-Andersen JA: Control, double-blind comparison of mepivacaine injection versus saline injection for myofascial pain. Lancet 8:499–501, 1980.
28. Gillstrom P, Ericson K, Hindmarsh T: Autotraction in lumbar disc herniation—a myelographic study before and after treatment. Arch Orthop Trauma Surg 104:207–210, 1985.
29. Godfrey KE, Kindig LE, Windell EJ: EMG study of duration of muscle activity in sit-up variations. Arch Phys Med Rehab, 58:132–135, 1979.
30. Goodman AG, Gilman LS, Gilman A: The Pharmacological Basis of Therapeutics, 6th ed. New York, Macmillan Publishiung Co., Inc., 1980, p. 686.
31. Gracovetsky S, Farfan H: The optimum spine. Spine, 11(6):543–573, 1986.
32. Gracovetsky S, Farfan H, Helleur C: The abdominal mechanism. Spine 10:317–324, 1985.
33. Harris FA: Facilitation techniques and technological adjuncts in therapeutic exercise. In Basmajian JV (ed): Therapeutic Exercise, 9th ed. Baltimore, Williams & Wilkins, 1984.

34. Haskvitz EM, Hanten WP: Blood pressure response to inversion traction. J Phys Ther 66(9): Sept. 1986.
35. Hinterbuchner C: Traction. In Rogoff JB: Manipulation, Traction, and Massage. Baltimore, Williams & Wilkins, 1980.
36. Hosea TM, Simon SR, Delatizky J, et al: Myoelectric analysis of the paraspinal musculature in relation to automobile driving. Spine 11:928–935, 1986.
37. Hoshina H: Spondylolysis in athletes. Phys Sportsmed 8:75–79, 1980.
38. Howe JF, Loeser JD, Collin WM: Mechanosensitivity of dorsal root ganglion and chronically injured axons: a physiological basis for radicular pain of nerve root compression. Pain 3:35–41, 1977.
39. Hutton WC, Stott JRR, Cyron BM: Is spondylolysis a fatigue fracture? Spine 2(3):Sept. 1977.
40. Jackson DW: Low back pain in young athletes: evaluation of stress reaction and discogenic problems. Am J Sports Med 7:364–366, 1979.
41. Jackson D, Leon W, Circincione R: Spondylolysis in the female gymnast. Clin Orthop 117:68–73, 1976.
42. Judovich BD: Lumbar traction therapy and dissipated force factors. Lancet 74:411, 1954.
43. Judovich BD: Lumbar traction therapy—elimination of physical factors that prevent lumbar stretch. JAMA 159:549, 1955.
44. Kirkaldy-Willis W, Farfan HF: Instability of the lumbar spine. Clin Orthop 615:110–123, 1983.
45. Klatz RM, Goldman PM, Pinchuk BG, et al: The effects of gravity inversion procedures on systemic blood pressure, intraocular pressure and central retinal arterial pressure. J Am Osteopath Assoc, 82:853–857, 1983.
46. Mannheimer JS, Lampe GN: Clinical Transcutaneous Electrical Nerve Stimulation. Philadelphia, F.A. Davis, pp. 210–212, 1984.
47. Lantz SA, Schultz AB: Lumbar spine orthosis wearing—restriction of gross body motions. Spine 11(8):1986.
48. Larsson U, Choler U, Lidstrom A, et al: Autotraction for treatment of lumbagosciatica. Acta Orthop Scand 51:791–798, 1980.
49. Lehman JF, DeLateur BJ: Therapeutic heat. In Lehman Jf (ed): *Therapeutic Heat and Cold*, 3rd ed. Baltimore, Williams and Williams, 1982, p. 531.
50. Lewit K: The needle effect in the relief of myofascial pain. Pain 6:83–90, 1979.
51. Lippitt AB: The facet joint and its role in spine pain: management with facet joint injections. Spine 9(7):746–750, 1984.
52. Liu YK, Goel VK, Dejong A, et al: Torsional fatigue of the lumbar intervertebral joints. Spine 10:894–900, 1985.
53. MacKenzie R: Mechanical Diagnosis and Treatment of Lumbar Spine Disorders. Spinal Publications, 1981.
54. Maigne R: Low back pain of thoracolumbar origin. Arch Phys Med Rehab 61: Sept. 1980.
55. Marshall LL, Trethewei ER, Curtain CC: Chemical radiculitis. Clin Orthop 129:61–67, 1977.
56. Mayer DJ, Price DD, Rafii A: Antagonism of acupuncture analgesia in man by the narcotic antagonist naloxone. Brain Res, 121:368–372, 1977.
57. McCall IW, Park WM, O'Brien JP, Seal V: Acute traumatic intraosseous disc herniation. Spine 10(2):1985.
58. McCarrol JR, Miller JM, Ritter M: Lumbar spondylolysis and spondylolisthesis in college football players. Am J Sports Med 14:404–405, 1986.
59. Melzack R, Stillwell DM, Fox EJ: Trigger points and acupuncture points for pain: correlations and implications. Pain 3:3–23, 1977.
60. Micheli LJ: Back injuries to dancers. Clin Sports Med 2(3):Nov. 1983.
61. Moffett JA, Chase SM, Porteck BS, Ennis JR: A controlled prospective study to evaluate the effectiveness of a back school in the relief of chronic low back pain. Spine 11(2):1986.
62. Mooney J, Robertson J: The facet syndrome. Clin Orthop 115:149–156, 1976.
63. Nachemson A: Intradiscal measurements of pH in patients with lumbar rhizopathies. Acta Orthop Scand 40:23–42, 1962.
64. Nachemson A: The lumbar spine: an orthopedic challenge. Spine 1:59, 1976.
65. Nordin M, Kahanovitz N, Verderame R, et al: Normal trunk muscle strength and endurance in women and the effect of exercises and electrical stimulation. Part I: normal endurance and trunk muscle strength in 101 women. Spine 112:105–118, 1986.
66. Nosse LJ: Inverted spinal traction. Ortho Diag 7(8–9):35–27, 1979.
67. Ortengren R, Anderson G, Nachemson A: Studies of relationships between lumbar disc pressure, myoelectric back muscle activity, and intra-abdominal (intragastric) pressure. Spine 6:98–103, 1981.

68. Oudenhoven RC: Gravitational lumbar traction. Arch Phys Med Rehab 59:510–512, 1978.
69. Panjabi M, Takata K, Goel V: Kinematics of lumbar intervertebral foramen. Spine 8(4):1984.
70. Partridge MJ, Walters CE: Participation of the abdominal muscles in various movements of the trunk in man, an EMG study. Phys Ther Rev 36:259–268, 1959.
71. Pountain GD, Keegan AL, Jayson MIV: Impaired fibrinolytic activity in defined chronic back pain syndromes. Spine 12:83–85, 1987.
72. Powell JW: Summary of injury patterns for seven seasons, 1980–1986. In NFL injury surveillance program, Dept. of Phys. Ed., San Diego Univ., San Diego, CA, 1987.
73. Reichmanis M, Becker RO: Relief of experimentally induced pain by stimulation at acupuncture loci. Comp Med East & West 5:281–288, 1977.
74. Rydevik B, Brown M, Lundborg G: Pathoanatomy and pathophysiology of nerve root compression. Spine 9:7–15, 1984.
75. Schmorl G, Junghann M: The Human Spine in Health and Disease. Grune & Stratton, New York, 1971.
76. Schnebel BF, Chowning J, Davidson R, Simmons J: A digitizing technique for the study of movement of intradiscal dye in response to flexion and extension of the lumbar spine (abstract). International Society for Study of the Lumbar Spine, 1987.
77. Selby D, Paris S: Anatomy of facet joints and its clinical correlation with low back pain. Contemp Orthop, 3(12):20–23, 1981.
78. Shealy CN: Facet denervation in the management of back and sciatic pain. Clin Orthop 115:157–164, 1976.
79. Sjolund BH, Eriksson MBE: Endorphins and Analgesia Produced by Peripheral Conditioning Stimulation. Raven Press, New York, 1979.
80. Sjolund BH, Terenius L, Eriksson M: Increased cerebrospinal fluid levels of endorphins after electro-acupuncture. Acta Physiol Scand 100–383, 1977.
81. Spencer IL, Irwin GS, Miller JA: Anatomy and fixation of the lumbosacral nerve roots in sciatica. Spine 8:672–679, 1983.
82. Stanitski CL: Low back pain in young athletes. Phys Sportsmed 10:77–91, 1982.
83. Stauffer TS: Gravity lumbar reduction. J Neurol Nursing 13(6):Dec. 1981.
84. Steiner ME, Micheli LJ: Treatment of symptomatic spondylolysis and spondylolisthesis with modified Boston brace. Spine 10:937–943, 1985.
85. Sunderland S: Nerve and Nerve Injuries, 2nd ed. New York, Churchill Livingstone, 1978.
86. Takagi H: Critical review of pain-relieving procedures including acupuncture: advances in pharmacology and therapeutics. II CNS pharmacology. Neuropeptides 1:79–92, 1982.
87. Takeshi T, et al: Selective lumbosacral radiculography and block. Spine 5(68):1980.
88. Travell J, Rinzter S: The myofascial genesis of pain. Postgrad Med 11:425–434, 1952.
89. Van Hoesen LB: Mobilization and manipulation techniques for the lumbar spine. In Grieve GP (ed): Modern Manual Therapy of the Vertebral Column. New York, Churchill Livingstone, 1986, pp. 733–739.
90. Walters CD, Partridge MJ: EMG study of the differential action of the abdominal muscles during exercise. Am J Phys Med 36:259–268, 1957.
91. Watkins LR, Mayer DJ: Organization of endogenous opiate and nonopiate pain control systems. Science 216:1185–1192, 1982.
92. Weinstein J: Mechanisms of spinal pain: the dorsal root ganglion and its role as a mediator of low-back pain. Spine 11(10):1987.
93. White AH: Injection techniques for the diagnosis and treatment of low back pain. Orthop Clin North Am 14(3):553–567, 1983.
94. Yong-King K, Kirkaldy-Willis WH: The pathophysiology of degenerative disease of the lumbar spine. Ortho Clin North Am 14(3):July 1983.

GARY S. FANTON, MD

REHABILITATION OF THE KNEE AFTER ANTERIOR CRUCIATE LIGAMENT SURGERY

Reprint requests to Gary S. Fanton, M.D., Sports, Orthopedic and Rehabilitation Medicine Associates, 3250 Alpine Rd., Portola Valley, CA 94025.

With a growing awareness of the functional limitations and alterations of athletic lifestyle imposed by an anterior cruciate ligament deficient knee, there has been a parallel trend toward more aggressive repair, reconstruction and rehabilitation of these injuries.[25,32] Medical advances in diagnosis, surgical technique, bracing, and rehabilitation, as well as a better understanding of the biomechanical and clinical consequences of a torn anterior cruciate ligament, have provided us with much more consistently successful results and greater patient satisfaction.[2,15,16,21,22,23,27,28] Instability, meniscal derangement, and arthritis have been better controlled through a well-organized surgical approach and a change in rehabilitation principles. These advances have resulted in a low rate of postoperative morbidity and reduced postoperative time required to return to work and athletic competition.

The following is our surgical rationale and rehabilitation "protocol" for the management of the patient with a repaired or reconstructed anterior cruciate ligament. Although the word protocol is used, it by no means implies that the patient, physician or physical therapist are confined to a time-restricted schedule of exercises. There is no rehabilitation "cookbook." In fact, a physician-directed rehabilitation program should provide specific guidelines by which the physical therapist plays a role instrumental in the patient's recovery. A clear understanding of the surgical procedure performed as well as experience and insight to tailor the rehabilitation program are imperative. Differences in patient goals, motivation, healing rates, and desired level of activity must be considered. The program should be closely monitored and adjusted to obtain the best results using therapy techniques that are based on sound biomechanical principles. Patient education and physician-therapist communication are also vital for a successful recovery. A patient who realizes the importance of his own active involvement in the rehabilitation process will achieve the most satisfaction with his operatively repaired knee.

SURGICAL RATIONALE

The first step in the appropriate management of any medical problem is a proper and complete diagnosis. It is usually quite simple to diagnose a torn anterior cruciate ligament after the initial history, physical examination and radiographs are performed.[17,39,40] Further investigation may be indicated if associated damage to articular structures is suspected. Very frequently, capsular or meniscal tears or chondral injuries are found in association with an acute or chronic anterior cruciate ligament tear.[5,24] Arthrography, computerized tomography or magnetic resonance imaging may be helpful.[4,40,30]

Examination of the knee under anesthesia and arthroscopy is considered the standard for confirmation and assessment of the degree of associated injuries and degenerative changes.[5,24] Meniscal repair, either open or arthroscopically assisted, is performed whenever possible.[1,6,14,19,38] Videotape documentation is not only helpful for patient education but also for re-evaluation of a potentially progressive degenerative process.

Based on extent of damage, degree of laxity, patient profile and preoperative discussion, a plan of operative versus nonoperative management is pursued. Our current approach is as follows: Younger, more active individuals who are athletically inclined are offered surgical repair and intra-articular augmentation or reconstruction. Older, non-athletically inclined individuals who place few demands on the knee, or those who cannot alter their work performance or lifestyle, are treated with nonoperative rehabilitation and, if necessary, bracing.

The greatest therapeutic controversy has centered on the young to middle-aged recreationally active population. We feel this group deserves special attention. In the past, a large percentage of these patients were treated with a "wait-and-see attitude," with the understanding that they might need to alter their activity status or have a surgical stabilization procedure at a later date, if necessary. It was felt that morbidity and risks associated with an intra-articular reconstructive procedure outweighed the benefits in this patient population. Our experience, however, agrees with that of Fetto and Marshall[9] in that patients with untreated anterior cruciate ligament tears have a very high rate of instability and dissatisfaction at five-year follow-up. In our experience, irreversible changes of articular cartilage damage, meniscal destruction or progressive laxity of secondary restraints often occur. We feel that the time interval between injury and surgical stabilization is very important and that surgery should be considered early in appropriate candidates. The procedure performed should be directed toward accurately restoring stability and preserving meniscal anatomy and function.

With this in mind, why hasn't there been a greater emphasis on early surgical management and rehabilitation? In the past, this may have been based on a lack of success using poorly performed or understood surgical techniques and inappropriate rehabilitation principles. Early range of motion, especially extension, was limited for the first few months, and this made physical therapy time-consuming and costly. Stability was frequently achieved secondary to stiffness rather than from reconstruction of a biomechanically intact ligament. A commitment of up to nine months of programmed therapy sessions understandably places a great burden on the actively employed or athletically inclined individual.

In the past few years, we have approached these problems with early anatomical stabilization, aggressive postoperative mobilization and rehabilitation. The risk of stiffness, adhesions, and patellofemoral disorders has been minimized without increasing the risk of graft failure, and the time frame to return to work or athletic activity has been greatly reduced. What were once goals to achieve at 9 to 12 months are now being realized in half that time.

OPERATIVE PROCEDURE

Our operative procedure combines both an interarticular and extra-articular reconstruction, and, as with any surgical procedure, attention to detail is of utmost importance. A central one-third patellar tendon graft appears to provide the strongest autogenous tissue to use in the interarticular reconstruction.[25,32] The graft must be placed isometrically and under proper tension. Using a patellar bone-tendon-bone intra-articular graft, failure usually occurs at a site of fixation. Therefore, a secure method of attachment of the graft is critical. Kurosaka et al.[20] have shown that using an interference fit with a 6.5 mm cancellous screw provides excellent fixation of the bone ends. This method will tolerate a load of up to 208 newtons and appears to be superior to other methods of graft fixation. A full ROM without graft impingement must also be confirmed intraoperatively, and a femoral-notch plasty to provide sufficient clearance is usually required.

An extra-articular procedure is always employed to provide additional security during the early phases of rehabilitation. In fact, we feel that it is probably the extra-articular reconstruction that protects our intra-articular procedure when an aggressive rehabilitation program is begun. In a sense, the extra-articular repair acts as a surgical "internal brace" by holding the tibia in derotation during muscle contraction, weight-bearing and, later, athletic activity. Several types of extra-articular reconstructions have been described, but, again, the importance of utilizing a technique that reliably holds the tibia back must not be overlooked. Our procedure routes the iliotibial band from distal to proximal behind the lateral collateral ligament, then deep to the accurate complex to which it is reinforced. It is then secured to the femur just proximal to Kaplan's extra-articular isometric point.

The importance of the extra-articular procedure to the early rehabilitation program is a key concept. A dilemma exists due to the fact that both rehabilitation of the patellofemoral joint and control of unwanted stress on the anterior cruciate ligament repair must be considered simultaneously in the postoperative program. Patellofemoral joint reaction forces increase greatly at flexion angles beyond 40 degrees when quadriceps force is applied against resistance.[10,11,31] Therefore, patellofemoral joint is best protected and rehabilitated using a quadriceps program from 30 degrees of flexion to full extension, especially if pre-existing chondromalacia is present. However, previous studies have also shown that considerable stresses are imposed on the anterior cruciate ligament repair when unimposed quadriceps activity against resistance is performed between 40 degrees and 0 degrees extension (Fig. 1). These studies are usually cited when strict immobilization, limited quadriceps activity, and limited range of motion are prescribed by a physician after cruciate reconstruction. With an extra-articular stabilization, we feel that the anterior tibial displacements during quadriceps activity are minimized at least for the first year after the reconstruction. This is partly based on past observations of reduced anterior tibial displacements in patients with anterior cruciate ligament stabilizations who had only an extra-articular procedure. With the extra-articular

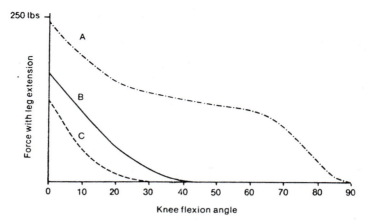

FIGURE 1. The anterior cruciate ligament resists anterior drawer forces beginning at approximately 40 degrees of flexion. These forces increase dramatically near complete knee extension and with the addition of distal leg weights. (A, Quadriceps force; B, anterior cruciate force with 7 pound weight on foot; C, anterior cruciate force during active leg extension.) (From Jackson DW, Drez D Jr (eds): The Anterior Cruciate Deficient Knee: New Concepts in Ligament Repair. St. Louis, C.V. Mosby Co., 1987, with permission.)

reconstruction "shielding" the intra-articular repair from excessive stress during quadriceps activity, terminal leg extensions and progressive resistive exercises can be utilized and should be encouraged even in the first few weeks after surgery to enhance strength, improve patellar tracking and promote an early normal gait pattern. Exercises near extension, rather than in deep flexion, may allow for strengthening of the thigh musculature without aggravation of patellofemoral pain or pressure syndromes.

Combined intra-articular and extra-articular cruciate ligament reconstruction is a complex procedure requiring meticulous surgical technique. But with a graft of satisfactory strength, fixation that is secure, and anatomic placement to ensure a tension-free range of motion, the physician should have the confidence to incorporate a rehabilitation program that allows a full, unimpeded active and passive range of motion as pain and swelling permit. This is a divergence from previous teachings. Physical therapists have been taught in the past that we rehabilitate anterior cruciate ligament reconstruction on the edge of danger—restrict motion and quadriceps muscle activity or the procedure will fail. This may have been true when primary suture repairs were performed or fixation techniques were inadequate, or perhaps when allografts of insufficient strength are utilized. Now that the consequences of restricting joint motion, including articular cartilage changes, decreased soft-tissue compliance, and prolonged muscle atrophy (especially type I fibers) are better understood,[3,7,12,13] our goals logically should be the opposite. Therefore, the approach to a patient with a torn cruciate ligament should reflect this change in concept.

REHABILITATION

With appropriate attention to the surgical procedure and a shift in emphasis to early quadriceps activity and weight-bearing, we have formulated an aggressive rehabilitation program that can achieve early full range of motion and strength, and promotes a more functional return to work and athletic endeavors.

Ideally, the rehabilitation process begins preoperatively. The patient is advised to see a physical therapist for a home instruction and strengthening program and to prepare for the upcoming surgery. He is also introduced to the exercise schedule that will be followed postoperatively. Although not always practical, preoperative counseling by the physical therapist is often helpful.

Several studies have supported the use of continuous passive motion (CPM) and immediate mobilization postoperatively. Research by Salter and others[29,33,34,35,37] has shown that CPM is well tolerated, promotes joint nutrition, prevents adhesions, and stimulates healing and regeneration of articular cartilage. It also reduces the post-surgical hemarthrosis and may help prevent infection.[29] The effects of joint immobilization are both clinically and physiologically apparent.[3,7,11] Enneking showed that the resulting extra-articular and pericapsular fibrosis restricts joint motion, and intra-articular fibrofatty proliferation of the fat pad and suprapatellar pouch encroaches and eventually obliterates the joint cavity. A decrease in muscle strength, enzymatic degradation and loss of contractility are rapid.[7,12,13]

Immediate Postoperative Phase

Immediately after the operation, the patient is placed in a compressive dressing and the continuous passive motion machine. In the recovery room, the CPM machine is set initially for a short arc of motion (usually 10 to 30 degrees) and is increased as tolerated by the patient or advised by the therapist on a daily basis. The range can be increased up to the full limits of the machine as quickly as possible. Full extension in the machine is encouraged and should not be restricted. While the patient is in the hospital, instructions are given for ankle and calf pumps, non-weight-bearing crutch walking, icing, and elevation. On the second postoperative day, the patient is instructed in knee flexion against gravity while lying prone, in reverse leg raises, and in assisted range of motion with the unoperated leg while sitting and lying prone. Co-contraction quadriceps and hamstring sets and patellar mobilization are started on the second postoperative day. A dual-channel TENS or electrical stimulation unit may be used postoperatively if desired but may be more effective for pain control rather than maintaining muscle tone or enzymatic activity. The patient is usually discharged on the third postoperative day.

During the first seven days after the operation, most of the patient's time should be spent in the CPM machine, except for exercises described above, meals, or bathroom privileges. When not in the CPM machine or doing exercises, the patient must have his knee secured in an immobilizer and continue non-weight-bearing crutch walking. The knee-flexion and range-of-motion exercises that were taught in the hospital should be performed for 15 to 20 minutes, twice daily. Physical therapy is begun during the second week and the CPM machine is continued at least 14 hours per 24-hour period. Quad sets and straight-leg-raising exercises are introduced along with four-quadrant hip exercises with the knee immobilizer. By the end of the second week, 0 to 90 degrees range of motion is expected in the CPM machine. At 12 days postoperatively, the sutures are removed.

Early Rehabilitation Phase

The second to sixth week postoperation is perhaps the most important window of time for obtaining a satisfactory range of motion, decreasing swelling and stiffness, and restoring patellar tracking. Success during this phase usually insures an excellent result and early functional return to activity. The knee immobilizer and crutches are continued during work or school, and the continuous passive-motion machine is used at night. Active, passive and active-assistive range of motion are instituted with no limitation on the range of motion unless otherwise indicated, such as after surgical repair of the medial collateral ligament or meniscus. Multiple-angle isometric and isotonic exercises against gravity for both the quadriceps and hamstrings are employed. The patient should be instructed to passively extend the knee at home on a daily basis to within 5 degrees of full extension but not to hyperextension. A prone resistive hamstring program can also be instituted during this time, as well as hip abduction, adduction and extension strengthening program. Active and passive patellar mobilization is also emphasized, as flexion is difficult and painful without proper patellar tracking. The most important goals in the first six weeks postoperatively are to enhance patellar mobility and to obtain as much motion as possible with no restriction on end-range of flexion or extension. The patient can usually discontinue the CPM machine at the end of the fourth postoperative week. Modalities used during the first few weeks include ice, electrical stimulation, interferential current and soft-tissue mobilization.

Early weight bearing is also begun during this rehabilitative phase. After the second postoperative week, the patient can begin a light weight-bearing program using crutches and the knee immobilizer set at 5 degrees. At three to four weeks postop, the knee immobilizer is discontinued, and a Neoprene sleeve with open hinges is substituted. This provides support and confidence without restricting motion. The patient can continue progressive weight bearing as tolerated with the use of his crutches, so that by the third week weight bearing as tolerated with one crutch is begun, and by the fourth or fifth week postoperatively most patients are independently ambulatory.

The rationale for early weight bearing, as early as 14 days postoperatively, is based on a renewed confidence that the surgical repair can tolerate the forces that are predicted or calculated on the anterior cruciate ligament during level walking. Information based on published work by Henning and others (Fig. 2) suggests that these forces are far below the ultimate ACL substitute strength, especially if a bone patellar tendon bone composite is utilized. These studies also provide the foundation for recommending an early aggressive mobilization and strengthening program. An even greater degree of confidence and security is achieved when the intraarticular procedure is combined with an extra-articular stabilization to "internally brace" the knee against unwanted anterior tibial displacements.

Rehabilitation with whirlpool and a stationary bicycle program from ROM, as well as a progressive resistive exercise program for hamstrings and quadriceps strengthening, are continued. Quadriceps concentric exercises should be performed with low resistance, and isokinetic equipment should be used only for hamstring strengthening until the fourth week postoperatively. This is best done by performing isokinetic exercises in the prone position with an extension block. By six weeks postoperatively a range of motion of 0 to 125 degrees is usually obtained.

Leg presses are a very useful component for strengthening after cruciate ligament surgery. Co-contraction of the quadriceps to promote knee extension and the hamstrings to promote hip extension helps protect the knee from unwanted anterior displacement of the tibia. A short arc leg-press machine, as well as supine leg presses with variable resistance, should be utilized. Quarter squats against gravity, free weights, or elastic tubing resistance are encouraged. The patient can work on resisted range of motion in a swimming pool using freestyle and back stroke at a submaximal level. Fins may be added at six weeks for increased resistance. Close attention by the therapist to restoring a normal heel-to-toe and swing-through gait patterns is very important. This will help enhance normal patellar tracking and

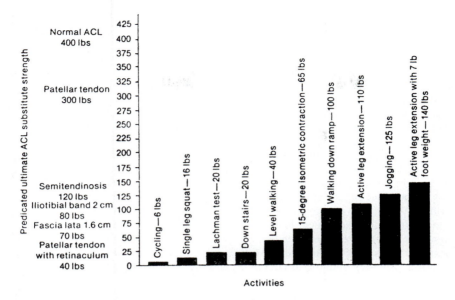

FIGURE 2. Anterior drawer forces are constantly present with normal daily living activities. This figure compares the expected ultimate anterior cruciate ligament graft strengths for commonly used replacement tissues (50% of original strength at time of insertion) to anterior drawer forces that represent calculated and or measured forces on the anterior cruciate ligament during specific activities. Calculations are based on a person weighing 150 pounds. (Anterior cruciate ligament substitute strengths are based on published data by Noyes et al. Anterior drawer forces on the anterior cruciate ligament are based on published work by Morrison et al., Smidt et al., Henning, and Paulos et al. From Jackson DW, Drez D Jr (eds): The Anterior Cruciate Deficient Knee: New Concepts in Ligament Repair. St. Louis, C.V. Mosby Co., 1987, with permission.)

improve range of motion in both flexion and extension. Early quadriceps and gastrosoleus tone is also promoted.

Intermediate Rehabilitation Phase

At or about the sixth week postoperatively, depending on the degree of swelling and range of motion, a strengthening and endurance phase begins. Leg presses, isokinetic leg curls and submaximal leg extensions through a full arc of motion with progressive resistance are continued. An aggressive program of active and passive ROM is continued if full range has not yet been obtained. Hip patterns and gastrosoleus rehabilitation are re-emphasized. Care should be taken at this phase of the rehabilitation to avoid any patellofemoral pain problems and to enhance patellar mobilization while restoring strength. A short arc quadriceps program from 30 degrees of flexion to full extension is helpful, particularly if the patient has considerable patellofemoral fibrosis, pre-existing chondromalacia, or pain in deep flexion. Again, the short-arc squat program and supine leg presses with variable resistance are most helpful. The sixth to tenth week emphasizes progressively increasing intensity, repetitions and resistance as the patient tolerates. The first isokinetic test can be performed at the tenth week if patellofemoral pain and swelling are minimal. The hamstring group is usually 90 to 100% of the contralateral side, with the quads at about 50 to 60%. High-speed (240–300 degrees/sec.) isokinetics and endurance are important for transition into the next phase.

Late Rehabilitation Phase

At the 10th to 12th postoperative week, the patient is fitted with a custom knee orthosis, and a full quadriceps and hamstring rehabilitation program is continued. There are essentially no limitations on the strengthening program at this phase, but again attention must always be kept on preventing patellofemoral joint pain. Once hamstring strength exceeds 90% of the opposite extremity and quad strength is at least 70%, then a functional program can be instituted. Swimming, cycling, rowing and leg presses are encouraged. Straight-ahead running is allowed, but because of the time course for ligamentous healing and maturation of grafts,[27] no jumping or cutting activities are allowed for the first 20 weeks.

Functional rehabilitation and sport-specific exercises should be encouraged prior to return to sporting activities to condition the musculature and promote coordination and endurance. Recent investigations suggest that the anterior cruciate ligament has mechanoreceptor nerve endings that may be important for position sense.[18,36] Therefore, proprioceptive training with a balance board and slide-board exercises, two-leg and one-leg hopping, and trampoline are useful for reconditioning. Most rehabilitation techniques utilize concentric one-plane concepts, yet rotational and eccentric modes are very important and must be included or rehabilitation will be incomplete. Backward running, linebacker drills, side-to-side, and carioca drills are useful. At or about the 14th week, the isokinetic test is repeated. We would like to see 100% hamstring strength and at least 80% quadriceps strength at this time. The patient is usually weaned off of the physical therapy program by the fourth month. Cutting, jumping, and contact sports are gradually instituted after six months, with the knee orthosis used to protect the anterior cruciate ligament repair for the first 18 months postoperatively. At that time, if the patient continues to have an excellent objective and subjective result, then the use of the custom brace may be optional, except for high risk sports such as skiing or football.

MODIFICATIONS OF THE REHABILITATION PROGRAM

Certain modifications may be required during the early postoperative period, depending on associated surgical findings. If the medial collateral ligament and posteromedial capsule are repaired, or a meniscorrhesis is performed, then the last 10 degrees of extension is limited for the first four weeks postoperatively, and the patient remains non-weight bearing during that period. Full range of motion and full weight-bearing are usually delayed until the sixth postoperative week. If a large chondral lesion is encountered, greater than 1 cm in diameter, then a staged surgical program of chondral drilling, continuous passive motion, and early non-weight-bearing mobilization for four to six weeks, followed by delayed reconstruction of the anterior cruciate ligament in two to three months, is recommended.

CONCLUSION

In conclusion, the fears that have been held in the past regarding the reconstruction and rehabilitation of the anterior cruciate ligament deficient knee have been overcome primarily because of a better understanding of surgical principles and rehabilitation techniques. Surgical stabilization can and should be recommended early in appropriate candidates and a postoperative program outlined and modified to suit the needs and progress of the patient. The physical therapist has a tremendous responsibility to be sure the patient goals are kept in perspective and to continually reinforce the motivation and understanding required by the patient for a truly successful result.

REFERENCES

1. Cassidy RE, Shaffer AJ: Repair of peripheral meniscus tears. A preliminary report. Am J Sports Med 9:209, 1981.
2. Chick RR, Jackson DW: Tears of the anterior cruciate ligament in young athletes. J Bone Joint Surg 60A:970, 1978.
3. Cooper RR: Alteration during immobilization and regeneration of skeletal muscle in cats. J Bone Joint Surg 54A:5, 919, 1972.
4. Crues JV, et al: Meniscal tears of the knee: Accuracy of MR imaging. Radiology 164:445, 1987.
5. DeHaven KE: Diagnosis of acute knee injuries with hemarthrosis. Am J Sports Med 8:9, 1980.
6. DeHaven KE: In Goldstein LA, Dickerson RC (eds): Atlas of Orthopedic Surgery, 2nd ed. St. Louis, C.V. Mosby, 1981.
7. Enneking WF, Horowitz M: The intra-articular effects of immobility of the human knee. J Bone Joint Surg 54A:5, 973, 1972.
8. Evans EB, et al: Experimental immobilization and remobilization of patellar knee joints. J Bone Joint Surg 42A:5, 737, 1960.
9. Fetto JF, Marshall JL: The natural history and diagnosis of anterior cruciate ligament insufficiency. Clin. Orthop 147:29, 1980.
10. Frankel VH, Nordin M: Basic Biomechanics of the Skeletal System. Philadelphia, Lea and Febiger, 1980.
11. Goodfellow J, Hungerford DS, Zindel M: Patellofemoral joint mechanics and pathology; functional anatomy of the patellofemoral joint. J Bone Joint Surg 58:B, 287, 1976.
12. Haagmark T, Eriksson E: Cylinder or mobile cast brace after knee ligament surgery. Am J Sports Med 7:1, 48, 1979.
13. Haagmark T, Eriksson E, Jansson E: Muscle fiber type changes in human skeletal muscle after injuries and immobilization. Orthopedics 9:181, 1986.
14. Hamberg P, et al: Suture of new and old peripheral meniscus tears. J Bone Joint Surg 65A:193, 1983.
15. Jacobsen K: Osteoarthritis following insufficiency of the cruciate ligament in man. Acta Orthop Scand 48:520, 1977.
16. Johnson RJ, Kettlekamp DB, Clark W, Leaverton P: Factors affecting late results after menisectomy. J Bone Joint Surg 56A:719, 1974.
17. Jonsson T, et al: Clinical diagnosis of ruptures of the anterior cruciate ligament. Am J Sports Med 10:100, 1982.
18. Kennedy JC, et al: The anatomy and function of the anterior cruciate ligament as determined by clinical and mophologic studies. J Bone Joint Surg 56A:223, 1974.
19. Krause WR: Mechanical changes in the knee after menisectomy. J Bone Joint Surg 58A:599, 1976.
20. Kurosaka M, Yoshiya S, Andrish JT: A biomechanical comparison of different surgical techniques of graft fixations in ACL reconstruction. Am J Sports Med 15:3, 225, 1987.
21. McDaniel WJ, Damerson TB: Untreated ruptures of the anterior cruciate ligament. J Bone Joint Surg 62A:696, 1980.
22. McDaniel WJ, Dameron TB: The untreated anterior cruciate ligament rupture. Clin Orthop 172:158, 1983.
23. Marshall JL, Olsson SE: Instability of the knee: A long term experimental study in dogs. J Bone Joint Surg 53A:1561, 1971.
24. Noyes FR, et al: Arthroscopy in acute traumatic hemarthrosis of the knee. J Bone Joint Surg 62A:687, 1980.
25. Noyes FR, Butler DL, Grood EJ, et al: Biomechanical analysis of human ligament grafts used in knee-ligament repairs and reconstructions. J Bone Joint Surg 66A:3, 344, 1984.
26. Noyes FR, McGinniss GH, Grood ES: The variable functional disability of the anterior cruciate ligament deficient knee. Orthop Clin North Am 16:1, 47, 1985.
27. Noyes FR, Matthews DS, Mooar PA, Grood ES: The symptomatic anterior cruciate-deficient knee; part II, The results of functional disability. J Bone Joint Surg 65A:163, 1983.
28. Noyes FR, Mooar PA, Matthews DS, Butler DL: The symptomatic anterior cruciate deficient knee; part I, The long term functional disability in athletically active individuals. J Bone Joint Surg 65A:154, 1983.
29. O'Driscoll SW, Kumar A, Salter RB: The effect of continuous passive motion on the clearance of hemarthrosis from a synovial joint. Clin Orthop R 176:305, 1983.

30. Pavlov H, et al: The accuracy of double-contrast arthrographic evaluation of the anterior cruciate ligament. J Bone Joint Surg 65A:175, 1983.

31. Reilly DT, Martens M: Experimental analysis of quadriceps muscle force and patellofemoral joint reaction force. Acta Orthop Scand 43:126, 1972.

32. Rovere GD, Adair DM: Anterior cruciate deficient knees: a review of the literature. Am J Sports Med 11:6, 412, 1983.

33. Salter RB, et al: Clinical application of basic research on continuous passive motion for disorder and injuries and synovial joints: a preliminary result of a reasonability study. J Orthop Res 1:325, 1984.

34. Salter RB, et al: The biological effect of continuous passive motion on the healing of full-thickness defects in articular cartilage. J Bone Joint Surg 62A:8, 1232, 1980.

35. Salter RB, Bell RS, Keely FW: The protective effects of continuous passive motion on living articular cartilage in acute septic arthritis. Clin Orthop 159:223, 1981.

36. Schultz, et al: Mechanoreceptors in human cruciate ligament: A histologic study. J Bone Joint Surg 66A:1072, 1984.

37. Skyhar MJ, Danzig LA, Hargons AR, Aileson, WH: Nutrition of the anterior cruciate ligament—Effects of continuous passive motion. Am J Sports Med 13:6, 415, 1985.

38. Tapper EM, Hoover NW: Late results after meniscectomy. J Bone Joint Surg 51A:517, 1969.

39. Torg JS, Conrad W, Kalen V: Clinical diagnosis of anterior cruciate ligament instability in the athlete. Am J Sports Med 4:84, 1976.

40. Woods GW, Stanley RF, Tullos HS: Lateral caspular sign: X-ray clue to a significant knee instability. Am J Sports Med 7:27, 1979.

JEFFREY A. SAAL, MD
MARK J. SONTAG, MD

HEAD INJURIES IN CONTACT SPORTS: SIDELINE DECISION MAKING

Reprint requests to Jeffrey A. Saal, M.D., Sports, Orthopedic and Rehabilitation Medicine Associates, 3250 Alpine Rd., Portola Valley, CA 94025.

The focus of this chapter is the proper management of head injuries in the athletic setting with particular attention to sideline decision making. Physicians will frequently find themselves dealing with an unconscious player at a football, rugby or lacrosse match and will be faced with immediate medical decisions. The injury protocol that is introduced in this chapter is directed at assisting the team physician in managing these injuries on the sideline. The main principles may be applied to other athletic head injuries as well.

Although only 5% of all football injuries involve a head injury,[6] these injuries account for 70% of all football fatalities.[29,47] Of the 1.5 million individuals that participate in football per year, over 80,000 of them will suffer a head injury.[24] It is estimated that 1 out of 8 collegiate football players sustains a head injury in their football college career.[17] The incidence of direct fatalities per 100,000 participants in high school and college football dropped from 1.39 and 2.22 per 100,000 participants from 1970 to 1975 down to .57 and .88 in 1976 to 1981, respectively.[29] A substantial further reduction is potentially possible with proper screening and sideline care.

The difficulty in sideline decision making is not in the obvious open head injury or comatose patient, who requires immediate emergency care and hospitalization, but rather in the mildly head injured athlete who is still conscious and wishes to return to the contest. The protocol presented in this chapter has been developed to assist the team physician in making rational decisions regarding appropriate care in an attempt to minimize further injury and sequelae from the head injury. This protocol has been developed as the result of an extensive review of the head injury literature,[8,14,24,45] integrated with the clinical experience of a large sports medicine medical group that serves professional, Olympic, collegiate, junior college and high school teams. Many opinions appear in the literature regarding the management of the head injured football player.[11,47,46,48] The following protocol is a conservative algorithm based upon currently available scientific data.

Due to the potential catastrophic nature of even mild head injuries, every head-injured athlete must be evaluated by a physician immediately following the injury, regardless of how mild the situation may appear. A follow-up evaluation on the sideline is necessary 15 minutes after the initial injury. In the interim, the team trainer or a responsible adult or player should be assigned to watch the injured athlete at all times. It is not the teammate's, the coach's or the athletic trainer's decision as to when the head-injured athlete may return to play, but rather it is solely the decision of the team physician. During practice sessions, when a physician is not immediately available, the burden of decision making falls to the trainer and/ or coach in attendance. Therefore, well-prepared and informed training and coaching staffs are imperative.

Clinical judgment must complement the guidelines outlined above. Prior to the athletic event, the team physician should know where the closest available telephone is and what hospital will be utilized in case of an emergency. Finally, ensure that there is a clear passageway for an ambulance to reach the field in case of an emergency.

MECHANISM OF BRAIN INJURY

It is estimated that 75% of fatal head injuries in football occur during tackling.[29] Other injury mechanisms have been identified that can result in a loss of consciousness (LOC).[38] A blow to the eye or neck can cause severe pain and result in LOC. A blow to the carotid sinus can block cerebral blood flow and result in LOC. Cases of post-traumatic cerebral thrombosis, following trauma to the neck vasculature, have been reported. Vertebral artery trauma can also occur with cervical rotation and hyperextension.

The most common catastrophic head injuries occur following the development of a subdural or epidural hematoma, an inner parenchymal bleed, or a basilar skull fracture. Subdural hematomas are not uncommon following "contre-coup" injuries, where there is tearing of cranial veins. Epidural hematomas often follow skull fractures across the path of the middle meningeal artery. Basilar skull fractures can present with periorbital ecchymosis ("raccoon eyes") or subcutaneous ecchymosis in the mastoid area   ("battle signs") or bulging tympanic membranes. Rarely a traumatic head injury will unmask a congenital or developmental problem, such as a brain tumor or arteriovenous anomaly.

PATHOPHYSIOLOGY OF BRAIN INJURY

Prior to the 1960s, brain injury was divided into two simple categories: concussion and contusion. Concussion, by definition, was described as a transient loss of consciousness not lasting more than a couple of minutes without evidence of structural damage to the brain and with complete neurological, behavioral and cognitive recovery resulting in absolutely no residuals. In contradistinction, a contusion represented a more serious injury, constituting the presence of a structural abnormality of the brain that could result in permanent neurological, behavioral, or cognitive deficits.[30,42] In 1941, it was demonstrated that LOC could only occur if the head was free to move.[9] High-velocity bullet injuries to the brain have been noted to frequently not cause LOC, while seemingly mild acceleration/deaccerlation type injuries can result in LOC.

In 1943, rotational shear strain of the brain contents was suggested as a mechanism of brain injury.[15] It has been demonstrated that there is actual neuronal damage that occurs in proportion to the number and strength of blows inflicted on experimental animals.[41] Elevated levels of creatine kinase isoenzyme (CK-BB) have been correlated with the extent of cerebral trauma.[32] Therefore, the result of a concussion of any degree might cause permanent loss of neuronal function, and the amount of such loss may be in proportion to the severity of the injury.

A second mechanism of linear or translational acceleration of the head can result in primary focal defects of the brain, resulting in inner parenchymal hemorrhages or cerebral contusions.[30] Local effects, in contradistinction to the rotational effects mentioned previously, often do not produce concussion or cause diffuse brain injury. Rotational injuries to the brain, such as diffuse stretching and shearing injuries to the nerve and vessels, most likely account for the loss of consciousness often seen in head injury.[41] The literature is still unclear if loss of consciousness is directly due to a rotational injury to the brain stem[21] where the reticular-activating system resides, or rather represents a diffuse cortical process.[31,1] Regardless, it appears that the acceleration/deceleration of the head following a tackle or a vertex blow will result in the commonly seen head-injured unconscious football player. This concept of rotational acceleration injury to the brain corresponds with the high incidence of head injuries noted on kickoffs, where opposing players collide at high velocities.

A graded set of clinical syndromes following head injury has been presented. Increasing severity of neurologic loss is caused by mechanically induced strains affecting the brain in a centripetal sequence of disruptive effects on function and structure.[31] Thus, in the mildest head injury, presenting with confusion and no loss of consciousness or amnesia, the superficial cortical and subcortical brain is damaged. In more severe injuries, involving amnesia, the diencephalic aspect of the brain (hippocampal gyri) is injured. Finally, the most severe injuries presenting with coma represent damage to the mesencephalic brain stem.

SEQUELAE OF HEAD INJURY

There is convincing evidence that cumulative mild head trauma results in progressive mental deterioration. Young adults studied after sustaining a second concussion revealed a reduced ability to process information.[13] Although controversial, there does appear to be a post-concussive syndrome,[23,40] consisting of headache, intermittent dizziness or vertigo, impaired short-term memory and concentration, emotional instability, and intolerance of noise.[14,27]

It is clear that even mild head injury can result in cognitive, behavioral, and psychosocial problems.[33] Whereas a stroke causes focal neurological damage, head injury results in widespread diffuse cortical damage that can manifest as mental status and personality changes.[7,12,19,20,22,23] It is apparent that a mildly head injured athlete who is evaluated on the side lines should be viewed as a possible brain injured athlete[34] who has a potential increased risk of catastrophic injury and permanent brain damage.

ATHLETIC HEAD INJURY PROTOCOL

Type I

LOSS OF CONSCIOUSNESS: None.

NEUROLOGIC SIGNS: None.

RETROGRADE AMNESIA: None.

POST-TRAUMATIC AMNESIA: None.

SYMPTOMS: Low-grade headache, dizziness without true vertigo, and mild unsteadiness of gait that clears quickly.

FOLLOW-UP EXAM: No change in orientation or neurologic signs 15 minutes after coming off the field.

RETURN TO PLAY CRITERIA: Once the player totally clears with absolutely no signs of significant headache, has no evidence of neurologic signs as discussed above, and has been observed for a minimum of one offensive series, the player can return to play.

MEDICAL FOLLOW-UP: A head-injury instruction sheet (Appendix A) should be given to all parents of high school students and they should be instructed regarding re-examination if post-traumatic amnesia should develop or any other localizing neurologic signs. On the collegiate level, the player should be checked the next morning in training quarters by the trainer for any signs of post-traumatic amnesia.

Type II

LOSS OF CONSCIOUSNESS: Momentary (seconds, if at all).

NEUROLOGIC SIGNS: None.

RETROGRADE AMNESIA: None (the player can remember the play as well as the hit).

POST-TRAUMATIC AMNESIA: None.

SYMPTOMS: Headache, unsteadiness of gait.

FOLLOW-UP EXAMINATION: At 15-minute intervals the player has been examined and there is no change in the development of post-traumatic amnesia and neurologic signs. The unsteadiness of gait is totally resolved and a mild headache persists.

RETURN TO PLAY CRITERIA: With total resolution of symptoms on repetitive examination, the player is able to return after an observation period of approximately 30 minutes (by the doctor's watch, not the game clock). The player should once again be re-examined after coming off the field following the first offensive-defensive personnel shift.

MEDICAL TREATMENT: Same as Type I.

Type III-A

LOSS OF CONSCIOUSNESS: None or momentary.

NEUROLOGIC SIGNS: None.

RETROGRADE AMNESIA: Present. The player is unable to remember the play or the hit (will eventually clear).

POST-TRAUMATIC AMNESIA: Will usually not develop. If it does, this will be classified as a Type III-B.

SYMPTOMS: Headache, dizziness without vertigo, unsteadiness of gait.

RETURN TO PLAY CRITERIA: Out for the game.

MEDICAL TREATMENT AND FOLLOW-UP: This player should be watched very closely on the sidelines. Careful instructions should be given to the parents regarding the neurologic signs to check throughout the night. At the collegiate level, an overnight stay in the health center, if available, would be appropriate. (Due to the dormitory and apartment living status of college students, the health center would be appropriate, whereas at the high school level, returning home with parents would be appropriate.)

Type III-B

LOSS OF CONSCIOUSNESS: Minutes.

NEUROLOGIC SIGNS: None.

RETROGRADE AMNESIA: Unable to remember play or hit (will eventually clear).

POST-TRAUMATIC AMNESIA: Will sometimes develop and subsequently clear.

SYMPTOMS: Headache, dizziness, some nausea without vomiting. Unsteadiness of gait. All these symptoms clear over 15 to 30 minutes.

FOLLOW-UP EXAMINATION: Careful observation on the sidelines using the buddy system and/or student trainer as described in previous sections.

RETURN TO PLAY CRITERIA: Unable to play on that day. The individual is able to play when all symptoms clear on a subsequent day, after medical follow-up and evaluation.

MEDICAL TREATMENT AND FOLLOW-UP: Close observation on the sidelines as described above. Overnight stay in the health center, if available; in lieu of that, careful instructions to a parent for evaluation. The athlete should be evaluated again the next morning. If dizziness remains and if headache is severe, or if retrograde amnesia is not cleared, and/or post-traumatic amnesia has developed, in-hospital evaluation by a neurosurgeon is appropriate. Transport can be either by ambulance or private car.

If retrograde amnesia does not clear by the end of the game, with a minimum waiting time of approximately 30 minutes, then the patient should be taken to the emergency room. If he clears in the emergency room, he can be discharged from the emergency room or stay in the hospital at the discretion of the hospital staff physician. If the player's amnesia does not clear while in the emergency room, he should be admitted and further neurosurgical evaluation is appropriate. If the problem resolves in the emergency room, with total clearing of retrograde amnesia, and the player is discharged from the hospital, an overnight stay in the health center, if available, is appropriate, or close observation by parents. If there is a living situation, such as living alone in an apartment, that is not conducive to appropriate neurologic recheck, the patient should stay in the hospital overnight for observation.

All players should be rechecked 24 hours later, either after discharge from hospital or in the event they are not kept in the hospital.

Type IV

LOSS OF CONSCIOUSNESS: 5–10 minutes.

NEUROLOGIC SIGNS: Sluggish pupillary reflexes and vestibular signs.

RETROGRADE AMNESIA: Does not remember the entire game day.

POST-TRAUMATIC AMNESIA: Often present.

SYMPTOMS: Headache, vertigo, disorientation, nausea with vomiting, lethargy, unsteadiness of gait.

FOLLOW-UP EXAMINATION: This player should be transported on a spinal board by ambulance to the emergency room for immediate neurosurgical evaluation. The player should not be discharged from the hospital until evaluated by a neurosurgeon and should not return to football play until cleared by the neurosurgeon. This is usually a season-ending and possibly career-ending type of head injury.

Type V

LOSS OF CONSCIOUSNESS: Player is unarousable.
NEUROLOGIC SIGN: Pupillary dilatation.
IMMEDIATE TRANSFER TO HOSPITAL ON A SPINAL BOARD WITH A CALL AHEAD TO THE EMERGENCY ROOM TO HAVE A NEUROSURGICAL TEAM WAITING FOR POSSIBLE DECOMPRESSION.

Recurrent Head Injury

RECURRENT TYPE II (three or more times):   The player is unable to participate in practice or in games until he is cleared by a neurosurgical and/or neurologic evaluation, which will probably include MRI and/or CT brain scanning.

RECURRENT TYPE III (more than once):   The player is through for the season. Neurosurgical examination is mandatory. Complete workup is necessary before the player is able to return to play the following season.

The same criteria for all the types discussed above pertain also to practice, where a physician is usually not in attendance. The coaches and/or trainers/student trainers should manage the medical triage in these situations.

Discussion of the Protocol

The terminology of concussion is notably absent from this protocol. A variety of definitions[24,30,42] attests to the difficulty of defining this nonspecific term and has led to its abandonment in our protocol. For most of this century, concussion was viewed as a transient and completely reversible neurological event caused by cerebral ischemia, secondary to vasoparalysis or circulatory compromise due to the instantaneous rise of intracranial pressure at the moment of injury.[42] As the cerebral ischemia theory has been disproven, so has the concept that even the mildest of head injuries or ''concussion'' is entirely reversible.

The length of post-traumatic amnesia has been correlated with the severity of a head injury,[16,18] and therefore it is a useful guideline for the on-the-field evaluation. The player is potentially at a great risk if he is permitted to return to play while suffering from post-traumatic amnesia. Retrograde amnesia is a frequent finding in all injuries that disturb consciousness, and therefore it is also a very important guideline in determining the severity of injury.[35] Apparently the longer the post-traumatic amnesia, the longer one will notice retrograde amnesia.[35] Mental status serial examinations are necessary to eliminate the possibility of missing the development of retrograde amnesia minutes after the initial blow.[52] Yarnell and Lynch discuss how often immediate memory (i.e., digit recall) remains intact, yet recently transpired events (i.e., the play, the score) are forgotten, and thus this should be tested.[51] It should be reemphasized that any focal neurological finding, vestibular finding, or facial bleeding (scalp, ear, nose or throat)[26] mandates the patient be taken immediately to the emergency room. Clinically, it is often hard to distinguish traumatic intracranial hematoma from a mild head injury, as both can initially present with normal mental status, normal neurological examination, and identical symptoms (headache, lethargy, vertigo).[14]

The physician must also be aware of concurrent spinal or internal organ injuries in a head-injured athlete. It is well established that occult spinal cord injuries occur in the head-injured population and vice versa.[49] If indeed a concurrent spinal injury is detected, a complete spine x-ray series is imperative, as there is a high incidence of noncontiguous spinal fractures.[43]

SUGGESTIONS FOR PREVENTION OF HEAD INJURY IN CONTACT SPORTS

Preseason or preparticipation physical examination by the team physician can be a valuable tool in screening potential head injury victims. In light of the established cumulative nature of head injury, it is important to establish if an athlete has suffered a previous athletic or nonathletic head injury. A recent fatality at a junior college in the Bay Area, following a relatively minor blow, could have been avoided if a pre-existing brain injury had been known. An athlete with a previous head injury is more likely to suffer greater consequences due to a second occurrence.[2,11,36] Neck strengthening for all athletes could potentially reduce the incidence of head injuries.[3,24]

The National Collegiate Athletic Association (NCAA) and the National Federation of State High School Athletic Associations implemented rule changes in 1976 that prohibited head tackling, spearing, and head-butting,[47] and in 1977 and 1978 allowed offensive players more liberal use of their arms for blocking.[2] These changes contributed to the dramatic reduction in head injury fatalities from 1975 to 1984, culminating in a current all time low.[28] Undoubtedly, further progress can be made with stricter officiating.

Diligent coaching with particular emphasis paid to tackling techniques[10] is the most advantageous way of diminishing head injuries. Greater involvement of the team physician in educating players, trainers, and coaches about head injury might reduce the reluctance of participants to actually report injuries.[11] Improved availability of qualified physicians on the side line can reduce the following alarming statistics: from 1970 to 1980 58% of Minnesota high school football players with loss of awareness were not evaluated by a physician.[11]

The National Operating Committee on Standards for Athletic Equipment (NOCSAE) introduced safety standards for collegiate (1978) and high school (1980) football helmets.[28] There continues to be a significant amount of literature suggesting improved helmet construction and fitting[3] could provide further protection for young athletes.

APPENDIX A: HEAD INJURY INSTRUCTION SHEET

A family member or friend has suffered a head injury. Although the athlete is currently alert, conscious, and shows no signs or symptoms of serious brain injury, a potentially catastrophic result can still occur, leading to permanent neurological deficit or even death. Occasionally, following even the mildest head injuries, blood will slowly accumulate causing compression of the brain (subdural hematoma) hours or even days after the initial injury. Thus, the following guidelines should be followed in conjunction with the physician's or trainer's advice.

(1) The injured athlete should never be alone for the first 24 hours after the injury.
(2) The athlete should be awakened every two hours in the evening to establish arousability and alertness.
(3) The following signs (physical findings) mandate immediate emergency room evaluation:

    A. Blood or watery fluid (cerebral spinal fluid) eminating from ears or nose.
    B. Unequal or dilated eye pupils.
    C. Weakness or clumsiness in arms or legs.
    D. Slurred or garbled speech.
    E. Asymmetry of the face.
    F. Expanding cranial lesion (increased swelling along scalp).
    G. Change in consciousness (hard to arouse, irritable or stuperous).

(4) The following symptoms (complaints) mandate immediate emergency room evaluation:

    A. Change in mental status (inability to concentrate or understand directions, alteration in alertness or consciousness).
    B. Double or blurred vision.
    C. Severe headache.
    D. Increased incoordination (clumsiness) or weakness.
    E. Vomiting.
    F. Loss of memory.
    G. Difficulty with speech.

Realize the above are only guidelines to assist you. If a sign or symptom develops that is new and is not mentioned above, err on the side of safety and have the athlete evaluated by a physician immediately.

Prepared by the Physicians of S.O.A.R.

REFERENCES

1. Adams H, Mitchell D, Graham D, Doyle D: Diffuse brain damage of immediate impact type: its relationship to "primary brain-stem damage" in head injury. Brain 100:489–502, 1977.
2. Albright J, McAuley E, Martin R, et al: Head and neck injuries in college football: an eight-year analysis. Am J Sports Med 13(3):147–152, 1985.
3. Alley R: Head and neck injuries in high school football. JAMA 188(5):418–422, 1964.
4. Annegers J, Grabow J, Groover R, et al: Seizures after head trauma: a population study. Neurology 30:683–689, 1980.
5. Bennett D, Fuenning S, Sullivan G, Weber J: Migraine precipitated by head trauma in athletes. Am J Sports Med 8(3):202–205, 1980.
6. Blyth CS, Mueller F: Football injury survey: Part 1: When and where players get hurt. Phys Sportsmed 45–52, September 1974.
7. Brooks D, Aughton M: Psychological consequences of blunt head injury. Int Rehab Med 1:160–165, 1979.
8. Cantu R: Guidelines for return to contact sports after a cerebral contusion. Phys Sportsmed 10(14):75–83, 1986.
9. Denny-Brown D, Russell WR: Brain 64:93, 1941.
10. Duff J: Spearing: clinical consequences in the adolescent. J Sports Med 2(3):175–177, 1974.
11. Gerberich S, Priest J, Boeon J, et al: Concussion incidences and severity in secondary school varsity football players. Am J Pub Health 73(12): 1983.
12. Gloag D: Rehabilitation after head injury-1: Cognitive problems. Br Med J 290:834–837, 1985.
13. Gronwall D, Wrightson P: Cumulative effect on concussion. Lancet 995–997, November 22, 1975.
14. Hockberger RS: Blunt head injury: a spectrum of disease. Ann Emerg Med 15(2):202–207, 1986.
15. Holbourn A: Mechanics of head injury. Lancet 438–441, Oct. 9, 1943.
16. Jennett B, Teasdale G: Predicting outcome in individual patients after severe head injury. Lancet 197:1031–1034, 1976.
17. Kulund D: The Injured Athlete. Philadelphia: J.B. Lippincott Company, 1982.
18. Levy D, Bates D, Caronna J, et al: Prognosis in nontraumatic coma. Ann Intern Med 94(3):293–301, 1981.
19. Lezak M: Living with the characterologically altered brain injured patient. J Clin Psychiatr 6–15, July 1978.
20. Lezak M: Subtle sequelae of brain damage: perplexity, distractibility, and fatigue. Am J Phys Med Rehab 57(1):9–15, 1978.
21. Lindenberg R, Freytag E: The mechanism of cerebral contusions. Arch Pathol Lab Med 69:440–469, 1960.
22. Lishman W: The psychiatric sequelae of head injury: A review. Psychological Medicine 3:304–318, 1973.
23. Long C, Novack T: Postconcussion symptoms after head trauma: Interpretation and treatment. Southern Med J 79(6):728–732, 1986.
24. Maroon J, Steele P, Berlin R: Clinical neurosurgery: Chapter 24: Football Head and Neck Injuries—An Update.
25. Matthews W: Footballer's migraine. Br Med J 326–327, May 6, 1972.
26. McCabe J, Angelos M: Injury to the head and face in patients with cervical spine injury. Am J Emerg Med 2(4):333–335, 1984.
27. Miller H: Accident neurosis. Br Med J 919–925, April 1, 1961.
28. Mueller F, Blyth C: Fatalities from head and cervical spine injuries occurring in tackle football: 40 years' experience. Clin Sports Med 6(1):185–196, 1987.
29. Mueller F, Blyth C: Fatalities and catastrophic injuries in football. Phys Sportsmed 10(10):135–138, 1982.
30. Ommaya A, Gennarelli T: Cerebral concussion and traumatic unconsciousness: correlation of experimental and clinical observations on blunt head injuries. Brain 97:633–654, 1974.
31. Ommaya A, Gennarelli T: Experimental head injury. Handbook of clinical neurology 23:67–90, 1975.
32. Phillips J, Jones H, Hitchcock R, et al: Radioimmunoassay of serum creatine kinase BB as index of brain damage after head injury. Br Med J 281:777–779, 1980.
33. Rimel R, Giordani B, Barth J, et al: Disability caused by minor head injury. Neurosurgery 9(3):221–228, 1983.
34. Russel R: Recovery after minor head injury. Lancet 1315, November 30, 1974.
35. Russel R, Nathan P: Traumatic Amnesia. Brain 69:280–298, 1946.
36. Saunders R, Harbaugh R: The second impact in catastrophic contact-sports head trauma. JAMA 252(4):538–539, 1984.

37. Schaffer L, Kranzier L, Siquieira E: Aspects of evaluation and treatment of head injury. Neurol Clin North Am 3(2):259–273, 1985.
38. Schneider R: Head and Neck Injuries in Football: Mechanisms, Treatment, and Prevention. Baltimore, Williams and Wilkins Co, 1973.
39. Snoek J, Bond M, Brooks N: Disability after severe head injury: Observations on the use of the Glasgow outcome scale. J Neurol Neurosurg Psychiatr 44:285–293, 1981.
40. Stevens M: Post-concussion syndrome. J Neurosurg Nurs 14(5):239–244, 1982.
41. Strich S: Shearing of nerve fibers as a cause of brain damage due to head injury: a pathologic study of twenty cases. Lancet 1:443–448, 1961.
42. Symonds C: Concussions and its sequelae. Lancet 2:1–5, 1962.
43. Tearse D, Keene J, Drummond D: Management of non-contiguous vertebral fractures. American Spinal Injury Association, San Francisco, CA, March 13–15, 1986, pp. 49–69.
44. Teasdale G, Jennett B: Assessment of coma and impaired consciousness. Lancet 81–83, July 13, 1974.
45. Thorndike A: Athletic injuries: prevention, diagnosis, and treatment. Philadelphia, Lea and Febiger, 1956.
46. Thorndike A: Serious recurrent injuries of athletes: contraindications to further competitive participation. N Engl J Med 247(15):554–556, 1952.
47. Torg J, Vegso J, Sennett B: The National Football Head and Neck Injury Registry: 14-Year Report on Cervical Quadriplegia (1971–1984).Clin Sports Med 6(1):61–72, 1987.
48. Vegso J, Lehman R: Field evaluation and management of head and neck injuries. Clin Sports Med 6(1):1–15, 1987.
49. Wilmont C, Cope N, Hall K, Acker M: Occult head injury: its incidence in spinal cord injury. Arch Phys Med Rehab 66:227–231, 1985.
50. Windle WF, Groat RA, Fox CA: Surg Gynecol Obstet 79:561, 1944.
51. Yarnell P, Lynch S: The "ding": amnestic states in football trauma. Neurology 23:196–197, 1973.
52. Yarnell P, Lynch S: Retrograde memory immediately after concussion. Lancet 863–864, April 25, 1970.

STEVEN J. ANDERSON, MD

THE PREPARTICIPATION EXAMINATION

Reprint requests to Steven J. Anderson, M.D., 6533 44th Ave., N.E., Seattle, WA 98115.

The preparticipation sports examination is one of the longest-standing traditions in sports medicine, yet it is also one of the most controversial.[1] The overall goals and purposes of the examination are generally agreed upon, but there is little or no consensus on its content, frequency, or format. This is due in part to the varying needs among athletes of different ages, different sports, and different states of physical well-being. Medical care providers introduce further variability through biases from their own areas of expertise. The lack of clear scientific data on effective risk factor identification and management further contributes to the confusion and controversy. As a result, our ability to use the preparticipation examination to reliably predict and prevent athletic injuries falls short of our otherwise high standards of care for athletes.

The purpose of this chapter is to help establish a rational basis for resolving the controversy and confusion that surrounds the preparticipation examination. Based on accepted goals, a system will be proposed to define what should and should not be included in the standard examination. Since individual needs and differences will continue to exist, attention will be focused on how the basic examination can and should be expanded to meet individual needs resulting from differences in age, sport, or health. The basis for these recommendations is found in the study of sports epidemiology. Known patterns of injury occurrence, risk factor identification, and preventive interventions are used to justify the following approach to the preparticipation exam.

GOALS

The goals of the preparticipation examination are outlined in Table 1. Individuals gen-

TABLE 1.   Goals of the Preparticipation Examination

1. Reduce life-threatening or disabling injuries by identifying predisposing risk factors
2. Recommend preparatory, preventive, and/or rehabilitative measures
3. Assist in matching participants with appropriate sport or position
4. Promote the role of exercise and physical fitness in overall health maintenance and disease prevention
5. Fulfill legal requirement

erally participate in sports for the enjoyment of competition, opportunity for self-improvement, and long-term fitness or health benefits. With these goals in mind, sports injuries—especially those resulting in death or permanent disability—are particularly sobering. The inherent risk of a given sport combined with the exhilaration of participation exposes athletes to physical stresses beyond what they would normally tolerate. The preparticipation examination has been utilized to help minimize these risks by predetermining those individuals whose risk may be excessive.[2-7] Excessive risk from the physical demands of sport may be due to recognized underlying medical conditions such as an acute infection or loss of a paired organ or a previously unrecognized underlying medical condition such as an asymptomatic cardiac lesion or an enlarged spleen.

For healthy individuals with no apparent excess risk due to underlying illness or disease, there are still anatomic variations that predispose to specific injuries in specific sports. Identifying extreme lower extremity malalignment in a prospective distance runner or rotator cuff weakness in a prospective swimmer or throwing athlete may help prevent injury and hence, loss of time, loss of performance, or loss in interest in a sport. By identifying sports-specific risk factors and detecting unrehabilitated past injuries, a specific pre-season preparatory, preventive, or rehabilitative program may facilitate safer, more successful, and more enjoyable sports participation.

Similarly, with goals of enjoyment, self-improvement, and long-term health motivating prospective athletes, the sports medicine specialist can help direct their patients toward sports or positions where the risk of injury and failure is not excessive. It is a far greater challenge for the sports physician to promote sports safety by finding what individuals *can do* rather than what they *cannot do*. Inappropriate or arbitrary restriction is no better than inappropriate clearance for the safety and health concerns of the athlete. A goal of the preparticipation examination should be to promote sport safety and physical fitness by finding safe ways for individuals to participate.

Medicine's goals of enhancing sports safety are shared by the legal profession. The preparticipation examination has become a legal requirement in most organized sports settings. This legal mandate is an ever-present incentive for us to do a better job of predicting and preventing sports injuries. Unfortunately, our ability to do so is less than perfect. There is a growing concern that medicine's "legal" responsibility for athletes' safety without total control of their risk may result in more global restrictions on sports participation. Obviously, an appropriate balance must be sought between the risks and benefits of sports, whereby eliminating risks does not require eliminating the sport.

It is hoped that this chapter will better define what can and cannot be accomplished with a preparticipation screening examination. By thoughtful application of our knowledge of sports injuries, risk factor analysis, and preventive interventions, we can help athletes make and accept responsibility for better decisions about the risks and benefits of their sports participation.

TABLE 2. Criteria for Inclusion in the Preparticipation Examination*

Relevant conditions to address in the preparticipation examination include:
1. Conditions that occur in the sports setting, are worsened by sports participation, affect sports performance, and/or lead to sports injury.
2. Conditions that can be reliably detected or predicted by reasonable and available means.
3. Conditions in which early detection and intervention favorably changes the risk.

*The history, physical examination and laboratory portions of the preparticipation examination are designed to gather information about a group of selected conditions. The conditions selected as most relevant to a sports preparticipation examination are defined by the three criteria listed above. Conditions that meet these criteria then determine what is justified in terms of content of the examination.

These criteria can be used to challenge or justify any element of the preparticipation examination. If one were to question the utility or value of any particular portion of the preparticipation examination, one would ask: What condition(s) can be identified by this procedure? Is this condition endemic in the sports population? Is it made worse by sports participation? Does it limit sports performance? and Does it increase the risk of sports injury? How reliable is the procedure for identifying this condition and does early identification and treatment favorably change the risk of problems? Each element of the examination should be able to stand up to this line of questioning.

CRITERIA FOR INCLUSION IN THE PREPARTICIPATION EXAMINATION

The goals of the preparticipation examination define a framework for organizing its contents. Specific criteria for determining content of the preparticipation examination are listed in Table 2. The preparticipation examination is basically a screening procedure designed to detect early, preclinical stages of a disease (in this case, sports injury) or risk factors that predict increased susceptibility to a disease. The content, therefore, should be based on conditions that occur in the sports setting and through which sports participation may lead to injury, disability, or even death. This should also include conditions which themselves are worsened by sports participation or those which affect sports performance. A ''sports relevant'' condition, therefore, may be anything from an unstable ankle in a basketball player, hypertension in a weight lifter, or a seizure disorder in a swimmer.

Other health screening procedures are indicated for the athletic age group such as early cancer detection through Pap smears, stool guaiacs, and prostate examinations.[8] However, the preparticipation sports examination is not intended as a substitute for a general physical examination, and the conditions detected by these procedures generally do not meet the criteria of being sports relevant.

To further illustrate the concept of sports relevance, parallels can be drawn to risk identification in other activities. For example, good vision is critical for an airline pilot and is a prerequisite for licensing. Having a good ear for pitch may also be desirable for a pilot but is not so essential for his optimal function as it would be for a musician. As a result, screening visual acuity in pilots is justified; screening for pitch discrimination is not.

Unfortunately, once a condition is deemed sports relevant, it still may not be reasonable to include it in the preparticipation examination. If expensive and invasive means are required to detect a condition or risk factor, the cost may not justify the benefit. An example is requirement of the U.S. Special Olympics and The Committee on Sports Medicine of the American Academy of Pediatrics to screen Down syndrome patients for atlantoaxial instability.[9] There is a 12–20% incidence of atlantoaxial instability in Down syndrome patients.[10,11] With this instability, Down syndrome patients are potentially at increased risk of cervical spine injury during participation in sports that place stress on the neck, including swimming, diving, high jump, or soccer. However, there are no reported cervical cord injuries among 500,000 Down syndrome participants over the last 15 years.[12] Nonetheless, clearance to participate requires flexion, extension, and neutral cervical spine radiographs plus an interpretation and consultation fee. This requirement has good intentions but poor medical justification. Ironically, if the cost of this evaluation prohibits enough would-be participants, the injury rate will remain low.

Similar questions may be raised about screening for cervical spine stenosis or instability in asymptomatic football players or wrestlers. Should a cervical myleogram, CT, or MRI be a routine part of their preparticipation examination? Underlying cardiac conditions raise the same concerns. A very small number of athletes each year will die from idiopathic hypertrophic subaortic stenosis (IHSS) and coronary artery anomalies. Does this justify performing echocardiograms or cardiac catheterizations on all prospective participants? Probably not. The prevalence of these conditions and the cost of detecting one instance does not justify routine screening. Because it is not feasible or practical to apply every available diagnostic test to every individual, we must resort to making thoughtful clinical judgments and must selectively apply advanced studies only when indicated.

An extension of this higher yield, cost-effective approach to sports injury risk detection involves a critical look at the statistical validity and reliability of our measures. To interpret any screening test in medicine—whether it is a reported symptom, physical finding, or laboratory value—requires an appreciation of the limits conferred by the sensitivity, specificity, and predictive value of that test or measure. For example, iron deficiency anemia is a sports-relevant issue. However, a finger prick hematocrit is not a sensitive measure of iron deficiency nor is it specific. A serum ferritin or free erythrocyte protoporphyrin is more sensitive and specific for iron deficiency. Again, however, we are challenged to justify the expense and invasiveness of a given test for everyone or determine a way to use it more selectively.

Finally, if a condition or risk factor is sports relevant and can be reliably and reasonably detected, this process should yield some benefit to the athlete. For example, tight hamstring muscles may predispose a running athlete to hamstring tears or patellofemoral pain.[13,14] This condition is easy to detect, and a stretching program to restore normal flexibility may decrease injury risk and even improve performance. Conversely, spending extra time to document conditions where early detection and intervention does not change the risk is difficult to justify. An example would be constitutional joint hypermobility. Joint injuries are common in all sports, and joint laxity is easily detected, making this a relevant and detectable condition. However, interventions such as special exercises or supportive braces have failed to eliminate complications of hypermobility. Thus, identifying constitutional joint hypermobility is of little benefit to the patient. Acquired joint laxity or increased laxity from previous injury is a different issue and has treatment implications unique to the cause.

Testing for proteinuria is an example of a screening procedure that fails to meet any of the criteria for inclusion in the preparticipation examination but nonetheless is still part of most examinations performed. The conditions that cause proteinuria are not disproportionately represented in the athletic population, are not necessarily worsened by sports participation, and are not associated with increased risk of sports injury. Furthermore, there is no evidence that early detection of proteinuria decreases the incidence or complications of chronic renal failure.[15] Benign proteinuria is common in those who exercise. The test done to detect proteinuria unfortunately lacks the specificity to differentiate the benign forms from the pathologic forms. This imprecision leads to performing more tests resulting in greater patient expense and anxiety in order to pursue abnormalities that may not be real and probably are not relevant.

APPLIED SPORTS EPIDEMIOLOGY

Medical issues relevant to athletes include injuries or illnesses acquired through sports participation, medical conditions affecting sports performance, and medical conditions affected by sports participation. Sports epidemiology is a study of these conditions. Minimizing the risk from these conditions is the essential purpose of the preparticipation examination. Therefore, these are the sports-relevant issues and the basis for determining what should be addressed in the preparticipation examination.

Many excellent papers and reviews are available on the epidemiology of sports injuries.[16–23] Generally, injuries are categorized by sport, age of participant, severity of injury, diagnosis, or body part injured. This information can be readily applied to individual examination settings for determining priority issues. For example, if one is faced with a group of 13-year-old prospective distance runners, the dilemma of "what to do" and "what to look for" is based, in part, on the data showing "what happens." The epidemiologic data relevant to this situation warrant specific attention to lower extremity injuries, footwear, and training regimens. Conversely, shoulder instability or ear infections do not appear to be significant issues for this group and do not warrant additional attention. A similar analysis can be used for highlighting priorities in each preparticipation situation.

Table 3[3] categorizes sports as contact versus noncontact and strenuous versus nonstrenuous. The injury type and injury frequency for each sport is what one would logically expect from the nature of the activity. Sports in which contact or collisions are an integral part are associated with a higher frequency of contusions, sprains, fractures, abrasions, and lacerations. Endurance athletes are at greater risk for tendinitis, bursitis, fasciitis, and stress fractures. Sports such as gymnastics, which place a premium on strength, speed, and agility but also require multiple repetitions of given movements, have an injury pattern with characteristics of both contact and endurance sports. The point to be made here is that there are predictable injuries for each sport. Identifying these injuries and focusing the preparticipation examination accordingly will maximize the yield and preventive benefits for each individual athlete.

The preparticipation examination also looks at underlying medical conditions that may affect or be affected by sports participation. Virtually any medical condition may affect physical performance.[24] However, those primarily involving the cardiovascular, respiratory, or neurologic system are most likely to have bearing on performance and hence, are more sports relevant. A partial list of such conditions includes asthma, exercise-induced bronchospasm, supraventricular tachycardia, and anemia. Furthermore, any acute infection causing fever or dehydration may compromise cardiac output or reserve. Certainly, the use or abuse of many drugs with effects on cardiovascular status, fluid regulation, or central nervous system function has potential bearing on athletic performance and injury risk. Fortunately, treatment of most of these conditions is available and effective in ameliorating any adverse effect on activity.

Other medical conditions both may affect sports participation and may themselves be worsened by the stresses and physical demands of sport. These include certain forms of structural heart disease, cardiac dysrhythmias, hemorrhagic disease, or loss of a paired organ. Conditions such as diabetes mellitus,[24] hypertension,[25,26] or epilepsy[27,28] are also influenced by physical activity. However, changes in their

TABLE 3. Classification of Sports*

Strenuous—contact
Football
Ice hockey
Lacrosse (boys)
Rugby
Wrestling

Strenuous—limited contact
Basketball
Field hockey
Lacrosse (girls)
Soccer
Volleyball

Strenuous—non-contact
Crew (rowing)
Cross-country
Fencing
Gymnastics
Skiing
Swimming
Tennis
Track and field
Water polo

Moderately strenuous
Badminton
Baseball (limited contact)
Curling
Golf
Table tennis

Nonstrenuous
Archery
Bowling
Riflery

*From Schaffer TE: The health examination for participation in sports. Pediatr Ann 7:27, 1978, with permission.

management can be anticipated and sports participation can usually safely occur. Guidelines for medical restrictions and disqualifying conditions are listed in Table 4.

When sports injuries are analyzed according to severity, those associated with permanent disability or death are obviously of greatest concern. The most common cause of sudden death in athletes is head and neck trauma[21] followed in frequency by heat injury. There are individuals who may be at excessive risk for these problems but, generally, prevention of these deaths takes place through modifying the risks of the sports environment—e.g., rules, techniques, protective equipment, and availability of fluids.

A subset of sudden deaths in sports involve those individuals with underlying pathologic conditions, of which the individual may or may not be aware. In the adult population, this most commonly is coronary artery disease. In younger athletes, the most common causes of sudden death due to underlying disease are IHSS, coronary artery anomalies, myocarditis, and conduction disorders.[18,19,30,31] Modifying the risk of death from these causes is a priority of the preparticipation examination.

TABLE 4. Disqualifying Conditions for Sports Participation

Conditions	Collision*	Contact†	Non-contact‡	Other§
General				
Acute infections:				
Respiratory, genitourinary, infectious mononucleosis, hepatitis, active rheumatic fever, active tuberculosis	X	X	X	X
Obvious physical immaturity in comparison with other competitors	X	X		
Hemorrhagic disease:				
Hemophilia, purpura, and other serious bleeding tendencies	X	X	X	
Diabetes, inadequately controlled	X	X	X	X
Diabetes, controlled	††	††	††	††
Jaundice	X	X	X	X
Eyes				
Absence or loss of function of one eye	X	X		
Respiratory				
Tuberculosis (active or symptomatic)	X	X	X	X
Severe pulmonary insufficiency	X	X	X	X
Cardiovascular				
Mitral stenosis, aortic stenosis, aortic insufficiency, coarctation of aorta, cyanotic heart disease, recent carditis of any etiology	X	X	X	X
Hypertension on organic basis	X	X	X	X
Previous heart surgery for congenital or acquired heart disease	‖	‖	‖	‖
Liver, enlarged	X	X		
Skin				
Boils, impetigo, and herpes simplex gladiatorum	X	X		
Spleen, enlarged	X	X		
Hernia				
inguinal or femoral hernia	X	X	X	
Musculoskeletal				
Symptomatic abnormalities of inflammations	X	X	X	X
Functional inadequacy of the musculoskeletal system, congenital or acquired, incompatible with the contact or skill demands of the sport	X	X	X	
Neurologic				
History or symptoms of previous serious head trauma or repeated concussions	X			
Controlled convulsive disorder	¶	¶	¶	¶
Convulsive disorder not moderately well controlled by medication	X			
Previous surgery on head	X	X		
Renal				
Absence of one kidney	X	X		
Renal disease	X	X	X	X
Genitalia				
Absence of one testicle	**	**	**	**
Undescended testicle	**	**	**	**

From American Medical Association: Medical Evaluation of the Athlete: A guide. Publication No. OP209. Chicago, 1979.

*Football, rugby, hockey, lacrosse, and so forth.

†Baseball, soccer, basketball, wrestling, and so forth.

‡Cross country, track, tennis, crew, swimming, and so forth.

§Bowling, golf, archery, field events, and so forth.

††No exclusions.

‖Each patient should be judged on an individual basis in conjunction with his cardiologist and surgeon.

¶Each patient should be judged on an individual basis. All things being equal, it is probably better to encourage a young boy or girl to participate in a noncontact sport rather than a contact sport. However, if a patient has a desire to play a contact sport and this is deemed a major ameliorating factor in his or her adjustment to school, associates, and the seizure disorder, serious consideration should be given to letting him or her participate if the seizures are moderately well controlled or the patient is under good medical management.

**The Committee approves the concept of contact sports participation for youths with only one testicle or with an undescended testicle(s), except in specific instances such as an inguinal canal undescended testicle(s), following appropriate medical evaluation to rule out unusual injury risk. However, the athlete, parents, and school authorities should be fully informed that participation in contact sports for youths with only one testicle carries a slight injury risk to the remaining healthy testicle. Fertility may be adversely affected following an injury. But the chances of an injury to a descended testicle are rare, and the injury risk can be further substantially minimized with an athletic supporter and protective device.

Risk of coronary artery disease can readily be evaluated with an assessment of weight, blood pressure, smoking history, family history, lipid levels, and an exercise ECG. Identification of the noncoronary cardiac conditions is more difficult.[30,32-34] For example, IHSS may be assymptomatic, with death being the first manifestation of disease. Fifty per cent of these patients have a positive family history for early cardiac death. Some, but not all, will have a history of syncope, chest pain, dizziness, or shortness of breath with exercise. The murmur associated with IHSS is a crescendo-decrescendo murmur that typically increases with maneuvers that increase contractility or decrease preload. The murmur will decrease with maneuvers that increase afterload or increase left ventricular outflow tract diameter. Associated ECG changes may include left ventricular hypertrophy or abnormal Q waves in II, III, and AVF, and cardiomegaly may be seen on chest x-ray. A thickened intraventricular septum or dynamic outflow obstruction by echocardiogram is diagnostic.

Unfortunately, there are no historical or physical features that reliably identify IHSS or predict who is at risk for sudden death. The same is true for coronary artery anomalies, myocarditis, and certain conduction disorders. That is, the patient may be asymptomatic at rest, have no reliable historical or physical predictors of disease, and may require more extensive and invasive laboratory testing to confirm the diagnosis. While clinical data may not reliably confirm these diagnoses, they may be helpful in deciding who needs further workup. Clearly, any individual with a family history of premature cardiac death, with a history of chest pain, syncope, or exercise intolerance, or with irregular rhythm or nonfunctional murmur deserves more detailed evaluation.

Sudden death and permanent disability from sports are fortunately rare. While the techniques for early identification and prevention are not perfect, the potential magnitude of the problem still justifies our assiduous attention to this risk.

PREDICTION OF SPORTS INJURIES

To this point, we have discussed how certain sports injuries or medical problems could be predicted based on the inherent nature of the sport and the presence of underlying medical disorders. There are also individual variations that are not necessarily disease states or even physical abnormalities but may, nonetheless, influence the risk for sports injury.[35,36] Being aware of such data provides further opportunity to enhance the safety of sports for each participant. These risk factors include physical immaturity, sex, ligamentous laxity, malalignment, and imbalances of muscle flexibility or strength.

Physical immaturity proves to be less of a risk factor than originally assumed.[37,38] Younger athletes with open growth plates are at risk for epiphyseal injuries. However, that risk has not been shown to be excessive among participants in organized sports.[39] Growth plate injury secondary to repetitive microtrauma has also been a concern but has not been demonstrated to occur disproportionately in athletes.[40-42] The injury risk that remains can be minimized by appropriate size and maturation grouping of participants and by using age appropriate guidelines for training and conditioning.[43]

The presence of physiologic immaturity raises concern about the young athlete's tolerance for strenuous aerobic training. Other than a greater susceptibility to heat-related illness[44] (which is entirely preventable), adolescent and pre-adolescent athletes' tolerance for exercise is equivalent to adult standards.[45]

It appears that the greatest risk endured by immature athletes is the psychological stress of training and competition.[38,46,47] Coaches, parents, peers, and adult role models create an environment with high expectations and often intimidating standards for performance. Not all athletes respond favorably to this form of "encouragement." The perception of failure may lead to low self-esteem, apathy, and drop-out from sports. Some studies indicate an increased susceptibility to musculoskeletal injury as a result of certain personality traits or injury proneness.[48] Clearly, this is an area where the psychologic risks and benefits need to be balanced on an individual basis for each athlete.

The regular participation of females in organized sports was delayed in part because of concern for their risk of injury. Studies have now shown quite clearly that for similar sports, the number of injuries and type of injury is no different between males and females.[49] Prepubescent males and females can safely compete with each other in all sports.[50-52] With puberty, males develop greater gains in strength and speed than females, creating an inequity in injury risk during contact and collision sports.

Ligamentous laxity or joint hypermobility has long been considered a risk factor for musculoskeletal injury.[35,53] Joint looseness has been seen in association with sprains and dislocations. However, well-designed prospective studies have shown no significant statistical correlation between indices of joint laxity and injury predisposition.[36] Joint instability from previous injury, in contrast to constitutional joint hypermobility, does lead to a greater risk of recurrent injury. Therefore, constitutional joint hypermobility does not warrant restriction from sports nor does it warrant protective measures such as taping. Conversely, acquired or asymmetric joint instability may require workup and treatment for a specific injury.

Malalignment of the lower extremity has been reported in association with an increased incidence of overuse injuries.[54,55] Extreme pes planus or pes cavus may be seen in association with an increased frequency of foot, ankle, and knee problems in runners. However, many of those with overuse injuries have normal anatomy and many patients with abnormal anatomy have no injury. Other anatomic variances such as femoral anteversion, tibial torsion, muscle tightness, and discrepancies in leg length need to be taken into account as do possible abnormalities in training or footwear. Therefore, restriction of activity based on malalignment alone is not justified. However, caution in the form of increasing awareness of early symptoms of injury, proper equipment, and proper training may be warranted.

Imbalances of muscle strength and flexibility are believed to be a predisposition to certain types of injuries.[56,57] Tight muscles may lead to muscle strains—particularly if a muscle is forced to stretch beyond its normal active limits. Tight muscles that restrict joint motion may also limit performance. For example, tight hamstrings will decrease stride length and result in a loss of running speed.

Imbalances between agonist-antagonistic muscle groups may also influence injury risk. A study involving college football players in whom hamstring/quadricep strength ratios were corrected to 0.6 or better showed a seven-fold decrease of hamstring strains compared with an uncorrected group.[58] Similar studies have been done in swimmers and tennis players, looking for imbalances between shoulder external rotators and internal rotators.[57,59] Preliminary data from these studies show that disproportionately weak external rotators are associated with an increased incidence of rotator cuff and impingement problems.

A history of previous injury is one predictor that encompasses many categories of risk but singularly identifies a group with extremely high likelihood of injury. In one study, up to 50% of the injuries in a 4-year period were reinjuries of the same type.[35] Presumably, this is because an initial injury resulted in residual joint laxity, muscle tightness, or weakness. Furthermore, if an abnormality of the training

TABLE 5.   Extrinsic and Intrinsic Factors in Sports Injuries*

Extrinsic factors	Intrinsic factors
Exposure	Physical characteristics
Type of sports, rules	Age
Playing time	Sex
Position in the team	Somatotype
Level of competition	Physical fitness
	Previous injury
Training	Muscle tightness
	Joint instability
Environment	Malalignment of the lower extremities
Type and condition of playing surface	
Weather conditions	
Time of day	Psychosocial characteristics
Time of season	
Equipment	
Protective equipment	
Footwear	

*From Lysens R, et al: The predictability of sports injuries. Sports Med 1:6, 1984, with permission.

program, equipment, or sports environment was contributory to the initial injury, a high recurrence risk would be expected unless the abnormality was corrected. Therefore, if any individual deserves a more detailed analysis of joint stability, range of motion, muscle flexibility, and strength as well as inquiry into training techniques and equipment, it would be someone with a previous injury.

The fact that injury risk is multifactorial limits the opportunity to isolate reliable predictors. The available information on risk factors is best used in combination with other risk data and in the context of the individual participant. The extrinsic and intrinsic risk factors in Table 5[35] collectively form a risk profile and a basis for planning injury prevention.

PREVENTIVE INTERVENTIONS

After establishing a risk profile for an individual based on the chosen sport, training regimen, and health/fitness characteristics, it is desirable to be able to offer ways to favorably modify that risk. Preventive interventions may be general or specific and may include a preseason general conditioning program, a resistance or weight training program, a warm-up/stretching program, proper equipment fitting or modification, or modification of the sport or sports environment.

With the mutiplicity of risk factors for injury, no single preventive intervention is going to eliminate risk. Furthermore, an attempt at injury prevention may work through more than one mechanism. A preseason general conditioning program is a good example. In an 8-year prospective study with high school football players,[60] the study group underwent a 5- to 6-week preseason conditioning program with emphasis on cardiovascular endurance, heat acclimatization, weight training, flexibility, and agility drills. When compared with a control group with no formal preseason program, the study group had 68% fewer early season knee injuries, 63% fewer surgical knee injuries, and 86% fewer anterior cruciate/medial collateral ligament tears.

Training error and doing "too much, too fast, too soon" is also associated with increased injury risk.[54] Perhaps for the same reason that a preseason conditioning program is successful, allowing time to build up to new physical demands gradually and preparing the body to withstand these demands may help in avoiding predictable injuries.

Resistance training has been shown to promote growth and/or increases in strength of ligaments, tendons, tendon/ligament connections to bone, and connective tissue sheaths within muscles—making these tissues more resistant to injury.[57,61] Identification of imbalances between agonist and antagonistic muscle groups may also identify athletes who would benefit from resistance training to correct the imbalances.[58,62] Data are available showing decreased injury rates after correcting weak wrist extensors in tennis players or weak shoulder external rotators in tennis players and swimmers.[57,63]

Stretching and warming-up surely function well as part of the psychologic preparation for athletic events. They may also enhance performance by increasing blood flow to muscles, increasing oxygen-hemoglobin dissociation, decreasing activation energy for energy-producing metabolic reactions, increasing speed of nerve conduction, increasing coronary blood flow, and serving as a rehearsal function.[14]

Only now are stretching and warm-up exercises being shown to decrease injury risk.[64] Warming-up increases muscle extensibility by increasing blood flow and decreasing viscosity. Warming-up also improves the elastic properties of tendons, ligaments, and other connective tissues. The response to stretching exercises is also enhanced with warm-up. Maximizing the freely available range of motion at a joint decreases the risk of injury if that joint is forced beyond its normal range. Improved flexibility is thought to be associated with decreased muscle/tendon strains. On a more chronic basis, improved muscle flexibility in the hamstrings and low back seems to decrease the risk of mechanical low back pain.

Clearly, there is a need for more research to establish optimal values for strength, strength balances, and flexibility in athletes as well as the optimal way to achieve and maintain these values. Preliminary data reviewed above need to be duplicated, then expanded upon. In the meantime, these studies can serve as a format for asking more in-depth questions about predicting and preventing other athletic injuries.

Equipment issues are relevant to this discussion, because sports equipment may be part of the cause or part of the cure for sports injury.[43] A football helmet may decrease impact to the head from contact but may also invite use of the head as a weapon and expose the neck to excessive stresses.[65] The equipment required for a given sport needs to be properly designed, properly fitted, and properly used to achieve its goals of injury prevention.[66] In youth sports, where often one set of equipment needs to be fit to a wide range of body types and shapes, improper fits are inevitable. Individuals nonetheless proceed with the false security of being protected, even if the equipment is malfitting and malfunctioning.

Some equipment may not be required by the sport but is still recommended because of a purported protective effect. This includes ankle taping or bracing, prophylactic knee bracing, mouth guards, and goggles or eye protection. Data on the effectiveness of such protective strategies are inconclusive.[67,68] Decisions about use should be individualized, and the limitations of effectiveness should be understood prior to participation.

A final application of sports equipment is to protect a past injury or allow safer participation during injury rehabilitation. Such equipment options may include tape for a sprained finger, a tennis elbow sleeve, a shoe insert, a neck roll, or a derotation brace for the knee. The effectiveness of such pieces of equipment depends on the specific injury diagnosed, state of recovery, exposure of the athlete, and the degree of protection conferred by the equipment. Again, such equipment use must be in the context of the specific injury, sport, and limitations of the equipment.

A final opportunity to prevent sports injury is directed more at the sport and sports environment than on the individual participant.[35,43,69] There are a variety of issues in this category which may be addressed. They include appropriate age and maturity matching of participants, rules, supervision, coaching, instruction in proper technique, availability of fluids, maintenance of fields or surfaces, restriction of activity in high temperature and high humidity conditions, and availability of first aid and an emergency plan. As an example, predictable shoulder and elbow problems in Little League baseball pitchers can be prevented by insisting that they pitch only 6 innings per week. Similarly, heat injury and dehydration in high school football players may be averted by scheduling summer practices during a cooler time of the day and having scheduled drinking breaks with appropriate fluids available.

Making such demands may seem awkward, but not making them may compromise the athlete. Physicians can involve themselves in promoting safety at this level by participating in committees that set rules and guidelines for participation or teaching first aid and emergency medical procedures to local coaches. This process inevitably improves the physician's appreciation of the risks of the sports environment and expands the physician's preventive influence beyond the confines of the office.

PERFORMING THE PREPARTICIPATION EXAMINATION

Similar to other health assessments, the preparticipation examination gathers information through a medical history, physical examination, and occasional laboratory study.[2-6] The stated goals of the preparticipation examination (Table 1), the criteria for inclusion in the examination (Table 2), and the available data on sports injury patterns, injury risk factors, and the success of preventive intervention collectively define the essential historical, physician examination, and laboratory elements of the preparticipation examination.

Medical History.   The medical history should focus on previous injuries, acute and chronic medical illnesses, cardiovascular disease, and a history of previous exercise intolerance. A previous injury is a strong predictor for subsequent injury. When present, a detailed search for evidence of residual pain, weakness, or dysfunction should occur. A history of past injury should also raise questions about general risk factors such as training error, anatomic or muscular imbalances, and equipment malfunction or misuse.

A medical review of systems is also indicated for the history portion of the preparticipation examination. This can take place by organ system (e.g., HEENT, respiratory, GI, GU, etc.) or disease process (infection, allergy, neurologic, etc.) but should be comprehensive and should include ongoing treatments. A history of medication use is critical because of the many potential effects on sports performance. Furthermore, many patients may remember a medication better than the problem for which it is prescribed.

The review of systems serves as a catch-all for identifying conditions that may or may not be relevant. For example, coughing after exercise may not be noteworthy to an athlete but may allow us to diagnose and treat exercise-induced bronchospasm. Similarly, a bee-sting allergy may be inconsequential to an athlete but allows planning for emergency, potentially life-saving care. We should not rely on the athlete to sort out what is and is not important.

TABLE 6.　Prioritizing Contents of the Preparticipation Examination

Information Source	Should be included in preparticipation examination:		
	All of The Time	With Specific Indication	Rarely, if Ever
Vital Signs (Ht, Wt, HR, BP)	X		
General Inspection	X		
HEENT		X	
Cardiovascular	X		
Respiratory		X	
Abdominal/lymphatic		X	
Genitalia			X
Skin		X	
Musculoskeletal	X		
Neurologic		X	
Laboratory (Hct, U/A)			X

Finally, the cardiac history warrants special attention in all athletes. Based on the histories of athletes who have experienced sudden cardiac death with sports, a high index of suspicion for cardiac disease should be raised when eliciting a positive family history for cardiac death under age 50, symptoms of chest pain, palpitations, dizziness, or syncope with exercise. The response to these questions may be more helpful than even the physical examination in revealing major cardiac risk—hence, they should be asked of all athletes.

Further recall of relevant information may be stimulated by questioning "memorable events." This includes questions such as, "Have you ever been hospitalized?" "Have you ever had surgery?" "Have you ever had x-rays taken?" "Have you ever worn a sling, cast, or used crutches?" or "Have you missed more than a week of school or work from illness or injury?"

Physical Examination.　The physical examination also has areas of general and specific relevance to athletes. The contents of the examination are justified based on what is sports relevant, what we can detect or predict, and what we can treat or prevent. Table 6 proposes a priority or ranking system for the various elements of the standard physical examination.

Every examination should consist of vital signs, height, weight, general inspection, a cardiovascular examination, and a musculoskeletal examination. The medical history and the chosen sport(s) dictate the areas of the body that should be emphasized.

Height and weight determinations are relevant in all athletes for purposes of selecting appropriate sports as well as their relation to overall growth, development, and nutritional status. A resting heart rate correlates with cardiovascular fitness and may be abnormal with cardiac or rhythm disorders, drug use, dehydration, or anemia. Blood pressure changes are also seen with disease states, dietary excesses, and drug use. High blood pressure may warrant restriction from primarily isometric sports or training programs. Temperature and respiratory rate determination are not routinely indicated.

A great deal can be learned from attentive observation and inspection of general body habitus. A maturity assessment is important in sport selection, matching, and injury risk. Nutritional status and body fat can be estimated, with implications for both performance and risk of heat injury. General inspection may reveal syndromic features. More common syndromes such as Down syndrome (trisomy 21) will be easily recognized but still may carry "hidden risk" of associated heart disease or atlantoaxial instability.[9] Recognition of less common and perhaps more subtle syndromes such as Marfan's syndrome may ultimately be life-saving.[70] Behavioral observation during the examination may provide useful information on readiness for sport, injury proneness, or sports "burnout."

Examination of the head and neck is generally a low-yield area of study in the asymptomatic athlete. Baseline pupil equality may be important to document in contact sports participants. Similarly, an athlete who wears contact lenses or requires glasses may be worth noting. Inspection of the outer ear and discussion of ear protection is relevant to a wrestler. Inspection of the middle ear and canal as well as discussing proper ear hygiene is relevant to a swimmer or diver. Examination of the nose, throat, and lymph nodes offers even fewer signs.

Percussion and auscultation of the chest in an asymptomatic individual has little proven value as a screening test. A history of exercise-induced bronchospasm, atopic disease, or cardiovascular disease may warrant a more detailed chest examination.

The cardiovascular examination, including pulses, rhythm, and heart sounds, is an essential part of all preparticipation examinations.[25,71–74] The goal of this portion of the examination should *not* be to discriminate subtle cardiac diagnoses but to identify those patients who need further workup before playing. A high index of suspicion for cardiac disease should be raised in patients with a family history of early sudden cardiac death, hypertension, stroke, or diabetes. As noted above, a history of exertional syncope, lightheadedness, or dyspnea on exertion is worrisome, as is a history of rheumatic fever or an "innocent murmur" that has been heard for 4 or more years. Physical findings that suggest disease include cyanosis, rales, hepatosplenomegaly, systemic hypertension, rate/rhythm disturbances, murmurs of grade IV or louder, diastolic murmurs, absent S1 with murmurs, fixed split S2, opening clicks, decreased or accentuated peripheral pulses, or certain "syndromic" features.

Because the comfort level for "clearing the heart" will vary with each examiner, the number of "worrisome features" leading to a cardiac referral also will vary. Generally speaking, if every patient referred for cardiac workup has significant disease, not enough patients are being referred.

The abdominal examination is another low-yield procedure without specific indication. A participant in contact sports with a history of mononucleosis, recent viral infection, or hematologic disorder may benefit from an assessment of liver and spleen size.

Examination of the genitalia and probing for asymptomatic hernias has little indication in the routine preparticipation examination. These procedures fail to meet the criteria for inclusion in the preparticipation examination but are still commonly done, often to the exclusion of an adequate musculoskeletal examination. A procedure that is unpleasant or embarrassing to the patient is not necessarily one that is thorough or appropriate.

If a patient is properly exposed during the preparticipation examination—shorts for males, shorts and swimsuit or halter top for females—the majority of the skin surface is available for inspection. Observing an atopic skin rash may precipitate further inquiry about exercise-induced bronchospasm. Jaundice may raise relevant questions about infectious hepatitis or the use of anabolic steroids. An active herpes simplex lesion or impetigo has implications for those in contact sports such as wrestling or rugby.[75,76]

TABLE 7. Sport-Specific Issues

Football	Neck/back, knee/ankle stability, shoulder
Wrestling	Neck, shoulder, nutrition, weight control
Track/cross-country	Lower extremity alignment, flexibility, training schedule, footwear
Swimming	Rotator cuff flexibility and strength, eye care, ear care
Ballet/gymnastics	Foot, ankle, spine, body fat, menstrual function
Throwing/racket sports	Shoulder, elbow, wrist

The musculoskeletal examination is another essential element of all preparticipation examinations, as most sports injuries involve the musculoskeletal system. Old injuries and risk factors for new injuries are easily detectable, and rehabilitative and preventive interventions are successful.[4,5,77] The examination should include the spine as well as the extremities. In general, each area should be checked for range of motion, strength, stability, and function. Abnormalities or asymmetries should be noted and used as the basis for rehabilitative or preventive measures. The history of previous injury and the demands of the selected sport or activity help focus the examination. Table 7 identifies some of these sport-specific issues.

Many key aspects of the neurologic screening examination are covered in other sections of the preparticipation examination. The medical interview and the other essential procedures allow the alert examiner to make a good, general assessment of central nervous system function, coordination, cerebellar function, and strength. Again, more detailed examination may be indicated by the history or the sport.

Laboratory Tests. By virtue of the criteria for inclusion in the preparticipation examination, routine screening laboratory tests are not justified. A hematocrit and urine dipstick for sugar and protein have been the traditional lab components of the examination. However, as previously noted, the sensitivity and specificity of these tests in aysmptomatic patients as well as the cost:benefit ratio for the patient does not warrant their regular use.

Resting electrocardiograms are fraught with the same limitations. There are many apparent ECG abnormalities that may be normal in the heart of an athlete.[78,79] Furthermore, many important ECG changes secondary to exercise stress may be missed on a resting study. For the ECG, like other laboratory studies, its use will be enhanced when ordered with specific indication or supplemented with a more precise test.

Other investigations outside the realm of traditional laboratory studies may be useful. For example, a body fat estimate may be useful for athletes in weight control sports, as a basis for nutritional or training recommendations or in assessing risk of heat injury. If available, pre-season Cybex evaluations looking for specific muscle asymmetries or imbalances may also help identify athletes at risk for selected injuries.[57]

TIMING AND FORMAT OF THE EXAMINATION

Each state and/or region has its own requirements for the frequency of the preparticipation examination. The minimum requirements are to have a comprehensive examination at the time of entry into sports at both the junior high and senior high school levels.[6,80] A preparticipation examination would also be ideally performed for any school-aged or adult patient who embarks on a new or different athletic endeavor. Annual updates may be brief unless there has been an intervening injury, medical problem, or change in sport.

Ideally the examination is performed 2 or more weeks before training begins. This allows some time for rehabilitation of old injuries, carrying out specific preventive or preparatory programs, and organizing further medical workup or diagnostic studies.

The examination format is optional but should be determined by its effectiveness in meeting the goals of the preparticipation examination.[81–83] Office examinations with one's private physician have the advantage of continuity and familiarity with the patient's past medical history. However, these examinations tend to be more variable in content and often are not sports-oriented. "Locker room" or "lineup" examinations have fallen out of favor because they are impersonal and superficial. A group or station examination involving a team of various sports specialists has the advantage of being comprehensive, sport-specific, and consistent in obtaining baseline data on injury states or injury risk.

DISPOSITION

The disposition defines how much leeway we are willing to give an athlete as they encounter the risks of the sports environment. It should translate what has been learned about injury risk and the opportunities for enhancing performance into specific tasks for the athlete. The disposition may fall into the following categories: (1) full, (2) full, pending further diagnostic studies or treatment, (3) limited, with specific modifications or restrictions, or (4) no participation. The disposition does not have to be an "all or nothing" statement. These intermediate options promote participation but actively involve the athlete in ways to make their own participation safer. Rarely is there an athlete who would not benefit from some safety or preparatory component attached to his or her clearance to play. It should be remembered that greater restriction does not necessarily imply greater safety. A major challenge to the sports physician is to advocate sports participation by finding a safe way for each individual to do so.

CONCLUSIONS

The goals of the preparticipation examination are to decrease injuries by identifying predisposing factors and recommending preparatory, preventive and/or rehabilitative measures. Sports safety and enjoyment is also promoted by helping to match each participant with an appropriate sport, position, and training regimen. The preparticipation examination consists of a medical history, physical examination, and occasional laboratory study. The contents of the examination are selected and justified by their relevance to the sports setting, ease of detection, and their response to preventive measures. Based on these criteria, the history portion of the preparticipation examination focuses on previous injuries, acute and chronic medical illnesses, and symptoms of cardiac disease or exercise intolerance. The essential components of the physical examination include vital signs, general body habitus, a cardiovascular examination, and a musculoskeletal examination. The history and physical examination should be expanded to evaluate disease-specific and sport-specific issues.

With commonly accepted goals and now, a system to critically evaluate and justify how best to meet these goals, the examination itself and examination format may vary without sacrificing effectiveness. The goal of safe sports participation will not be reached simply by taking away potential dangers. Affirmative steps to enhance sports safety will better serve the aspirations of each participant. The preparticipation sports examination provides an excellent opportunity to practice, promote, and insure the goal of safety in sport.

REFERENCES

1. Moore M: Preparticipation examinations: Just a "lick and a promise." Phys Sportsmed 10:113, 1982.
2. Strong WB, Linder CW: Preparticipation health evaluation for competitive sports. Pediatr Rev 4:113, 1983.
3. Schaffer TE: The health examination for participation in sports. Pediatr Ann 7:27, 1978.
4. McKeag DB: Preseason physical examination for the prevention of sports injuries. Sports Med 2:413, 1985.
5. Runyan DK: The pre-participation examination of the young athlete: Defining the essentials. Clin Pediatr 22:674, 1983.
6. Blum RW: Preparticipation evaluation of the adolescent athlete: Timing and content of the examination. Postgrad Med 78:52, 1985.
7. Tennant FS, et al: Benefits of preparticipation sports examinations. J Fam Pract 13:287, 1981.
8. Woo B, et al: Screening procedures in the asymptomatic adult: Comparison of physicians' recommendations, patients' desires, published guidelines, and actual practice. JAMA 254:1480, 1985.
9. American Academy of Pediatrics, Committee on Sports Medicine: Atlantoaxial instability in Down syndrome. Pediatrics 74:152, 1984.
10. Semine AA, et al: Cervical-spine instability in children with Down syndrome (trisomy 21), J Bone Joint Surg 60A:649, 1978.
11. Peuschel SM, et al: Atlanto-axial instability in children with Down syndrome. Pediatr Radiol 10:129, 1981.
12. Golden GS: Controversies in therapies for children with Down syndrome. Pediatr Rev 6:116, 1984.
13. Ekstrand J, et al: The frequency of muscle tightness and injuries in soccer players. Am J Sports Med 10:75, 1982.
14. Shellock FG, Prentice WE: Warming-up and stretching for improved physical performance and prevention of sports-related injuries. Sports Med 2:267, 1985.
15. Feld LG, et al: Evaluation of the child with asymptomatic proteinuria. Pediatr Rev 5:248, 1984.
16. Garrick JG, Requa RK: Injuries in high school sports. Pediatrics 61:465, 1978.
17. Zaricznyj B, et al: Sports-related injuries in school-aged children. Am J Sports Med 8:318, 1980.
18. Luckstead EF: Sudden death in sports. Pediatr Clin North Am 29:1355, 1982.
19. Northcote RJ, Ballantyne D: Sudden death and sport. Sports Med 1:81, 1984.
20. Mueller FO, Blyth CS: Annual survey of catastrophic football injuries: 1977–1983. Phys Sportsmed 12:122, 1984.
21. Bruce DA, et al: Brain and cervical spine injuries occurring during organized sports activities in children and adolescents, Clin Sports Med 1:495, 1982.
22. Clement D, et al: A survey of overuse running injuries. Phys Sportsmed 9:47, 1981.
23. DeHaven K: Athletic injuries in adolescents. Pediatr Ann 7:704, 1978.
24. Bar-Or O: Pediatric Sports Medicine for the Practitioner: From Physiologic Principles to Clinical Applications. New York, Springer-Verlag, 1983.
25. American Academy of Pediatrics, Policy Statement: Cardiac evaluation for participation in sports. News and Comments, 1978.
26. Nudel DB, et al: Exercise performance of hypertensive adolescents. Pediatrics 65:1073, 1980.
27. Committee on Children with Handicaps: The epileptic child and competitive school athletics. Pediatrics 42:700, 1968.
28. AMA Committee on the Medical Aspects of Sports: Epileptics and contact sports. JAMA 229:820, 1974.
29. AMA Committee on Medical Aspects of Sports, Publication No. 0138-590K: 7/74-3M, p. 209. Chicago, American Medical Association.
30. Starek PJK: Athletic performance in children with cardiovascular problems. Phys Sportsmed 10:78, 1982.
31. Tunstall-Pedoe D: Exercise and sudden death. Br J Sports Med 12:215, 1979.
32. Maron BJ, et al: Sudden death in patients with hypertrophic cardiomyopathy: Characterization of 26 patients with functional limitation. Am J Cardiol 41:803, 1978.
33. Orinius E: Prognosis in hypertrophic obstructive cardiomyopathy. Acta Med Scand 206:289, 1979.

34. Arbogast RC, White RS: Idiopathic hypertrophic subaortic stenosis. Am Fam Physician 24:97, 1981.
35. Lysens R, et al: The predictability of sports injuries. Sports Med 1:6, 1984.
36. Jackson DW, et al: Injury prediction in the young athlete: A preliminary report. Am J Sports Med 6:6, 1978.
37. Micheli LJ: Pediatric and Adolescent Sports Medicine. Boston Little Brown, 1984.
38. Schaffer TE (ed): Schering Symposium on Sports Medicine: The uniqueness of the young athlete. Am J Sports Med 8:370, 1980.
39. Pappas AM: Epiphyseal injuries in sports. Phys Sportsmed 11:140,1983.
40. Kozar B, Lord, RM: Overuse injury in the young athlete: Reasons for concern. Phys Sportsmed 11:116, 1983.
41. Micheli LJ: Overuse injuries in childrens' sports: The growth factor. Orthop Clin North Am 14:337, 1983.
42. Caine DJ, Linder KJ: Growth plate injury: A threat to young distance runners? Phys Sportsmed 12:118, 1984.
43. Goldberg B, et al: Children's sports injuries: Are they avoidable? Phys Sportsmed 7:93, 1979.
44. Committee on Sports Medicine: Climatic heat stress and the exercising child. Pediatrics 69:808, 1982.
45. Shephard RJ: Physical Activity and Growth. Chicago, Year Book Medical Publishers, 1982.
46. Simon JA, Martens R: Children's anxiety in sport and non-sport evaluative activities. J Sport Psychol 1:160, 1979.
47. Purdy DA, et al: Stress among child athletes: Perception by parents, coaches, and athletes. J Sport Behavior, 1982, p. 32.
48. Bramwell ST, et al: Psychosocial factors in athletic injuries: Development and application of social and athletic readjustment rating scale (SARRS). J Human Stress 1:6, 1975.
49. Garrick JG, Requa RK: Girls sports injuries in high school athletics. JAMA 239:2245, 1978.
50. Committee on Pediatric Aspects of Physical Fitness, Recreation, and Sports: Competitive athletics for children of elementary school age. Pediatrics 67:927, 1981.
51. American Academy of Pediatrics: Committee on Pediatric Aspects of Physical Fitness, Recreation, and Sports: Participation in sports by girls. Pediatrics 55:563, 1975.
52. Haycock CE, Gillette JV: Susceptibility of women athletes to injury: Myth vs. reality. JAMA 236:163, 1976.
53. Godshall RW: The predictability of athletic injuries: An eight-year study. J Sports Med 3:50, 1975.
54. James S, et al: Injuries to runners. Am J Sports Med 6:40, 1978.
55. Mann R, et al: Running symposium. Foot and Ankle 1:190, 1981.
56. Grace TG: Muscle imbalance and extremity injury: A perplexing relationship. Sports Med 2:77, 1985.
57. Fleck SJ, Falkel JE: Value of resistance training for the reduction of sports injuries. Sports Med 3:61, 1986.
58. Heiser TM, et al: Prophylaxis and management of hamstring muscle injuries in intercollegiate football players. Am J Sports Med 12:368, 1984.
59. Falkel JE, et al: Shoulder external rotation strength and endurance deficits in swimmers. Submitted for publication.
60. Cahill BR, et al: Effect of preseason conditioning on the incidence and severity of high school football knee injuries. Am J Sports Med 6:180, 1978.
61. Hage P: Weight training reduced sports injuries. Phys Sportsmed 11:20, 1983.
62. Abbott HG, Kress, JB: Preconditioning in the prevention of knee injuries. Arch Phys Med Rehabil 50:326, 1969.
63. Hawkins RJ, et al: Impingement syndrome in athletes. Am J Sports Med 8:151, 1980.
64. Hubley-Kozey CL, Stanish WD: Can stretching prevent athletic injuries? J Musculoskel Med 1:25, 1984.
65. Clark K: Football head and neck injuries. Interschol Athlet Admin 7:9, 1980.
66. Gieck J, et al: Fitting of protective football equipment. Am J Sports Med 8:192, 1980.
67. Teitz CC, et al: Evaluation of the use of braces to prevent injury to the knee in collegiate football players. J Bone Joint Surg 69A:2, 1987.
68. Gieck J, et al: The prevention and treatment of ankle injuries. Am J Sports Med 4:136, 1976.
69. Feldman E, Jackson DW: Sports injuries in young athletes: steps to prevention. J Musculoskel Med 1:25, 1984.
70. Cantwell JD: Marfan's syndrome: Detection and management. Phys Sportsmed 14:51, 1986.
71. Galioto FM: Identification and assessment of the child for sports participation: A cardiovascular approach. Clin Sports Med 1:383, 1982.
72. Liebman J: Diagnosis and management of heart murmurs in children. Pediatr Rev 3:321, 1982.

73. Salem DN, Isner JM: Cardiac screening for athletes, Orthop Clin North Am 11:687, 1980.
74. Grossman M, Baher BE: Current cardiology problems in sports medicine. Am J Sports Med 12:262, 1984.
75. Snook GA: How I manage skin problems in wrestlers. Phys Sportsmed 12:97, 1984.
76. White WB, Grant-Kels JM: Transmission of HSV type I infection in rugby players. JAMA 239:2245, 1978.
77. Rice SG: Sports medicine. JCE Pediatr 21:13, 1979.
78. Ferst JA, Chaitman BR: The electrocardiogram and the athlete. Sports Med 1:390, 1984.
79. Lichtman J, et al: Electrocardiogram of the athlete: Alterations simulating those of organic heart disease. Arch Intern Med 132:763, 1973.
80. Committee on School Health: School health examinations. Pediatrics 67:576, 1981.
81. Harvey J: The preparticipation examination of the child athlete. Clin Sports Med 1:353, 1982.
82. Durant RH, et al: The preparticipation examination of athletes: Comparison of single and multiple examiners. Am J Dis Child 139:657, 1985.
83. Linder CW, et al: Preparticipation health screening of young athletes: Results of 1268 examinations. Am J Sports Med 9:187, 1981.

INDEX

Note: Page numbers of issue and article titles are in **boldface** type.

STATE OF THE ART REVIEWS (STARs)

SUBJECT	FREQUENCY	PRICE (U.S.)	PRICE (Foreign)	PRICE (Single)
☐ CARDIAC SURGERY	Triannual	84.00	93.00	36.00
Subscription year begins in October (Oct., Feb., June)				
☐ NEUROSURGERY	Biannual	75.00	84.00	42.00
☐ OCCUPATIONAL MEDICINE	Quarterly	64.00	74.00	29.00
☐ PHYSICAL MED & REHAB (PM&R)	Quarterly	62.00	68.00	28.00
☐ SPINE	Triannual	75.00	87.00	32.00
Subscription year begins in September (Sept., Jan., May)				

☐1988 subscription ☐ 1987 subscription ☐ Single issue

Check subject title above.

Title _____

I enclose payment: ☐ Check ☐ Visa ☐ MasterCard

Credit Card # _____ Exp. Date _____

Name _____

Signature _____

Title _____

Street Address _____

Company/Hospital _____

City/State/Zip _____

Send order to:

HANLEY & BELFUS, INC.

210 South 13th Street / Philadelphia, PA 19107 / 215-546-7293

STATE OF THE ART REVIEWS (STARs)

SUBJECT	FREQUENCY	PRICE (U.S.)	PRICE (Foreign)	PRICE (Single)
☐ CARDIAC SURGERY	Triannual	84.00	93.00	36.00
Subscription year begins in October (Oct., Feb., June)				
☐ NEUROSURGERY	Biannual	75.00	84.00	42.00
☐ OCCUPATIONAL MEDICINE	Quarterly	64.00	74.00	29.00
☐ PHYSICAL MED & REHAB (PM&R)	Quarterly	62.00	68.00	28.00
☐ SPINE	Triannual	75.00	87.00	32.00
Subscription year begins in September (Sept., Jan., May)				

☐1988 subscription ☐ 1987 subscription ☐ Single issue

Check subject title above.

Title _____

I enclose payment: ☐ Check ☐ Visa ☐ MasterCard

Credit Card # _____ Exp. Date _____

Name _____

Signature _____

Title _____

Street Address _____

Company/Hospital _____

City/State/Zip _____

Send order to:

HANLEY & BELFUS, INC.

210 South 13th Street / Philadelphia, PA 19107 / 215-546-7293

STATE OF THE ART REVIEWS (STARs)

SUBJECT	FREQUENCY	PRICE (U.S.)	PRICE (Foreign)	PRICE (Single)
☐ CARDIAC SURGERY	Triannual	84.00	93.00	36.00
Subscription year begins in October (Oct., Feb., June)				
☐ NEUROSURGERY	Biannual	75.00	84.00	42.00
☐ OCCUPATIONAL MEDICINE	Quarterly	64.00	74.00	29.00
☐ PHYSICAL MED & REHAB (PM&R)	Quarterly	62.00	68.00	28.00
☐ SPINE	Triannual	75.00	87.00	32.00
Subscription year begins in September (Sept., Jan., May)				

☐1988 subscription   ☐ 1987 subscription   ☐ Single issue

Check subject title above.   Title _____

I enclose payment: ☐ Check ☐ Visa ☐ MasterCard   Credit Card # _____ Exp. Date _____

Name _____   Signature _____

Title _____   Street Address _____

Company/Hospital _____   City/State/Zip _____

Send order to:
HANLEY & BELFUS, INC.
210 South 13th Street / Philadelphia, PA 19107 / 215-546-7293

STATE OF THE ART REVIEWS (STARs)

SUBJECT	FREQUENCY	PRICE (U.S.)	PRICE (Foreign)	PRICE (Single)
☐ CARDIAC SURGERY	Triannual	84.00	93.00	36.00
Subscription year begins in October (Oct., Feb., June)				
☐ NEUROSURGERY	Biannual	75.00	84.00	42.00
☐ OCCUPATIONAL MEDICINE	Quarterly	64.00	74.00	29.00
☐ PHYSICAL MED & REHAB (PM&R)	Quarterly	62.00	68.00	28.00
☐ SPINE	Triannual	75.00	87.00	32.00
Subscription year begins in September (Sept., Jan., May)				

☐1988 subscription   ☐ 1987 subscription   ☐ Single issue

Check subject title above.   Title _____

I enclose payment: ☐ Check ☐ Visa ☐ MasterCard   Credit Card # _____ Exp. Date _____

Name _____   Signature _____

Title _____   Street Address _____

Company/Hospital _____   City/State/Zip _____

Send order to:
HANLEY & BELFUS, INC.
210 South 13th Street / Philadelphia, PA 19107 / 215-546-7293